Internet Directories

ISBN 0-13-974452-5

Prentice Hall Series in
Computer Networking and Distributed Systems
Radia Perlman, editor

Internet Directories

How to Build and Manage Applications for LDAP, DNS, and Other Directories

Bruce Greenblatt

Prentice Hall PTR
Upper Saddle River, NJ 07458
www.phptr.com

Library of Congress Cataloging-in-Publication Data Available

Editorial/Production Supervision: *MetroVoice Publishing Services*
Acquisitions Editor: *Mary Franz*
Editorial Assistant: *Noreen Regina*
Marketing Manager: *Bryan Gambrel*
Buyer: *Maura Goldstaub*
Cover Design: *Anthony Gemmellaro*
Cover Design Direction: *Jerry Votta*
Art Director: *Gail Cocker-Bogusz*
Series Interior Design: *Meg Van Arsdale*
Project Coordinator: *Anne Trowbridge*

 © 2001 Prentice Hall PTR
Prentice-Hall, Inc.
Upper Saddle River, NJ 07458

Prentice Hall books are widely used by corporations and government agencies for training,
marketing, and resale.

The publisher offers discounts on this book when ordered in bulk quantities.
For more information, contact Corporate Sales Department, phone: 800-382-3419;
fax: 201-236-7141; e-mail: corpsales@prenhall.com
Or write: Prentice Hall PTR
　　　　　Corporate Sales Department
　　　　　One Lake Street
　　　　　Upper Saddle River, NJ 07458

Printed in the United States of America
10　9　8　7　6　5　4　3　2　1

ISBN 0-13-974452-5

Prentice-Hall International (UK) Limited, **London**
Prentice-Hall of Australia Pty. Limited, **Sydney**
Prentice-Hall Canada Inc., **Toronto**
Prentice-Hall Hispanoamericana, S.A., **Mexico**
Prentice-Hall of India Private Limited, **New Delhi**
Prentice-Hall of Japan, Inc., **Tokyo**
Pearson Education Asia Pte. Ltd.
Editora Prentice-Hall do Brasil, Ltda., **Rio de Janeiro**

*To my wife Cynthia, without whose love and support
I would have never been able to finish this book.*

Contents

Figures

Tables

Acknowledgments

Radia Perlman, while we were colleagues at Novell, first suggested that a survey of the various Internet Directory technologies would make a good topic for a book. Mary Franz at Prentice Hall took on the project and helped guide the project over the two years (and a bit). Corinne Gregory's excellent technical editing helped turn my often incoherent statements into more understandable coverage of the topic. Barbara Cotton's copyediting and Scott Suckling's page composition skills gave a level of consistency to the formatting of the book and figures that makes the book easier to read.

The book would not have been nearly as accurate in the technical sense without the contributions of many reviewers, most of whom I never had the opportunity to meet. Special thanks to the Electronic Messaging Association (EMA) and Susan May for letting me adapt and extend the article that I co-authored with Ms. May for the March/April 1997 issue of *Messaging Magazine* as Chapter 7 of this book.

I would also like to thank the many contributors to the standardization efforts of Internet Directories that I've met through the mailing lists and the meetings of the Internet Engineering Task Force (IETF). The consistent pressure that is applied to implement and use directories has brought Internet Directories to the state that they are in today.

## CHAPTER 1

Introduction

Imagine that a little girl is walking along a path through the forest on the way to her grandmother's house. In addition to the beautiful red riding hood that she is wearing, she is carrying a large picnic basket full of food for her grandmother. Suddenly, a large wolf accosts the girl. He indicates that he will take the food the rest of the way for her. She's tired and there is still a long way to go in order to get to her grandmother's house, so the girl wants to believe the wolf. However, rumors abound that wolves are not always the most trustworthy creatures. How is one to know whether or not to trust the wolf? If only there were some reliable third party available that could provide some guidance. Suddenly, the girl has an inspiration. She pulls her palm-size computer out of the picnic basket, connects to the Trustworthy Wolf Registry on the Internet, and asks the friendly wolf for his identification card. She slides the card through the reader on her computer. The wolf's identification information is transmitted to the registry, which in turn validates that he is indeed trustworthy. She then feels safe in handing over the basket and providing the wolf with directions to her grandmother's house.

In this modern revision of the classical fairy tale, Little Red Riding Hood has made use of a directory service in order to retrieve information about the wolf based upon certain known properties that he provided on his identification card. This story is not too far-fetched (except for the talking wolf part). The Internet provides all of the necessary underpinnings in order to make it a reality. Directories can provide most of these underpinnings. Directories allow for the look up of information in well-known formats, and this lookup can be done in such a way that there is some guarantee of the reliability of the information's source. In this book, we will provide detailed descriptions and definitions of many different types of directories that are available on the Internet. We will show how the different components which make up the directory communicate, and describe the interaction among different types of Internet directories. Furthermore, we will show several different types of applications that can be built on top of directories.

WHAT IS DRIVING INTERNET DIRECTORIES?

The future utilization of Internet directories in Internet applications is potentially, if not inevitably, explosive. This is due to the fact that businesses are moving away from proprietary mechanisms to run their network as they connect to the Internet. The corporate networks are now running the same TCP/IP-based *networking* protocols that are used on the Internet. In the corporate network, directories are responsible for making available information about network accessible resources such as host machines, printers, users, etc. Directories are now available as integrated components of modern network infrastructures furnished by major network operating system providers (e.g., Windows NT, NetWare, and most versions of Unix).

A directory provides a set of names and properties in such a way that users can easily search them. Each name and its associated properties are collected together as a directory entry. All directories provide functions for their users to allow for retrieval of the entries based on the name of the entry. Some directories provide functions that allow users to retrieve entries based on properties of the entry in addition to the name.

Directories operate in client-server mode; directory clients submit service requests to directory servers and directory servers handle the requests and provide responses to the directory clients. The core services provided by a directory server include property or attribute-based information storage, manipulation, and retrieval. The most frequently utilized and, hence, most essential directory service is *property* or *attribute-based information retrieval*. Other services provided by a directory server, i.e. data addition, deletion, and modification services, exist to support this primary service and are considered ancillary to the information retrieval service. There are several different directories that are used on the Internet. One prevalent example of an Internet directory is the Domain Name System (DNS). The primary goal of the DNS directory service is to provide for the mapping of Internet host names to IP addresses. By making this service available, users are able to refer to computers and other network-connected devices by easy-to-remember names, rather than numeric address formats that are used internally by the Internet Protocol suite. Several other Internet directory services are also used extensively on the Internet.

WHO IS THE TARGET AUDIENCE OF THIS BOOK?

Throughout this book, the explanations of the various Internet directory technologies have been supplemented by making extensive use of examples. Thus, administrators seeking to deploy either a directory or a modern application that is in some way dependent on an Internet directory will find the material contained in this book helpful. Similarly, software developers desiring to create an application that is to be integrated with an Internet directory will find the treatment of technology, as well as the data organization in the examples, helpful in their efforts.

WHAT BACKGROUND IS NEEDED TO UNDERSTAND THIS BOOK?

This book assumes the reader has a basic background in computer science. Most computer professionals will find the majority of this book easy to understand. Computer programming experience will be very helpful in understanding Chapter 7, *"Building an LDAP Browser in Java."* It is not assumed that the reader has a deep understanding of computer networking. It is helpful, however, to have experience in using Internet applications, such as a Web browser.

This book provides tutorial information on several different Internet directory technologies. Background material in computer networking and security is provided at appropriate points to provide a complete treatment of the Internet directory technology being discussed. This background material is provided for those with limited backgrounds in those areas.

HOW TO OBTAIN DOCUMENTATION ON THE INTERNET

The Internet Engineering Task Force (IETF) provides the specifications that define the protocols that are used on the Internet. The IETF notes on its web site (located at http://www.ietf.org), "The IETF is a large, open, international community of network designers, operators, vendors, and researchers concerned with the evolution of the Internet architecture and the smooth operation of the Internet." The IETF publishes its specifications in documents that are known as Requests for Comments

(RFCs). RFCs document various aspects of computer communications, mainly in the area of protocols that are to be used for the exchange of information between two (or more) Internet hosts. These protocols fall into three main categories: Network Layer, Transport Layer, and Application Layer.

An example of a Network Layer protocol is Internet Protocol (IP). Examples of Transport Layer protocols are Transport Control Protocol (TCP) and User Datagram Protocol (UDP). These layers will be summarized in the next chapter. Examples of Application Layer protocols are LDAP and SMTP.

RFCs are freely available from a number of sites around the world, including the IETF's own web site mentioned above. The work of the IETF that has yet to be published as RFCs is available from these same sites in the form of Internet drafts. Drafts are work-in-progress documents that are either being investigated by one of the many working groups of the IETF, or are individual contributions.

An important item to note about the documentation concerning the Internet that differs from the documentation concerning many other standards-making bodies is this: the IETF documents are always free and, with only very rare exception, contain no patented or copyrighted information or ideas. Documentation from virtually every other standards body (e.g., ITU, ANSI, IEEE, ECMA, etc.) is prohibitively expensive to obtain. The IETF views this expense as a barrier to the implementation of standards, and encourages implementations far and wide. As evidence of this strategy, RFC 2026 (the Internet Standards Process) defines the various types of RFCs and the stages in which they proceed. It defines the conditions that must exist before an RFC can proceed from the first level (Proposed Standard) to the first level on the IETF standards track (Draft Standard type RFC): "A specification from which at least two independent and interoperable implementations from different code bases have been developed, and for which sufficient successful operational experience has been obtained, may be elevated to the *Draft Standard* level." Other standard bodies typically introduce their standards prior to any implementation experience.

ORGANIZATION OF THIS BOOK

This book contains nine chapters organized into three parts, arranged as follows:

1. Part I serves as the book's introductory portion. Chapter 1 sets out the purpose, target audience, and required background for the book. Chapter 2 serves as a continuation of the introductory portion of the book. It provides a tutorial on computer networking for those unfamiliar with the protocols that define the way information is moved between Internet hosts. A short primer on security is given as well. It also provides short descriptions of some of the more important Internet directories, in addition to a few examples of how directories can be used.

2. Part II provides detailed definitions of several Internet directories and the protocols that they use. Chapter 3 discusses the Domain Name System (DNS). Chapter 4 presents the Lightweight Directory Access Protocol (LDAP). Chapter 5 discusses several text based internet directory services such as Finger, Whois, and Whois++. Chapter 6 introduces back end directory protocols that are used by the directory servers themselves.

3. Part III studies the applications of Internet directories. Chapter 7 examines directory management which involves how the directory can be used to administer other applications. In addition, it involves a treatment of how the directory itself may be managed. Chapter 8 describes how to build an LDAP browser using the Java programming language. Chapter 9 provides a detailed description of building applications that use the directory. Several detailed examples of applications that make use of DNS and LDAP are provided. Chapter 10 gives an overview of two major directory servers that implement LDAP, Novell Directory Service and Microsoft Active Directory.

## CHAPTER 2

An Overview of Directories and the Internet

A DIRECTORY FOR THE DOGS

As an example of a typical directory request that illustrates property-based information retrieval, consider a directory that contains information about dogs. Imagine that a directory client wants to know about breeds of dogs that are black and weigh less than 20 pounds. In this situation, the directory client would present two facts that it knows about objects that are in the directory:

☞ Weight < 20 pounds
☞ Color = Black

The directory server that the client contacts is expected to return information about all dog breeds of which it is aware, that have a weight property that is smaller than twenty, and a color property equal to black. The precise information that is returned depends upon the type of directory service, and what information is available, but would include other properties of the people that matched the request, such as breed name, height, weight, etc. Figure 2.1 shows this interaction between the directory client and the directory server.

There are numerous kinds of directories that have been defined by the Internet. Most directory services are identified by the protocol that is used to communicate between directory clients and directory servers,

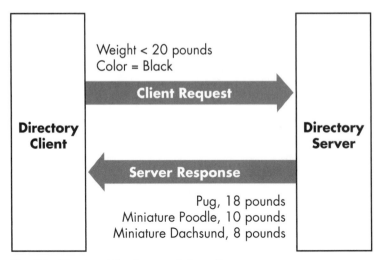

Fig. 2.1 Directory/client server interaction

even though there may be other protocols that are defined by this service that allow for communication among the directory servers. These server-to-server communication protocols are often termed *back end* protocols.

Compare this notion of directories to that of the widely used Internet search engines. The directory allows the client to supply some properties and proposed values, and the server returns matching entries and actual values from those entries. The search engine is specifically designed to go to pages on web sites that want to be searchable and reads them, using hypertext links on each page to discover and read a site's other pages. Then, using this information, the search engine has a program that creates a huge index (sometimes called a "catalog") from the pages that have been read. This index or catalog can then be searched by users to find web sites of interest. The typical search engine then allows the user to supply some words and returns some web pages that it has searched that have some type of match with the supplied words. Notice that in the directory the client request has a definite property-value structure, while the search engine request is relatively unstructured.

A Security Primer

This section introduces network security. Network security provides safeguards against various threats that may be targeted against computer networks. As directories are a network application service, they could be prime targets for these threats. Typical attacks against a directory involve the theft of information that is stored in the directory and the denial of service to a directory client. If a rogue user gains access to the directory, then that user may be able to change the directory information and cause the directory to provide incorrect answers to the clients' queries.

In order to provide a complete directory service some level of network security must be provided. But what parts of security are relevant to directories? Users need to prove who they are since some data that the directory stores is marked with access control information indicating who is allowed to read and write it. In some systems, proof of users' identities is accepted by just trusting the IP address from which the request comes, or by sending a password across the network, neither of which is secure. A better way is through cryptography, in which you provide knowledge of a secret without divulging it. Using cryptographic techniques allows a directory client to prove to the directory server that it knows the password without ever sending the password across the network. Thus, even if there is an eavesdropper on the connection between the client and the server, the user's password is still safe.

Authentication is the process of determining whether someone or something is, in fact, who or what it claims to be. It is often the case that a directory client must be authenticated to the directory server before being granted access to the directory information. Secure forms of authentication involve the process in which you provide knowledge of a secret without divulging it. There are two types of secrets: the first type is where both sides (i.e., the client and the server) know the same secret. The other type is known as public key schemes, in which each user has a pair of keys, one public and one private, which are mathematically related such that you can verify if someone knows the private key by using the public key. Authentication is the primary use of security in directory systems.

Various security mechanisms that are used by directories are introduced here. A complete discussion of network applications can be found in Kaufman, Perlman, and Speciner's book, *Network Security: Private Communication in a Public World*.[1] The most basic tool used in network security is *encryption*. Encryption allows data to be modified into a form that allows it to be hidden from unauthorized people. The encrypted form of the data is known as the cipher data. Decryption is the process that these authorized people use to transform the cipher data back into the original data. Authorized people encrypt and decrypt data by making use of *keys*

---

[1] Published by Prentice Hall PTR, 1995.

that are used by the encryption or decryption process. A key is a short piece of data that is known only to the authorized people. Keeping the key secret allows the encryption algorithms to be published. The typical use of encryption in directories is to keep certain data private as it is transferred across the network between the directory client and server. There are a large number of encryption algorithms that can be used to provide this privacy; the most widely used algorithms fall into two categories:

☞ *Public-key* algorithms use a pair of keys that are created in a special process that allows one key to be used in encryption, and the other key to be used in decryption. One of the keys is kept secret (the *private* key), and the other key is made widely available (the *public* key).

☞ *Secret-key* algorithms allow only a single key to be used for both encryption and decryption.

A few notes about these two types of encryption algorithms:

☞ Public-key algorithms are substantially slower than secret-key algorithms. In fact, public-key algorithms are so much slower that they are rarely used for encrypting data that is larger than a few kilobytes.

☞ The keys used in public-key algorithms are much larger than the keys used in secret-key algorithms. The key used in the popular RSA public-key algorithm defined in RFC 2437 is normally 256 bytes to provide adequate security. The key used in the popular RC5 secret-key algorithm defined in RFC 2040 is normally only 8 or 16 bytes.

☞ Great care must be taken in transmitting the key used in the secret-key algorithm among authorized users. If any unauthorized users gain access to the key, then any data encrypted using that key has been compromised.

Secret-Key Encryption

The most common secret-key encryption algorithms operate on a fixed length segment of data at a time, usually 8 or 16 bytes. The algorithms take this data segment in combination with the secret key as input data in order to produce the encrypted data. The encrypted data is almost always the same size as the input, plain text data. When the data to be encrypted is longer than the segment that the algorithm is designed to accept, the plain text data is broken into several blocks which are encrypted one at a time. For example, if a document to be encrypted is 100 bytes long, and the encryption algorithm operates on data blocks that are 8 bytes long, then the document would be divided into 13 blocks. Note that the last block of data would not be 8 full bytes, but only 4 bytes long. In order to decrypt the data, the algorithm uses the encrypted data along with the same secret key that was used in the encryption.

Some algorithms are defined to encrypt each block independent of all the other blocks of data. Alternatively, the algorithm can use the results of a previous block in the input to the encryption of the next block. The details of any particular encryption algorithm are beyond the scope of this book. However, it can be assumed that if a document has been encrypted with a strong secret-key encryption algorithm, then the encrypted data may be safely transmitted across the Internet. As long as only the originator and the intended recipient know the key used in the encryption process, any malicious intruders that may intercept the document cannot decrypt the document.

Public-Key Encryption

Two keys are required, in public-key encryption algorithms. One key is used in the encryption process, and another key is used in the decryption process. In public-key technology, the two keys must have some sort of special relationship to each other, and be generated by a special mathematical process at the same time. Each pair of keys belongs to a user. The user will publish one of the keys (i.e., the public key) in order to make it available to other users. The second key (i.e., the private key) is kept confidential and not made available to anyone else. For example, if Alice wants to send Bob a secret message, she would retrieve Bob's public key (perhaps from a known directory) and use it to encrypt the message. Once the message has been encrypted, only Bob can decrypt it using his private key. Thus, even though Alice knows the public key, the plain text data, and the encrypted data, she still cannot derive Bob's private key. This is due to the special mathematical relationship between the two keys. In one popular encryption algorithm, the attempt to derive the private key would require the potential attacker to factor a large number. This large number is in the range of the size of the key. If the key is 1024 bits, then the attacker would have to factor a number in the range of 2^{1024} power, which is a number with more than a hundred decimal digits and, therefore, nearly imposssible to guess or derive.

Public keys should be widely published. If Alice published her public key so that it is widely available, anybody who needs to send her encrypted data can easily retrieve Alice's key and securely send her information. A good way of publishing public keys is by storing them in a directory. A directory client can provide Alice's e-mail address, and the directory server will be able to perform the lookup to find the entry in the directory, which contains Alice's public key, and return it to the end user.

Message Digests, Digital Signatures, and Authentication

Another security algorithm of special interest is the message digest algorithm. A message digest algorithm takes any size document as input (i.e., the message) and produces a fixed size data block as output. This fixed size data block is called the *message digest*. For example, the popular MD5 message digest algorithm is described in RFC 1321: The MD5 Message Digest Algorithm. MD5 produces a 16-byte message digest of its input. The message digest is also called a fingerprint because of the analogy to a person's fingerprint. Just as it is extremely difficult to find two people with the same fingerprint, it is also extremely difficult to find two documents that produce the same MD5 message digest. A good message digest algorithm has the property that it is computationally infeasible to produce two messages having the same message digest. Similarly, it is also computationally infeasible to produce any message having a given prespecified target message digest.

A message digest algorithm must have these properties to be useful in the creation of digital signatures. If Alice wants to create a digital signature for a document, she must first create the message digest of the plain text document. Then Alice will create the digital signature using her private key. She can then send the plain text document along with the document's signature to Bob. Bob can verify the digital signature by first creating the message digest of the plain text document. Then he will verify the digital signature using Alice's public key. If the decrypted digital signature and the message digest that Bob created are identical, then Bob has *verified* Alice's signature. In verifying the digital signature, Bob is guaranteed of two facts:

☞ The document that Bob received is precisely the document that Alice sent, and it has not been altered en route.
☞ The document was actually sent by Alice and no one else. This is due to the fact that no other person could have created the digital signature since it required the use of Alice's private key, and only Alice has access to her private key.

Digital signatures are especially useful in directories for the purpose of authentication. The digital signature process can be used in this scenario. Once the client connects to the server, the server provides the client with a piece of data that the client must sign. Once the server verifies the signed data, the server is assured of the identity of the client, and the client can continue operating on the directory. Additionally, digital signatures are also useful so that the information in the directory can be signed. This allows the directory clients to trust the information in the directory (especially if the information has been signed by a trusted agent).

THE INTERNET

Now that the basic concepts of directories have been introduced, the concepts of the Internet that are important to directories can be discussed. The Internet refers specifically to the original network that was funded by the United States Department of Defense Advanced Research Projects Agency (DARPA) known as ARPANET. Since its inception in the late 60s the ARPANET has evolved to a network that connects millions of hosts across the world. These hosts are all connected by protocols that are known as the TCP/IP suite of protocols. When an Internet-like network is contained inside an enterprise, it can also be called an intranet.

This section will not attempt to explain the entire Internet suite or protocol stack. That will take the perspective of viewing the Internet stack from the perspective of a directory, and discussing what parts of the Internet Suite directories use. For example, the services offered by the Internet Protocol (IP) and the Internet Core Message Protocol (ICMP) are not directly used by directory services, and so won't be discussed. However, an understanding of the Transport Control Protocol (TCP), Transport Layer Security (TLS, also known as Secure Sockets Layer or SSL), and the User Datagram Protocol (UDP) are directly used by directory services, and thus will be introduced. However, before discussing these services specifically, it is important to understand how TCP/IP works so that the features that are available to the Directory are known.

The suite of protocols used by the Internet is known as the TCP/IP suite because the principal protocols used by Internet applications to communicate are the Transport Control Protocol (TCP) and the Internet Protocol (IP). The TCP/IP suite of protocols is typically viewed as a stack, in which one layer is piled upon another. This is an indication that the layers at the top of the stack make use of services at the layers toward the bottom of the stack. A view of a portion of the TCP/IP stack is shown in Figure 2.2.

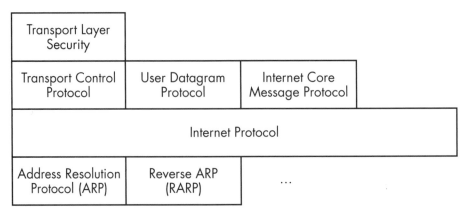

Fig. 2.2 Upper layers of the Internet Protocol Stack.

In this figure, each layer in the stack provides a set of services that are available to the layers that reside logically on top of it. TLS directly makes use of the services provided by TCP, but does not use any of the services that are offered by UDP or ICMP. Furthermore, TLS is generally ignorant of the services that are offered by the IP layer, and does not directly make use of those services. Internet applications, such as web browsers, connect to Internet servers, such as web servers, by creating a connection known as a *socket* between the application and the server. A socket can be viewed as a pipeline between the application and the server through which data may be exchanged once it is created.

The creation of a socket is very analogous to the dialing of a telephone call. Once the telephone number is entered, the destination line rings, and when the receiving party answers the ringing telephone on their end, a telephone connection is established. In order to create a socket connection between two entities on the Internet, the calling party (known as the client) enters an Internet address (the format of which will be discussed shortly). This Internet address is made by some process running on the client's machine which attempts to make a connection to some process that is running on the machine named by the given Internet address. If there is any process listening for connections on the destination machine, then the connection can be established. All of the Internet transports that are used in Internet directories (i.e., TCP, UDP, and TLS) make use of sockets for communication between clients and servers, but use different types of sockets. However, the sockets for all of the transport types have similar behavior. Thus, when they are used for the simple transport of data between the client and the server, the different socket types can be used by the directory entities in virtually the same way.

During the attempt to create a socket, the client and server go through a process known as *handshaking*. During the handshaking process, the client and server each exchange some information before the socket can be created. If either side is not satisfied with the information that is provided by the other side (known as its peer), then the attempt to create the socket is broken off, and no socket connection is created. For example, a socket server may be configured in such a way that it only allows sockets to be opened by clients from a specified set of hosts. During the handshaking process the client and server exchange their address information. If the client's address is not one of those that the server is configured to accept, then the server will reject the client's attempt to create the socket.

During any handshaking process at the Internet Transport Layer, the client and server exchange information in order that (among other things) they may be able to identify each other. In the real world, people identify each other by any number of means—names, telephone numbers, electronic mail addresses, etc. In the Internet, peer entities are able to identify each other by several different means, but by far the two most common mechanisms are Internet addresses and Internet host names. The following section presents an overview of the upper layers of the TCP/IP stack, from the top of the stack first, since those layers are directly used by the directory.

THE TLS LAYER

A very simplified view of the handshaking that occurs in the TLS layer is shown in Figure 2.3.

In this view of the handshaking that occurs during the attempt by a TLS client to open a socket with a TLS server, both the client and the server send two pieces of information across the network prior to a successful TLS socket creation. The client initiates the handshaking when it sends a special message defined by TLS, known as a *client hello*. This message contains various parameters that define those kinds of TLS services that are being requested. For example, the TLS client can request that the connection be encrypted by any of several different means. It can also request that any data being passed across the socket is to be compressed. The client hello message also includes some randomly generated data that aids in the creation of the encrypted connection. The server responds to a client hello with another special message that is defined by TLS, known as a *server hello*. The main piece of information that is included in the server hello message is information that is unique

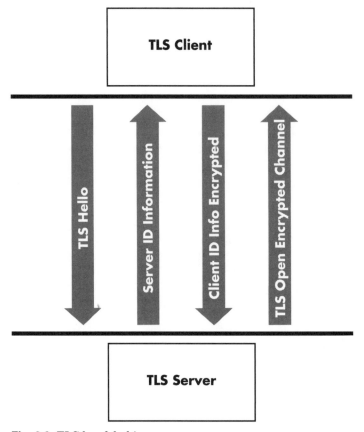

Fig. 2.3 TLS handshaking

to the server, known as a *certificate*. The server presents its certificate in such a way that the client can verify that it really does belong to the server. This verification is known as *authentication*. The precise details of how this authentication works are not particularly important to the functions of Internet directories, but a short overview of the authentication process will be discussed in Chapter 4, "Directory Management." The important feature of this first stage in the handshaking process is that it has allowed the TLS client to verify that the TLS server to which it has connected is indeed the one that it intended to contact.

Once the client has authenticated the server, the second phase of the TLS handshaking can begin. The objectives of the second phase are to allow the server to authenticate the client, and for the creation of an encryption key that allows all data passed across the TLS session to be kept confidential. If the server requested client authentication in its server hello message, then the client is obligated to provide its certificate information in the subsequent message. At this time the client uses the random data that it provided in the client hello message along with information that is in the server certificate to generate the encryption key. Simultaneous to this, the server is performing the same process, thus guaranteeing that the client and server have generated the same key, often known as a *shared secret*. If the server is satisfied with the client certificate information that the client has provided, then it provides a response that indicates that the connection has been opened successfully. (Keep in mind that this explanation of a TLS connection creation has been greatly simplified, and, while accurate, many details have been omitted.)

THE TCP LAYER

TCP is the Transport Control Protocol. It takes care of providing a reliable connection between two Internet nodes (e.g., hosts). For example, TCP nodes synchronize with each other and number each packet that is sent between them. For each packet that is sent from one host to the other, an acknowledgment is returned. If a host does not receive an acknowledgment for a sent packet, that packet is presumed to have been lost and is retransmitted. The TCP handshaking and socket setup process is much simpler than that of TLS. When a TCP client wishes to open with a TCP server, the client transmits a special message that indicates it wishes to *synchronize* sequence numbers with the server. This message, known as a SYN message, is the first step in the TCP handshaking. The steps in the TCP handshaking are illustrated in Figure 2.4 (taken from RFC 793, which defines TCP).

RFC 793 describes this process, known as the *3 way handshake,* as follows: The TCP client begins by sending a SYN segment indicating that it will use sequence numbers starting with 100. Next, the TCP server sends a SYN and acknowledges the SYN it received from the TCP client. Note that the acknowledgment field indicates that the TCP server is now expecting to hear sequence 101, acknowledging the SYN, which occupied sequence 100. Finally, the TCP client responds with an empty segment containing an ACK for the TCP server's SYN. With this third message, the TCP client and server have successfully negotiated a socket connection.

The synchronizing of the TCP sequence numbers is particularly important to the reliability of the TCP layer. As RFC 793 indicates, the TCP must recover from data that is damaged, lost, duplicated, or delivered out of order by the IP layer. This is achieved by assigning a sequence number to each octet transmitted, and requiring a positive acknowledg-

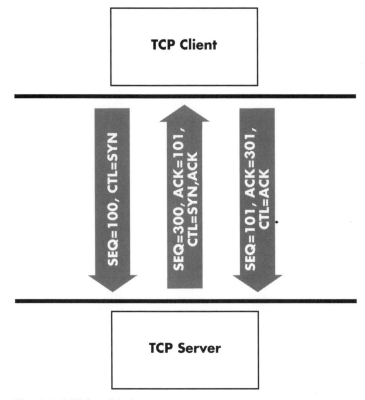

Fig. 2.4 TCP handshaking

ment (ACK) from the receiving TCP. If the ACK is not received within a timeout interval, the data is retransmitted. At the receiver, the sequence numbers are used to correctly order segments that may be received out of order and to eliminate duplicates. Damage is handled by adding a checksum to each segment transmitted, checking it at the receiver, and discarding damaged segments.

THE UDP LAYER

TCP is an inherently reliable protocol (using the above notion of reliability). This is due to the fact that packets are sent again when lost or somehow damaged in transit. Its companion protocol, User Datagram Protocol (UDP), is considered to be an inherently unreliable protocol. This unreliability is due to the fact that the guarantees of TCP are not made by UDP. UDP does not recover from data that is damaged, lost, duplicated, or delivered out of order by the IP layer. UDP does not have a handshaking process that takes place. UDP is designed for situations in which all that is needed is a single message and a single response. Thus, no ongoing connection between a UDP client and server is maintained. UDP is defined in RFC 768, which indicates that UDP provides a procedure for application programs to send messages to other programs with a minimum of protocol mechanisms. Applications requiring ordered reliable delivery of streams of data should use TCP. UDP operates by the UDP client opening a socket to a UDP server and sending some data across the socket. The UDP server replies to this request with whatever data is appropriate, and the UDP socket is then closed.

TYING THE LAYERS TOGETHER

Most hosts that are reachable on the Internet have been assigned one or more Internet Protocol (IP) addresses, and usually have been assigned a host name as well.[2] The IP is the numeric form, while the host name is the textual form. For convenience, the numeric addresses are normally represented textually in the *dotted notation* form, e.g., 127.0.0.1, rather than as the raw 32-bit or 64-bit number. Humans prefer the host name, as the names generally have some intrinsic meaning. For example, the web site for the Prentice Hall publishing company is located on the Internet host *www.prenhall.com*. Host names are the text strings that appear on the right side of the "@" in electronic mail address. For example, the author can be reached via e-mail at: bgreenblatt@directory-applications.com.

Version 4 of IP, which is the current ubiquitously deployed version, allows for the IP address to be 32 bits, which is large enough to hold approximately four billion different addresses. The recently approved version 6 of IP allows for 64 bit addresses, which is large enough to hold over four quintillion (i.e., 4.6×10^{18}) addresses.

In addition to knowing the name or address of the server on which it wants to open a socket, the client must also know the number of the port to which the server is connected. To allow for many processes within a single host to use TCP communication facilities simultaneously, the TCP provides a set of addresses or *ports* within each host. Concatenated with the network and host addresses from the IP layer, this forms a socket. This definition, taken directly from RFC 793, indicates that the purpose of the TCP port is to allow for many servers to operate on the

---

[2] Modern techniques allow hosts to participate on the Internet without having an IP address (or host name) assigned to them.

same Internet host at the same time. A TCP port is identified by an integer. In order to make this happen, each server must listen to a different incoming port. If a server attempts to listen on a port to which another server is already listening, TCP will return an error to the second server that indicates that the port is busy. Both UDP and TLS support the same implementation of port numbers, in that only one server is allowed to listen on a port at a time. Historically, Internet application services have reserved ports when they were defined. The Internet Assigned Numbers Authority (IANA) keeps track of all port numbers that have been assigned. Some of the more notable assignments for service contact ports are named in Table 2.1.

Table 2.1 Port Number Assignments for Some Internet Protocols

Protocol Name	TCP Port	UDP Port	TLS Port
Telnet	23	23	992
SMTP	25	25	465
DNS	53	53	
Whois	43	43	
Whois++	63	63	
Finger	79	79	
Http	80	80	443
Ldap	389	389	636
Rwhois	4321	4321	

Note in the above table that not all Internet application protocols have been assigned TLS ports. Port numbers are divided into three separate ranges:

☞ Well Known Ports—numbered from 0 through 1023
☞ Registered Ports—numbered from 1024 through 49151
☞ Dynamic or Private Ports—numbered from 49152 through 65535

Thus, DNS uses a well-known port while Rwhois uses a registered port. The distinction between these two port types is minor, in that typically only processes or programs that are run by the most privileged users can listen on a well-known port number. If a service has a well-known or registered port assignment, then clients of that service can assume that the default configuration of the server has the server listening on the assigned port. Thus, finger clients normally assume that there is a finger server listening on port number 79 on most Internet hosts, and that there is never a server that doesn't understand the finger protocol listening on that port. This means that when the finger client attempts to open a socket to a finger server, it will try port 79, and it will both succeed and talk to a finger server, or there will not be a finger server active on that server. It will never be the case that the finger client will attempt to open the socket, and that there is a server listening on port 79 that does not understand the finger protocol (for example, a web server).

More information on the definition of the Internet may be found in the Internet document, FYI 20, entitled "What is the Internet?" as well as any number of other published references.

INTERNET DIRECTORIES

Recall from our earlier discussion that a directory is an application service that primarily performs property-based information retrieval. Directories store objects of various types. Each object that is stored has properties. For example, dog objects have properties, such as color, breed, height, weight, age, etc. A directory that contains objects of this type would allow clients to retrieve information about dogs based on the properties that have been defined.

As they relate to the Internet, directories perform various necessary and useful functions. For example:

- ☞ They allow for the resolution of host names to underlying IP address.
- ☞ They allow for the creation of an Internet Public Key Infrastructure (PKI) in order to allow for the secure exchange of information across an insecure network.
- ☞ They allow for controlled access to resources across a distributed network.
- ☞ They allow for location of a server based upon the type of the service (e.g., electronic mail) rather than upon the name of the server.
- ☞ They allow for the exchange of index information among themselves in order to facilitate the routing of queries to the appropriate server. This function allows each server to have some knowledge about the data that is contained on many other servers.

Directories provide many useful services for the Internet. But the Internet also provides many useful functions for directories. TCP provides a reliable means of transporting data from client to server. TLS allows for the directory to provide a secure means of transporting data from client to server. TLS also allows the directory peers to provide a strong means of identifying each other, rather than simply passing user IDs and passwords across the network.

The previous section provided an overview of the Internet, and the notion of Directories as a service that allows for property-based information retrieval has been touched upon. Putting the Internet and directories together yields the concept of the Internet directory. An Internet directory is a service that has *property-based information retrieval* as its primary function, and uses one or more of the *Internet transports* (TLS, TCP, or UDP) as its native means for communication between the client and server. The two most prominent Internet directories are the Domain Name System (DNS) and the Lightweight Directory Access Protocol (LDAP).

DNS

DNS is an Internet standard that is defined in RFCs 1034 and 1035. The primary goal of the DNS directory service is to provide for the mapping of Internet host names to IP addresses. In terms of the property-based information retrieval concept, the objects that are stored in the DNS directory are Internet hosts. The properties that are available for retrieval are host names and IP addresses. DNS clients, known as *resolvers,* send requests to DNS servers. In the DNS, resolvers typically provide a server with a host name, and the server provides the resolver with the IP address that corresponds to the provided host name. The growth in the Internet was the impetus for the development of DNS. As the number of hosts attached to the Internet grew beyond several hundred in the early 1980s, scalability problems with the previous mechanism for providing the name to address mapping were exposed.

As described in RFC 1035, prior to the implementation of DNS, host name to address mappings were maintained by the Network Information Center (NIC) in a single file (HOSTS.TXT) which was copied by all hosts [RFC-952, RFC-953]. The total network bandwidth consumed in distributing a new version by this scheme was proportional to the square of the number of hosts in the network; the outgoing FTP load on the NIC host was considerable. Explosive growth in the number of hosts didn't bode well for the future. Furthermore, the network population was also changing in character. The timeshared hosts that made up the original ARPANET were being replaced with local networks of workstations. Local organizations were administering their own names and addresses, but had to wait for the NIC to change HOSTS.TXT to make alterations visible to the Internet at large. The proposals for the replacement of this mechanism varied, but a common thread was the idea of a hierarchical name space, with the hierarchy roughly corresponding to organizational structure, and names using "." as the character to mark the boundary between hierarchy levels. The implementation of DNS met the requirements with a distributed database of information rather than a centrally administered hosts file. The distributed administration of directory administration devised by DNS was to become a hallmark for virtually all of the Internet Directory services that were to follow. The implementation and protocols involved in DNS will be discussed in significant detail in a subsequent chapter.

LDAP

The Lightweight Directory Access Protocol (LDAP) was defined as a result of the desire to pursue implementation of the X.500 series of recommendations of the International Telecommunications Union (X.500) on the part of Defense Advanced Research Projects Agency (DARPA). X.500 defines several different models and protocols that are used in the implementation of directories. The most notable protocol defined by X.500 is the Directory Access Protocol (DAP). DARPA wanted to deploy directories based on the X.500 series, but their implementation was slow in coming. DARPA decided to fund a research project at the University of Michigan that would result in the definition of a different version of DAP that would be significantly easier to implement, but would still retain the core features of the X.500 model. The end product of this research project was LDAP.

An early definition of LDAP was experimental in nature, and the first widely implemented definition of LDAP was LDAP version 2, as defined in RFC 1777. Due to deficiencies in the areas of security, internationalization, and extensibility, a third version of LDAP was defined in RFC 2251. RFC 2251 indicates key aspects of this version of LDAP:

☞ All features of LDAPv2 (RFC 1777) are supported. The protocol is carried directly over TCP or other transport, bypassing much of the session/presentation overhead of X.500 DAP (which is defined on top of the OSI protocol stack).

☞ Most of the data that is passed between LDAP clients and servers can be encoded as ordinary strings (X.500 uses various binary data types to encode its information).

☞ Referrals to other servers may be returned when the server initially contacted by the LDAP client does not have enough information in order to completely fulfill the client request.

☞ Any mechanism may be used with LDAP to provide security services that can be used in the authentication step between the client and the server.

☞ Attribute values and distinguished names have been internationalized to allow for any character (e.g., in the Chinese character set) to be used in LDAP strings.

☞ The protocol can be extended to support new operations, and controls may be used to extend existing operations.

☞ Clients publish schemas in the directory for use so that the types of information that are available for retrieval are available as part and parcel of the normal information that is published by LDAP servers.

The last point is especially interesting. In the context of Internet directories, the schema defines the types of objects and the properties of those objects that are available for retrieval by clients. Since LDAP clients are the ones that are capable of publishing the information that appears in directories, it is only natural that the clients are allowed to publish (and retrieve) the schema for that information. While appearing natural, this innovation is new in version 3 of LDAP, and allows clients to be able to find out about new types of objects that are stored in the directory, and to determine the precise syntax that is used in the properties of these new types of objects. This notion of dynamic schema discovery is a marked difference between LDAP and earlier directories. In DNS, resolvers are expected to have full knowledge of the various types of records that are maintained by DNS servers. There is no defined way in the DNS scheme of things for resolvers to understand new record types on the fly.

INTERNET DIRECTORY REQUIREMENTS

In the previous sections of this chapter, various functions of Internet directories have been discussed, but the fundamental requirements for a directory service has only been touched on. In traditional software development, the requirements gathering phase is the first part of developing software and it defines the external behavior of the software system to be built. In terms of Internet directories, the requirements indicate the features of the clients that are made available to their users. Note that not all directory services implement all of these requirements. For example, as we mentioned previously, DNS does not implement schema discovery. This section is meant to describe, in a general way, the types of features that are available in many Internet directory services, in order to distinguish them from other types of application services.

The foremost requirement of an Internet directory service is to allow for property-based information retrieval. Regardless of the type of information that is stored in the directory, each object that is stored has various properties, and the directory service must allow for clients to retrieve this information based on these properties.

Data Storage

Internet directories store their data in such a way that the properties and protocol that are used fit in naturally with the rest of the Internet. For example, multimedia objects are typically represented in the Internet by making use of the MIME (Multipurpose Internet Mail Extensions) structure. MIME was first defined as a way to transport various types of binary data across the Internet in electronic mail messages. However, it has come to be used in numerous protocols that need to define ways to transport multipart, possibly binary data. For example, MIME is used not only in electronic mail, it is also used in LDAP, the Common Index Protocol (CIP), the Hypertext Transport Protocol (HTTP) used in the World Wide Web, and many other Internet application protocols.

In the original days of the Internet, data was assumed to be stored in the United States (U.S.) version of the ASCII character set. U.S. ASCII represents each character as a single byte, the high order bit of which is always zero. The resulting 128 different characters that are defined by U.S. ASCII include the 26 upper and lowercase letters, the 10 digits, and various other punctuation and control characters. Of course, information that is transported across the Internet needs to include characters from many different cultures outside the US. For example, European and Oriental characters are not represented in U.S. ASCII. The French word "çiel" can't be represented using U.S. ASCII, since the character 'ç' is not one of the 128 characters defined by ASCII. In order to represent such kinds of information, the Universal Character Set (UCS) repertoire was devised. UCS character sequences are normally represented on the Internet by using the specification known as UTF-8. UTF-8 is defined in RFC 2279, which is titled, "UTF-8, a transformation format of ISO 10646." The International Organization for Standardization (ISO) standard numbered 10646 defines the multibyte character set known as UCS.

UCS characters are either two bytes long or four bytes long, and they use the full range of possible two or four byte values.

The point of UTF-8 is that it encodes UCS characters as a sequence of one or more 8-bit ASCII characters. UTF-8 defines an encoding mechanism that has the characteristic of preserving the full U.S. ASCII range. It also provides a mechanism for encoding characters outside of this range in more than one byte. Table 2.2 (taken directly from RFC 2279) summarizes the format of these different octet types. The letter "x" indicates bits available for encoding bits of the UCS-4 character value.

Table 2.2 UTF-8 Character Encoding

UCS-4 range (hex.)	UTF-8 octet sequence (binary)	Number of 8 bit characters needed
0000 0000-0000 007F	0xxxxxxx 1	
0000 0080-0000 07FF	110xxxxx 10xxxxxx	2
0000 0800-0000 FFFF	1110xxxx 10xxxxxx 10xxxxxx	3
0001 0000-001F FFFF	11110xxx 10xxxxxx 10xxxxxx 10xxxxxx	4
0020 0000-03FF FFFF	111110xx 10xxxxxx 10xxxxxx 10xxxxxx 10xxxxxx	5
0400 0000-7FFF FFFF	1111110x 10xxxxxx ... 10xxxxxx	6

Thus, the UTF-8 encoding of the word "Directory" is precisely the same as the original ASCII encoding of that same word. Some other examples from RFC 2279 of character encoding are:

☞ The UCS-2 sequence "A<NOT IDENTICAL TO><ALPHA>." (0041, 2262, 0391, 002E) may be encoded in UTF-8 as follows:

```
41 E2 89 A2 CE 91 2E
```

☞ The UCS-2 sequence representing the Hangul characters for the Korean word "hangugo" (D55C, AD6D, C5B4) may be encoded as follows:

```
ED 95 9C EA B5 AD EC 96 B4
```

☞ The UCS-2 sequence representing the Han characters for the Japanese word "nihongo" (65E5, 672C, 8A9E) may be encoded as follows:

```
E6 97 A5 E6 9C AC E8 AA 9E
```

☞ Since UTF-8 encoding is the Internet Standards track definition for international character representations, when representing data outside of the US-ASCII character set, Internet directories should make use of UTF-8 encoding for that data, as specified in RFC 2279.

Protocol Usage

The protocols that are used in Internet directories should be carried directly on top of an Internet transport, i.e., TCP, UDP, or TLS. Native integration of applications with the TCP/IP stack makes integration with future enhancements to this stack more likely to be smooth. For example, TLS has been designed in such a way that creation and deletion of TLS sockets is done in virtually the same way as the creation and deletion of TCP sockets. For example, even though TLS had not yet been invented at the time that LDAP v2 was released, LDAP v2 clients have no problem in changing from the use of TCP to access directory servers to using TLS to access those same directory servers. LDAP v2 clients thereby gained the advantage of encrypted sessions, server authentication, and other TLS provided services without any change at all in the LDAP protocol definition.

Distributed Operation

Internet directories should operate in a distributed manner in such a way as to allow consistent access to their information throughout the Internet. Not all Internet hosts are uniformly available from any site on the Internet. This is due to a wide variety of factors, not the least of which are geographic considerations and other bandwidth-related concerns. However, access to directory information should not suffer from these problems. It must be possible to allow multiple directory servers to provide services for the same set of objects. This allows directory clients to access whichever directory server is most conveniently located. In order to illustrate this requirement, consider Figure 2.5.

The point here is that any of the clients can present their query ("What breeds of black dogs weigh under 20 pounds?") to any of the servers and expect to get the same answer back. Due to geographical and other bandwidth considerations, the timing will be different for each of the clients working with each of the servers. Therefore, Internet directory servers are required to cooperate in order to present a uniform view of the data they manage to Internet directory clients. Historically, directory servers that do support the notion of information sharing or replication have defined their own information sharing protocols that are

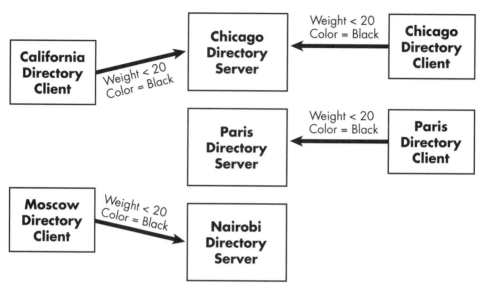

Fig. 2.5 Directory replication

specific to one type of directory (e.g., DNS, X.500, etc.). RFC 2651 defines the Common Indexing Protocol (CIP). CIP allows directory servers to share and publish much of the information that they contain, and CIP is not limited to any particular protocol.

Because directory servers cooperate to provide a service, they will often not be able to fulfill a client request. In this situation, the directory server that is being queried may be able to refer the client to another directory server that can be consulted with this query. This notion of *referrals* is illustrated in Figure 2.6.

In this figure the directory client first submits its query about small black dogs to the Chicago directory server. The Chicago directory server is unable to fulfill this request, and refers the directory client to the Paris directory server. The directory client *chases* the referral that is provided, and presents the same query to the Paris directory server. In this instance, the Paris directory server is able to fulfill the client's request, and furnishes an appropriate response. Thus, a referral is an indication by a directory server that it does not have the information needed to return that desired result. The referral contains that information needed by the directory client for it to be able to contact some other directory server. Directories can gather knowledge of the information that is held by other directory servers. This knowledge can be manually gathered by the directory administrator, or it can be automated by the use of back end directory protocols.

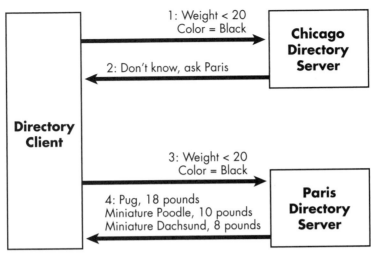

Fig. 2.6 Directory Referrals

WHITE PAGES SERVICE

One of the main uses for a directory on the Internet is for the provision of an Internet White Pages Service (IWPS) in which the client furnishes some properties of a user that it knows about, and the service responds with various types of address information about this user. In the context of the telephone system, a white pages book, in which a list of names are arranged alphabetically, is often used. If the white pages client knows the name of a listed telephone subscriber, then the white pages service will supply the client with a telephone number and possibly a street address. An IWPS, as a special type of white pages service that is located on the Internet, is intended to provide Internet-related addressing information. In the IWPS, the principal addressing information that is to be returned by the IWPS server is the electronic mail address of a user. Other types of related information can also be returned. For instance, RFC 2148 "Deployment of the Internet White Pages Service" describes in great detail the requirements for an IWPS, and RFC 2218 "A Common Schema for the Internet White Pages Service" defines the data that is to be maintained by an IWPS server. A small subset of the user properties that are defined by RFC 2218 is:

E-mail
Certificate
Home Page

Given Name
Surname
Organization
Country
Personal Phone
Personal Fax

From the list above, it can be seen that some of the properties are those that are generally provided by the IWPS client in a request (e.g., Given Name, Surname, Country), while others are generally provided by the IWPS server in its response (e.g., E-mail, Certificate, Personal Phone). For example, an IWPS client in a search for someone's electronic mail address could provide:

Given Name = "John"
Surname = "Smith"
Organization = "Prentice Hall"

while the IWPS server would respond with *john.smith@prenhall.com*. An IWPS was historically connected with electronic mail packages, and often called an address book service. An IWPS has been confused by many with the directory service itself. This important distinction is made between a service and an application of that service. The directory service is a general-purpose property-based information retrieval service, while an IWPS is a special purpose service optimized for retrieval of user's addressing properties.

A Simple Directory

Consider as an example of a directory service a system that converts IP addresses into host names. This directory fits the definition that is being used for a directory (a property-based information retrieval service). The service will operate as a client server application protocol. The client, when attempting to retrieve a host name for a known IP address, will open a socket to the Internet host that corresponds to that IP address. The service operates equally well on TCP, UDP, or TLS. Once the socket has been successfully opened, the client uses the protocol to request the host name for the server that accepted the incoming socket. The server responds to this request by sending its host name and closing the socket connection.

The property that the client knows about is the IP address of the server, and the property that it is attempting to retrieve is the host name of the server. The question for the protocol designers was: "what information does the client need to present to the server in order to relay the information request?" It turns out that once the client opens the socket no further information needs to be transmitted by the client. So, the client only needs to indicate that it is ready for the server to transmit the data. This can be represented in the protocol as the sequence of ASCII characters, carriage return, and line feed. The hexadecimal representation of this in the protocol that is transmitted over the socket is "0D0A." Once the server receives this data, it is expected to respond with its host name. While this example may seem a bit contrived, it turns out (as will be seen later) that this protocol really exists as a subset of the Internet finger protocol. Try using a telnet application to connect to port 79 on an Internet host (the finger port), and hitting the enter key. If a finger server is listening, it should tell you the host name.

CHAPTER SUMMARY

This chapter provided a general purpose definition of a directory as a *property-based information retrieval system*. This definition will be used throughout the book. A simple example of a directory was given. This chapter defined computer and network security as they are used by directories. Additionally, the various upper layers of the Internet protocol stack were defined. Finally, a quick overview of some of the important directories was given.

With this foundation of computer networking and security, as well as a quick overview of some directories and their applications, we can progress into more detailed definitions in the chapters to come. The following chapters will give detailed descriptions of DNS, LDAP, and many of their applications, as well as shorter overviews of some other Internet directories.

## CHAPTER 3

Domain Name System

The Domain Name System (DNS) is defined in RFC 1034 and 1035, and was the first Internet directory service that was widely deployed. The rationale for the creation of DNS was to solve the problem of host-name-to-IP address resolution on the Internet. Prior to the existence of DNS, Internet hosts relied upon the existence of a local file that contained a list of host-name-to-IP address mappings. No host ever had to look beyond this one file to find the IP address that corresponded to the host name of some other Internet host. The problem with this model was due to the fact that this "hosts" file was centrally administered for the entire Internet, and each time a new host was added to the Internet, a new host file had to be generated and distributed to each Internet host. This solution was becoming completely unmanageable at the time of DNS's creation, as the number of hosts connected to the Internet was increasing daily, beyond the few hundred Internet connected hosts that were in existence in the early '80s.

Local area networks were being installed at various sites that increased the number of hosts by several hundred at a time. The administrators of these networks wanted to be able to administer their own IP address spaces without having to notify the entire Internet every time any change to their network hosts was made. Any time a host was added to the network, removed from the network, or had its IP address changed, the administrator had to notify the entire Internet. In response to this pressure, DNS was proposed as the replacement of the centrally administered host file scheme. The implementation of DNS met the requirements with a distributed database of information rather than a centrally administered hosts file. As was noted before, the distributed administration of directory administration devised by DNS was to become a hallmark for virtually all of the Internet directory services that were to follow.

DNS is administered in a distributed manner that allows each organization that is connected to the Internet to administer its own namespace. Furthermore, DNS allows for many different types of information to be associated with each Internet-connected host. Each piece of information that is associated with an Internet host corresponds to one of the DNS defined record types. For example, the most common record type that is used in DNS is the *address record*, which lists a host name and the corresponding Internet address. Another common record that is found in DNS is the *start of authority resource record* that gives the network administrator's contact information (e.g., name and electronic mail address). The number of resource record types that are available for retrieval via the DNS defined protocols has continued to grow since DNS was first implemented.

DNS HIERARCHY

The information that is stored in the DNS distributed database, known as the DNS namespace, is organized in a hierarchical manner that is typically illustrated as a tree structure, as in Figure 3.1 (taken from RFC 1034).

This figure shows the Internet hosts structured in a manner that is similar to a typical corporate organizational chart. In this hierarchy, the root is typically represented by the symbol ".", as are the connections between levels in the hierarchy. Thus, the three leaf host names at the bottom of the diagram are given the names: *mail.isi.edu, news.isi.edu,* and *www.isi.edu.* Each box in the DNS hierarchy is known as a domain. The administration for that domain is responsible for administering all domains beneath it in the DNS hierarchy. Thus, the administrators at *isi.edu* are responsible for handling the naming of all of *isi.edu's* subdomains (e.g., *mail.isi.edu, news.isi.edu* , and *www.isi.edu*).

Not only are the administrators responsible for the naming of the hosts within their subdomains, they are also responsible for assigning an IP address to each of the hosts. Even though modern techniques allow the IP address for most hosts to be assigned automatically, the DNS database must still be updated when the IP address is assigned to a host. DNS provides the mechanisms whereby system administrators are able to allow other systems to discover these host-to-IP address mappings.

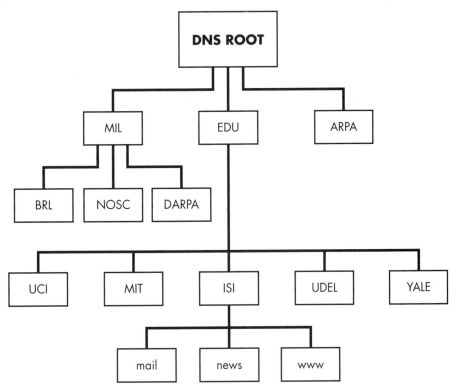

Fig. 3.1 DNS hierarchy.

DNS RESOURCE RECORDS

The standardized format for the resource data associated with a particular host name is known as a *resource record*. DNS specifies the format of a resource record as it is passed across the network. DNS does not specify the format of a resource record in the system administrator's local file system.

A common misconception about DNS is that the resource record formats and files that are associated with the DNS server, Berkeley Internet Name Domain (BIND), actually form part of the DNS protocol. This is due to the fact that BIND is the most common implementation of DNS servers that is used on Internet hosts. Even though the BIND format is based upon the original format that was centrally administered and then distributed about the Internet prior to DNS, it is not specifically part of any DNS standardized protocol. The BIND format is also used in the DNS standard as the "textual expression of resource records." DNS servers do not necessarily use this as their storage format. As an example of the textual expression, consider the following resource record that represents the mapping of a fictitious host name, *bruce.greenblatt.com,* to its IP address as given in the textual expression in Table 3.1:

Table 3.1 Textual Resource Record Format

Name	Record type	IP address
Bruce.greenblatt.com	A	10.0.2.27

Taken by itself, this resource record indicates that the host named by *bruce.greenblatt.com* can be found at the IP address 10.0.2.27. The field between the host name and the IP address indicates the record type, which in this case is the "address" or "A" record type. Different resource record types identify different properties that are stored in DNS. These types are defined in various RFCs, including the RFCs that define the DNS standard (1034 and 1035). All of the different standardized resource record types are listed at the web site of the Internet Assigned Numbers Authority (IANA). Some of the more useful resource record types are listed in Table 3.2.

Table 3.2 Common DNS Resource Records

Record Type	Numeric Identifier	Meaning
A	1	Host address
NS	2	Authoritative name server
CNAME	5	The canonical name for an alias
SOA	6	Start of a zone of authority
WKS	11	Description of a well known service
PTR	12	A pointer to some other domain name
MX	15	Mail exchange record
TXT	16	Comments and other unformatted textual data
RP	17	Responsible person
SIG	24	Security signature used in DNS Security Extensions (RFC 2065)
KEY	25	Security key used in DNS security extensions
SRV	33	Service type record (RFC 2052)
NAPTR	35	Naming authority pointer (RFC 2168)
IXFR	251	Incremental zone transfer (RFC 1995)
AXFR	252	Transfer on an entire zone

As might be surmised from the missing numeric identifiers in the above table, there are many other resource record types that have been defined, but those listed are most common.

DNS CLIENT/SERVER OPERATION

DNS is implemented as a distributed service that operates in a client-server manner. DNS provides three main features:

☞ Standard formats for resource data.

☞ Standard methods for querying the database.

☞ Standard methods for name servers to refresh local data from name servers that are from outside of the local domain. For example, allow the *yale.edu* domain to get an update of DNS resource records from the *mit.edu* domain.

DNS clients are known as *resolvers*, and DNS servers are known as *servers*. Note that DNS does not define a mechanism to enter data into the DNS database. It only provides the mechanism that allows the servers to provide the data to resolvers and to other servers. Typically, a DNS server provides some mechanism for the system administrator to create and modify the local copy of the master files. An administrator is only allowed to modify information for the hosts for which he has responsibility. For example, using the domain names from the hierarchy depicted in Figure 3.1, the administrator for *mit.edu*'s domain would not be allowed to make changes to the DNS information for the *yale.edu* domain.

When passing across the network between a DNS resolver and a DNS server, the textual format mentioned in Table 3.1 is not used. Instead, a more compressed binary format is used. In this instance, the binary format for this resource record would appear simply as the 32-bit representation of the IP address. In order to understand how this transformation is made, consider Figure 3.2.

In this figure, the operation of DNS in its simplest form is shown. A single resolver queries a single name server that is able to determine the appropriate response by searching its local database of resource data. In the normal deployment, every computer in the network contains a DNS resolver, and there are several name servers deployed in the network as well. DNS defines a concept known as *recursion*. Recursion allows a DNS query to be forwarded from one name server to a second name server.

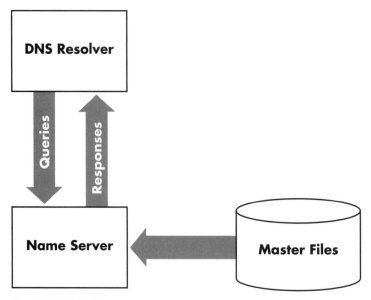

Fig. 3.2 DNS client/server operation.

The second name server returns a response to the first name server, which will finally return the result to the resolver. Theoretically, the second name server could have operated recursively as well. In this case, it would have forwarded the query to a third name server instead of answering the query itself. The administrator generally configures whether or not the name server acts recursively. The administrator also configures the other name servers to which recursive queries are forwarded. Figure 3.3 illustrates recursive query support.

In this situation, the resolver issues a query. The name server in its domain does not have sufficient information in its database to answer the query. This name server then acts in the role of a resolver and submits a new query to another name server that it thinks might have the answer to the original query. This new name server will eventually return a response to this query that the original name server uses to formulate its response to the original query.

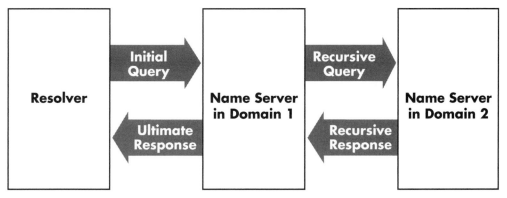

Fig. 3.3 DNS recursive query.

STRUCTURE OF DNS DATA

The reason that the address record above is translated into the 32 bit IP address—and that the host name doesn't need to appear—is due to the overall format of the resource records in the DNS query/response protocol. All resource records share the same general format in the protocol, which is shown in Figure 3.4.

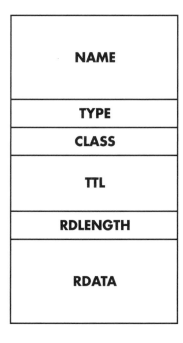

Fig. 3.4 DNS resource record structure.

The definitions of the fields that make up the resource record from RFC 1035 are as follows:

- ☞ NAME: an owner name, i.e., the name of the node to which this resource record pertains.
- ☞ TYPE: two bytes containing one of the resource record TYPE codes.
- ☞ CLASS: two bytes containing one of the resource record CLASS codes.
- ☞ TTL: a 32-bit signed integer that specifies the time interval (in seconds) that the resource record may be cached before the source of the information should again be consulted. This is the Time To Live (TTL) for the record.
- ☞ RDLENGTH: an unsigned 16-bit integer that specifies the length in octets of the RDATA field.
- ☞ RDATA: a variable length string of octets that describes the resource. The format of this information varies according to the TYPE and CLASS of the resource record.

Consider again the "A" resource record given in Table 3.1.

Table 3.3 Sample Resource Record Layout

Field Name	Field Value	Comment
Name	*bruce.greenblatt.com*	Host that "owns" the data.
Type	1	The numeric identifier for an "A" record is 1. See Table 3.2.
Class	1	This is an Internet resource record.
TTL	604800	Check for an update of this record in a week.
RDLENGTH	4	RDATA is four bytes long.
RDATA	0x0A00021B	32-bit representation of 10.0.2.27.

Notice that the DNS format for the A record uses the 32-bit representation of the IP address. The dotted notation for IP addresses is just a convenience to allow them to be read more easily by humans. They are translated into a 32-bit integer representation for various uses by computers, such as in the protocol used between DNS resolvers and name servers. IP version 4 uses this 32-bit representation of IP addresses, while version 6 of IP uses a 64-bit representation. Each decimal number in the dotted notation encodes one byte of the 32-bit address. So,

10.0.2.27 would be represented as the 32-bit hexadecimal value 0x0A00021B. Hexadecimal uses base 16 digits (0-9 then A-F), and it takes two hexadecimal digits to make up one 8-bit byte.

The resource records comprise one element of the queries and responses that are exchanged between the resolver and server. These queries and responses share a common format as in Figure 3.5.

This common format is known in the DNS protocol as a *message*. Each of the sections has a meaning as defined in RFC 1035. The header section is present in all DNS messages. It describes the meaning of the message, and which of the following four sections is also present. The header section follows the format shown in Figure 3.6.

Header
Question
Answer
Authority
Additional

Fig. 3.5 DNS query response format.

ID							
Q R	OPCODE	A A	T C	R D	R A	Z	RCODE
QDCOUNT							
ANCOUNT							
NSCOUNT							
ARCOUNT							

Fig. 3.6 DNS message header format.

The fields are defined as follows:

☞ ID: The ID (Identifier) field contains a 16-bit resolver assigned identifier for the message. This is needed in situations where the resolver has more than one query outstanding to servers. The server copies the ID field from the query into the response, and the resolver uses the ID field in the response message to match it up with the query message that had previously been submitted.

☞ QR: The QR (Query/Response) field is 1 bit long, and indicates whether the message contains a query (0) or a response (1).

☞ OPCODE: The OPCODE (OPeration CODE) is a 4-bit field that is used in queries to identify the type of query. This field almost always has the value 0 to indicate a standard query. Other values for the OPCODE are: 1 for an inverse query and 2 for a server status query. Inverse queries will be defined later in the section on PTR records. Status queries are an experimental service that was never defined in the DNS standard. Values 3 through 15 are reserved by DNS for future use.

☞ AA: The AA (Authoritative Answer) bit is set to 1 in a response if the responding name server is authoritative for a domain name in the question.

☞ TC: The TC (TrunCation) bit is set to 1 if the message has been truncated due to an inadequacy of the transmission channel to handle the length of the message. This is normally only seen in a response. For example, if DNS is being used over UDP, and a transfer of all of the "A" records for the ".com" domain is requested, then the TC bit would more than likely be set. This is due to the fact that the large number of top-level domains would not fit in a single UDP packet.

☞ RD: The RD (Recursion Desired) bit is set in queries when the resolver desires recursive query support. Name servers are not required to support recursion. If a name server does support recursion, then it will act as a resolver to some other name server, and submit a new query on behalf of the initial resolver. The name server only acts in this recursive manner if it does not have the answer to the query locally.

☞ RA: A name server sets the RA (Recursion Available) bit in responses to indicate that recursive support is available.

☞ Z: The 4-bit Z (Zero) field is always 0, and is reserved for future use.

☞ RCODE: The RCODE (Response CODE) field contains the response code from the name server. RCODE is zero if no error occurred. Otherwise, RCODE contains one of several DNS defined error codes.

☞ QDCOUNT: The QDCOUNT field is an unsigned 16-bit integer indicating the number of entries in the question section.

☞ ANCOUNT: The ANCOUNT field is an unsigned 16-bit integer indicating the number of entries in the answer section.

☞ NSCOUNT: The NSCOUNT field is an unsigned 16-bit integer indicating the number of entries in the authority section.

☞ ARCOUNT: The ARCOUNT field is an unsigned 16-bit integer indicating the number of entries in the additional record section.

The question section describes the query that the resolver is submitting to a server. The question section contains three fields: a query class (QCLASS), a query type (QTYPE), and a query domain name (QNAME). The QCLASS field is a two-byte field that indicates the class of the query, and in practice is always IN for Internet queries. The QTYPE field indicates the type of the query and contains the type of resource record or records that is requested. For example, if the resolver were interested in an address or "A" record, then the QTYPE field would hold the value 1. Other values for the type will be discussed later at some length. The QNAME field contains a domain name represented as a sequence of labels, where each label consists of a length byte followed by that number of bytes. The domain name terminates with the zero length byte for the null label of the root.

As an example, consider the query that the resolver would submit to the server asking for the "A" record for the host named by "bruce.greenblatt.com." The header section fields would be set as shown in Table 3.4.

Table 3.4 Sample DNS Query

Field Name	Field Value	Comments
ID	0	Unique identifier for the query
QR	0	0 indicates query
AA	0	Only applies to responses
TC	0	Only applies to responses
RA	0	Only applies to responses
RCODE	0	Only applies to responses
RD	1	Allow for recursive operation
Z	0	Always 0!

Table 3.4 Sample DNS Query (continued)

Field Name	Field Value	Comments
QDCOUNT	1	Only one entry in the question section
ANCOUNT	0	Only applies to responses
NSCOUNT	0	Only applies to responses
ARCOUNT	0	Only applies to responses
QCLASS	1	Internet Class
QTYPE	1	Numeric identifier for "A" record
QNAME	"bruce.greenblatt.com"	Domain names to search for. Null domain name would also be present.

This query is enclosed in hexadecimal as shown in Table 3.5.

Table 3.5 Hexadecimal Encoding of the DNS Query

Header Section	0000 0100 0001 0000 0000 0000
Question Section	1462 7275 6365 2E67 7265 656E 626C 6174 742E 636F 6D00 0001 0001

Note that in the question section, 1462 7275 6365 2E67 7265 656E 626C 6174 742E 636F 6D, the ASCII encoding of the string is "bruce.greenblatt.com." This query can be represented in Figure 3.7, which omits many of the unneeded fields of the query.

A similar request from the resolver to get "all" records would use the special QTYPE value of 255. This would allow the resolver to receive all DNS resource data that is associated with the host "bruce.greenblatt.com." This query would keep all but the QTYPE field of the question section the same, and change it to have the value 255. The response from the server would be represented as shown in Figure 3.8.

OPCODE = STANDARD, ID = 0
QCLASS = IN, QTYPE = "A", **QNAME = "bruce.greenblatt.com"**
<empty>
<empty>
<empty>

Fig. 3.7 DNS query for an "A" resource record.

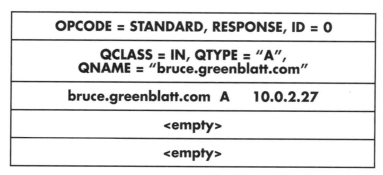

OPCODE = STANDARD, RESPONSE, ID = 0
QCLASS = IN, QTYPE = "A", QNAME = "bruce.greenblatt.com"
bruce.greenblatt.com A   10.0.2.27
<empty>
<empty>

Fig. 3.8 DNS response containing an "A" resource record.

Notice that the question is copied from the query into the response. The hexadecimal representation of this DNS message displayed in Table 3.6.

Table 3.6 Hexadecimal Encoding of the DNS Response

Header section	8000 0100 0001 0001 0000 0000
Question section	1462 7275 6365 2E67 7265 656E 626C 6174 742E 636F 6D00 0001 0001
Answer section	1462 7275 6365 2E67 7265 656E 626C 6174 742E 636F 6D00 0100 0109 3A80 040A 0002 1B

This illustrates the conversion of the graphical display of the DNS message (which is significantly easier for most humans to read) into the hexadecimal format which is used in the actual DNS protocol. For the remainder of the chapter, only the graphical format will be used.

This chapter has shown how DNS can be used to provide a property-based information retrieval system. So far, the only properties that have been mentioned are host names and IP addresses. The object that these properties belong to is an Internet Host. There are many more properties which can be retrieved via DNS that are of interest.

It is the responsibility of the name server in DNS to provide answers to the questions that resolvers ask. In DNS, these answers take the form of a set of resource records. Not only is the name server expected to provide the answer, it is also expected to know where to find the answer when its local database does not contain the appropriate resource records. This is due to the fact that the typical resolver is configured with the location of only one name server, and if this one name server does not have the appropriate resource record, then the resolver will be unable to get the resource record.

The text up until now has assumed that the questions the resolvers are allowed to ask are restricted to retrieving the IP address corresponding to a host name. But, as Table 3.2 implies, resource records can contain many other pieces of information other than just the IP address mapping. It is important to note that in DNS any resource record is describing some property about an Internet host or domain. The Internet host to which a resource record refers is given in the Name section of the resource record as shown in Table 3.4 (page 46).

SOA Records

A resource record that provides several pieces of useful information is the Start Of Authority (SOA) resource record. The SOA RDATA field layout is shown in Figure 3.9.

As do all resource record definitions given here, the SOA record makes up the RDATA portion of the resource record as shown in Figure 3.4. The SOA resource record gives information about the naming authority for a host name. This naming authority is responsible for administering a particular zone of DNS. The header fields of the SOA record are described in Table 3.7.

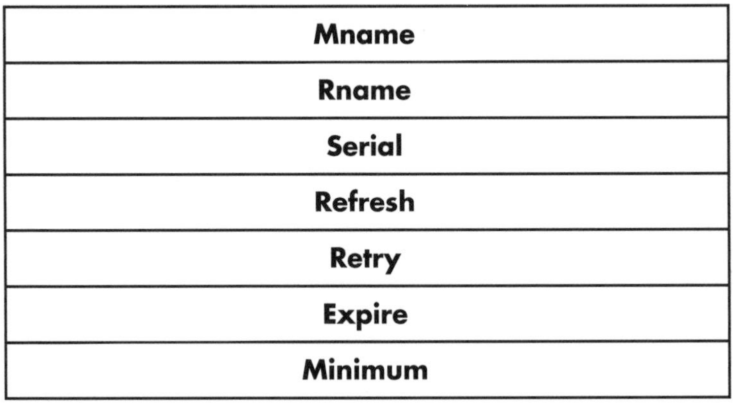

Mname
Rname
Serial
Refresh
Retry
Expire
Minimum

Fig. 3.9 SOA resource record.

Table 3.7 Fields in the SOA Resource Record

Field Name	Description
Mname	Name of the host on which this resource record was created.
Rname	The e-mail address for a contact point for this host.
Serial	The number of times the host information has been changed, which is in effect the version number (32-bit number).
Refresh	How often the zone information should be updated in seconds (32-bit number).
Retry	How long to wait, in seconds, before retrying to refresh the data for this zone (32-bit number).
Expire	How long, in seconds, until the data for this zone is no longer good (32-bit number).
Minimum	The minimum time, in seconds, that a name server should hold this resource record before refreshing it. This is known as the "Time To Live" (TTL).

The TTL is an important concept in DNS, and is DNS's attempt to guarantee that all information retrieved from it is current. The TTL associated with a resource record assures that a name server does not cache the data associated with the record forever. The TTL field in resource records gives the number of seconds that a name server is allowed to hold the data. After the TTL period, the name server is expected to discard the information in the resource record and get new data from the authoritative name server. Some resource records even have a TTL value of zero, which insures that this information is never cached, and must be retrieved from the authoritative name server each time the information is requested by a resolver. The SOA record is one such resource record. The TTL field in the RDATA field of an SOA resource record is information that applies to the other resource records in the zone to which the SOA refers. There is only one SOA record for any particular zone.

NS Records

The NS resource record gives information about the name servers that are available in a particular domain. DNS requires that all zones be supported by more than one name server. In any zone of DNS there is one primary name server, and one or more secondary name servers. Secondary name servers acquire their DNS information from the primary name server in their domain. This allows for easier administration of name servers. The primary name server bootstraps itself with information from its local database. The secondary name servers bootstrap themselves with information that they retrieve from the primary name server. This transfer of information between name servers is known in DNS as a zone transfer. As DNS resource records expire (their TTL expires), the secondary name servers will periodically query the primary name server to keep their information current. The use of secondary name servers is shown in Figure 3.10.

The resolver can submit queries to either the primary name server or the secondary name server. Normally, resolvers use the secondary name server. The primary name server is used to distribute updates to all of the secondary name servers. It is common to have many secondary name servers for a single domain. Resolvers in different parts of the domain will use different secondary name servers. This allows administrators to attempt to balance the amount of queries that are submitted across all of the name servers so that no one name server is overburdened. The DNS administrator will only update the information in the primary name server. The updates will later be reflected on the secondary name servers after the next zone transfer.

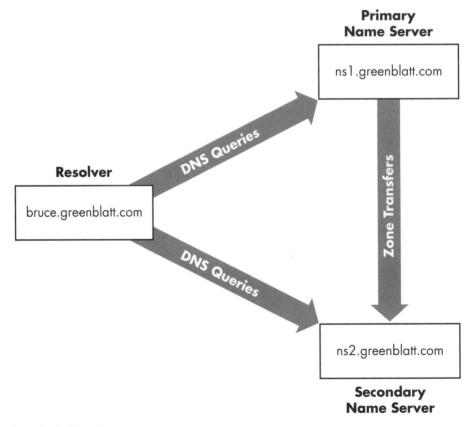

Fig. 3.10 Use of secondary name servers.

In DNS the NS RDATA field has the format that contains only one field that gives the host name that is authoritative for the specified domain. This means that since there is always more than one DNS record for a particular domain, there is always more than one host that is authoritative for a particular domain as well. A typical request reply exchange for the NS record is shown in Figure 3.11.

In Figure 3.11 it is shown that in response to the resolver's request for NS records, two separate resource records are returned in the answer section of the DNS message. Even though it is omitted in the figure, the

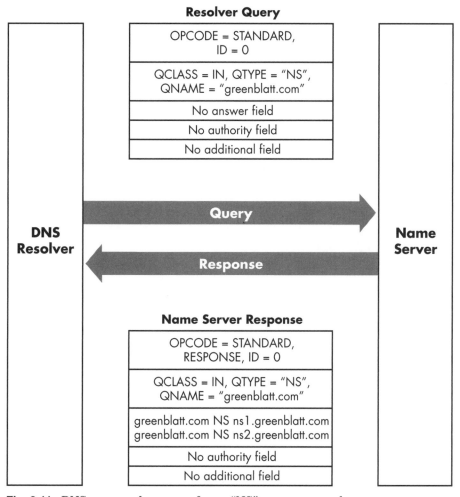

Fig. 3.11 DNS query and response for an "NS" resource record.

CLASS of the resource records is IN. One might wonder what the real purpose of the NS record is in DNS, since it was previously mentioned that most resolvers are statically configured with the IP address of a primary and secondary name server. It is often the case that resource records from "foreign" domains must be retrieved. This situation normally arises for resolvers that are attached to name servers.

Consider the situation for a resolver in one domain (greenblatt.com) that needs the "A" resource record of a host in a second domain (prenhall.com). If the record is not in the greenblatt.com name server's database, then the information should be retrieved from the name server for prenhall.com. The problem with this is that ns.greenblatt.com does not know the name server to contact in the prenhall.com domain. So, ns.greenblatt.com would attempt to contact the name server for a more knowledgeable domain; in this case, the name server for the .com domain could be contacted. So, ns.greenblatt.com, acting in the role of a resolver, would contact the .com name server and query for the "NS" record for the prenhall.com domain. Then ns.greenblatt.com would request the "A" record for whatever server is acting as prenhall.com's name server. Assuming that this name server is ns.prenhall.com, ns.greenblatt.com contacts ns.prenhall.com (again, acting in the role of a resolver) and requests the "A" resource record that the original resolver had requested. Upon receiving this information, ns.greenblatt.com finally returns the resource record to the original resolver. This is illustrated in Figure 3.12.

In this illustration, the results coming back are not shown. The results to the operations labeled 2, 3, and 4 do get returned to the appropriate resolvers in the numerical order of the labels. Queries 2 and 3 should be issued as separate DNS messages. This is due to the fact that there is no way of knowing what host might be the name server for the prenhall.com domain. The prenhall.com name server need not be in the prenhall.com domain at all. So, ns.greenblatt.com must first find the name server for prenhall.com, and then once this host name is known, its IP address is retrieved from the "A" record.

After ns.prenhall.com returns the result for query number 4 to ns.greenblatt.com, the result of query number 1 is returned to the original resolver. Depending upon the configuration of the name server at ns.greenblatt.com when it contacts ns.prenhall.com, it might request more information than was originally requested by the resolver. For example, query number 4 could make a request for all the records associated with test.prenhall.com, or perhaps request a zone transfer for the domain prenhall.com. By doing this, the name server would be able to add resource information to its database, and is able to answer subsequent queries itself, without having to refer to other name servers.

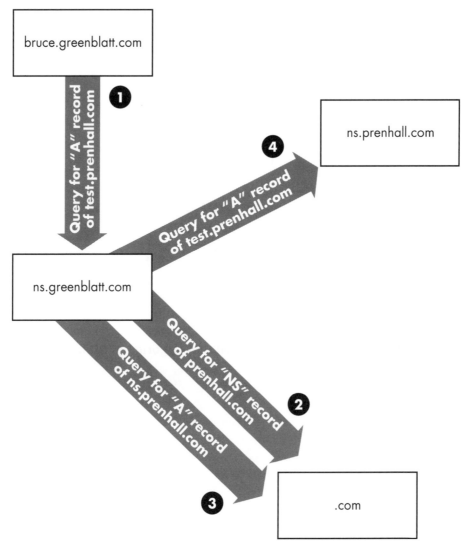

Fig. 3.12 DNS operating in a distributed fashion for the retrieval of an "NS" resource record.

In making the request to the .com name server, it is possible that ns.greenblatt.com would be likely to receive a *referral result*, rather than an actual answer. A referral occurs when a name server is unwilling or unable to act recursively, and instead points the resolver to another name server. A recursive result is illustrated in Figure 3.13.

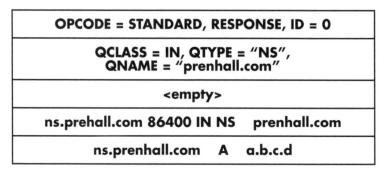

| OPCODE = STANDARD, RESPONSE, ID = 0 |
| QCLASS = IN, QTYPE = "NS", QNAME = "prenhall.com" |
| <empty> |
| ns.prehall.com 86400 IN NS   prenhall.com |
| ns.prenhall.com   A   a.b.c.d |

Fig. 3.13 DNS recursive result format.

Notice that the answer is empty in this DNS message. This is the indication in DNS to the resolver that it has received a referral, and that the name server is not going to perform a recursive query on behalf of the resolver. In addition, the header section of this message may also turn off the RA bit indicating that recursion is not available.

CNAME Records

CNAME records are among the most common records that appear in DNS. A CNAME record is present for a host name that is actually an alias for some other host name. This situation arises when more than one host name refers to the same physical node. If mail.prenhall.com and www.prenhall.com (prenhall.com's mail server and web server) are actually located on the same machine (services.prenhall.com) then there might be two CNAME records in prenhall.com's domain, as shown in Table 3.8.

Table 3.8 Sample CNAME Resource Records

Owner Name	Class	Record Type	RDATA Value
mail.prenhall.com	IN	CNAME	services.prenhall.com
www.prenhall.com	IN	CNAME	services.prenhall.com

This is an indication that these three host names all refer to the same underlying node. Thus, a query for the "A" record for any of the three of these host names would return precisely the same IP address. In response to the query for the "A" resource record for www.prenhall.com, the name server returns both the CNAME record and the corresponding "A" record in the answer section. The RDATA format for a CNAME record is simply the host name of the alias. Thus, the RDATA of the CNAME record for the host www.prenhall.com would contain the host services.prenhall.com.

WKS Records

An interesting resource record that is unfortunately not widely deployed is the WKS (Well Known Services) record. This resource record is intended to describe the various services that are deployed on a particular host (e.g., e-mail, directory, web services). The WKS resource record contains the RDATA format as shown in Figure 3.14.

The address field is the 32-bit IP address of the server. The protocol field is the 8-bit Internet protocol number. The format of an IP packet is reasonably complex, and a complete discussion of the format is described in RFC 791 and in numerous, excellent texts on computer networks.[1] It is simplified substantially in Figure 3.15.

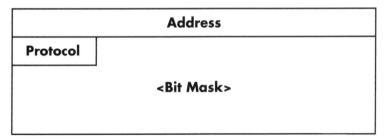

Fig. 3.14 WKS resource record RDATA format.

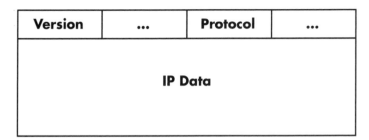

Fig. 3.15 IP packet format.

---

[1] One excellent reference that includes a discussion of IP is *Interconnections, Second Edition: Bridges, Routers, Switches, and Internetworking Protocols*, by Perlman, Radia.

Note that numerous fields in the IP packet have been omitted in the above figure. The version field appears first and indicates which version of IP is being used. The current widely deployed version of IP is 4. The field in the IP packet that is of interest here is the protocol field. This field identifies the upper layer protocol that is used in the data portion of the packet. For example, TCP uses protocol number 6, while UDP uses protocol number 17. So, if the protocol field of an IP packet is 6, then the IP data would contain a TCP packet.

The bit mask of the WKS resource record defines what services appear on this host. Each WKS has a registered well-known port number with IANA. Recall that the well-known ports are numbered from 0 to 1023. The first bit in the bit mask corresponds to port zero, the second bit to port one and so on, until bit number 1024 corresponds to port 1023. Thus, if a host has services for supporting SMTP, LDAP, HTTP, and DNS over TCP, then the protocol field would have the value 0x06, and the bit mask would have bits 26, 54, 81, and 390 set to one, and all other bits set to zero. The bit mask is always a multiple of 8 bits long, and should never be more than 1024 bits (or 128 bytes long). In the above example, the bit mask would need to be only 49 bytes long, as that would be enough to accommodate 390 bits. Similarly, if the host also supported LDAP and DNS over UDP, then the protocol field would have the value 0x11, and the bit mask would have bits 54 and 390 set.

It is interesting to ponder why the WKS resource record was never widely used. Probably, because it places a large burden on the administrator to keep all of the WKS records updated for a domain. This is especially the case when one considers the fact that most DNS administrators configured that domain by text editing their host files. Given such a mechanism that is prone to error, the administrator would naturally want to make as few entries and changes as possible. As more and more application services would become available, and possibly move from one host to another, the administrator would be constantly updating the host files. The other problem is that most applications never consulted the DNS to look up the WKS records, but instead required the application client to be statically configured with the name of the application server.

For example, an e-mail client could make use of the local resolver to find the WKS records in the local domain for SMTP (for electronic mail submission) and POP (for electronic mail retrieval) servers, but this rarely (if ever) happens. Instead, the user must dutifully enter the names of the SMTP and POP servers in order to configure the e-mail client appropriately. Service type (SRV) resource records (which will be discussed shortly) are another (later) attempt to use DNS to help configure clients.

PTR Records

The PTR resource record was defined in the original DNS RFC. The PTR resource record includes a pointer from one point in the DNS name space to another. In the case of the PTR record, it was designed to enable inverse address to host name lookups. In this situation, the PTR record would point to the specially defined domain name "IN-ADDR.ARPA." This domain name is used exclusively for inverse IP address to host name lookups. The PTR record has the exact same format as a CNAME record, which is that the RDATA portion only includes the domain name that is pointed to be the owner of the record. See Figure 3.16 for the RDATA of the PTR records.

A PTR type query is used to get the resource record (RR) with the primary name of the host. For example, a request for the host name corresponding to IP address 1.2.3.4 looks for PTR RRs for domain name "4.3.2.1.IN-ADDR.ARPA." One of the problems in inverse lookups for most implementations of name servers is that they rely upon the DNS administrator to create the PTR records that look like the following examples from 1034 (see Table 3.9).

Table 3.9 PTR resource record example

Owner Name	Type	PTRDNAME
52.0.0.10.IN-ADDR.ARPA	PTR	C.ISI.EDU
73.0.0.26.IN-ADDR.ARPA	PTR	SRI-NIC.ARPA
65.0.6.26.IN-ADDR.ARPA	PTR	ACC.ARPA
51.0.0.10.IN-ADDR.ARPA	PTR	SRI-NIC.ARPA

One might imagine that the maintenance cost of the PTR records is not troublesome, since every time a host moves or is added the administrator need only update the "PTR" record at the same time that the "A" record has to be updated. Unfortunately, in common implementations of name servers, nothing forces "PTR" records and "A" records to be synchronized. It is better for the IN-ADDR.ARPA namespace to be missing rather than inaccurate. PTR records are supposed to point to the primary host name rather than to an alias (the alias is indicated by the CNAME record), so they only appear occasionally in the host file, since

```
|  PTRDNAME  |
```

Fig. 3.16 PTR resource record RDATA format.

most hosts that are known are aliases rather than primary names. All of these factors contribute to the fact that PTR queries will often not return any data at all since the administrator has made the decision not to create these resource records in the host file. Hopefully, modern name servers will be able to automatically infer the existence of a "PTR" record from the existence of an "A" record, which will remove the burden of the maintenance of PTR records from the DNS administrator. Similarly, DHCP servers, which allow for the dynamic assignment of IP addresses, could automatically update the DNS database whenever an IP address assignment is made or deleted.

TXT Records

TXT records exist in the DNS in order for the DNS administrator to provide unformatted comments about a particular host or domain. The RDATA format of the TXT record simply holds the text of the comment, as indicated in Figure 3.17.

The TXT DATA that is found can indicate virtually anything, but the precise meaning (if any) is completely dependent upon the domain in which it is found. TXT records commonly include data about the location of the host, what it is used for, and any other comments that are appropriate for the host. For example, a TXT record could be used to indicate which port number a particular application service is using. Recalling the Simple Directory (SD) service of the previous chapter, assume that upon installation, the server inserts a TXT record of the form: "SD: nnnn," where the number nnnn refers to the port number upon which the SD server for that host is listening. Thus, when an SD client wants to contact the SD server for a particular host, it would first get the TXT records for that host, and look for one that had the prefix "SD:". If such a TXT record were found, the SD client would then attempt to open a socket on the indicated port number. Thus, SD makes clever use of DNS so that it does not have to register a well-known port number with IANA. On the down side, because SD is dependent upon the existence of TXT records, which may be deleted by administrators or overwritten by other applications, it is a little dangerous to depend upon the long term existence of these records. Thus, the SD server should continuously check the DNS to ensure that the appropriate information is still intact.

TXT-DATA

Fig. 3.17   TXT resource record RDATA format.

The TXT DATA is normally formatted as a sequence of character strings enclosed in quotes. Within the quotes, any character can appear, except the quote mark itself, which must be preceded by the backslash character ('\'). So, the following TXT records might appear (see Table 3.10).

Table 3.10 Text Resource Record Example

Owner Name	Class	Type	TXT Data
Greenblatt.com	IN	TXT	"If you see Bruce, say \"HI!\""

RP Records

RP records were defined in RFC 1183 after the publication of the original DNS standard. The problem they solve is to allow the person responsible for a particular host or domain to be found. The information that is given for this responsible person is the e-mail address. The format of the RDATA section for an RP resource record is shown in Figure 3.18.

Table 3.11 shows an example of the use of an RP record according to RFC 1183.

Table 3.11 Sample RP Resource Records

sayshell.umd.edu	A	128.8.1.14	
	MX	10	sayshell.umd.edu
	HINFO	NeXT UNIX	
	WKS	128.8.1.14	tcp ftp telnet smtp
	RP	louie.trantor.umd.edu	LAM1.people.umd.edu
LAM1.people.umd.edu	TXT	("Louis A. Mamakos, (301) 454-2946, don't call me at home!")	

mbox-dname
txt-dname

Fig. 3.18 RP resource record RDATA format.

The host "sayshell.umd.edu" has, among other records, an RP record that has the mbox-dname of "louie.trantor.umd.edu." This is the DNS representation of an e-mail address. To obtain a real e-mail address, substitute an @ for the first period in the name. In this case, this results in the e-mail address of "louie@trantor.umd.edu." The second part of the RDATA for the RP record is a pointer to the TXT record of some other domain name, which in this case is "LAM1.people.umd.edu." This is an indication that, in situations when more information about the responsible person is needed, it can be found by retrieving the TXT records for the name given. In this situation, the subsequent retrieval of the TXT record yields the actual name and phone number of the administrator. The RP record shows the interaction between resource records for one host and the resource records for another host. This interaction is more complex than that used in the CNAME records. In the CNAME record, one host name is used just as a substitution for another host name.

MX Records

The MX record is designed to facilitate the routing and delivery of SMTP-based electronic mail. The Simple Mail Transfer Protocol (SMTP) is defined in RFCs 821 and 822. SMTP is the Internet standard mechanism for sending and formatting electronic mail. SMTP operates in a client/server manner. An SMTP client (also known as a sender-SMTP) contacts an SMTP server (also known as a receiver-SMTP) when it has a message to send. Once an SMTP client opens a connection with an SMTP server and identifies itself (with the "MAIL FROM" command), it lists the intended recipients for the message by their e-mail addresses (with the "RCPT TO" command). A typical SMTP conversation is represented in Table 3.12.

Table 3.12 Typical SMTP Conversation

Client or Server	Command	Comment
Client command	MAIL FROM:<bruce@greenblatt.com>	Client identification
Server response	250 OK	Command accepted
Client command	RCPT TO:<alice@greenblatt.com>	First recipient
Server response	250 OK	Command accepted
Client command	RCPT TO:<bob@greenblatt.com>	Second recipient
Server response	550 No such user here	Error code
Client command	RCPT TO: <louie@trantor.umd.edu>	Third recipient
Server response	251 User not local; will forward to <louie@trantor.umd.edu>	Command accepted
Client command	...	Continue with more recipients and message text.

Some of the message recipients are not local to the SMTP server. For those recipients (in this case <louie@trantor.umd.edu>) that are not local, the SMTP server must relay the message to some other servers. In order to relay the message the SMTP server must contact some other SMTP server that will be able to deliver the message to the intended recipient. In some cases, there may be more than one relay step along the way, and a single message may be relayed amongst several SMTP servers before it reaches its ultimate destination. In this case, let's assume that this SMTP server will contact the SMTP server that is responsible for delivering the messages for the host: trantor.umd.edu. It finds out which server to use by consulting DNS in order to retrieve the MX record for trantor.umd.edu.

The MX record is also known as the Mail eXchange record. Its RDATA section has the following format (see Figure 3.19).

The preference field is a two-byte integer that indicates the preference given to this resource record with respect to other MX records with the same owner. The exchange field contains the name of a host that is willing to act as an exchange for this owner name. The MX record allows for a scheme of routing electronic mail that allows for a level of indirec-

Preference
Exchange

Fig. 3.19 MX resource record RDATA format.

tion. In the original scheme, if you had mail that needed to go to a user on a particular host (e.g., phil@prenhall.com), you just opened a socket to prenhall.com on the SMTP port and started executing the SMTP protocol to get your mail delivered to Phil. This scheme is unacceptable for several reasons. It places a single point of failure for e-mail delivery on prenhall.com. If it is ever unavailable, mail for the entire domain doesn't get delivered. For large domains, it places a heavy burden for routing electronic mail on a single host.

For these reasons (and others), an indirect scheme of routing electronic mail was devised. In order to deliver mail to users on a host (e.g., prenhall.com) instead of opening a socket directly to prenhall.com, the MX records for prenhall.com are retrieved. These records might appear as those seen in Table 3.13.

Table 3.13 Sample MX Resource Records

Host Name	Class	Type	Weight	Mail host
Prenhall.com	IN	MX	10	mail1.prenhall.com
Prenhall.com	IN	MX	15	mail2.prenhall.com
Prenhall.com	IN	MX	20	mail.isp.net

In this example, there are three MX records for the domain prenhall.com. They are listed in the order of preference. Hosts named in MX records are to be contacted in the order of their preference, from the numerically lowest preference to the numerically highest preference. So, when attempting to deliver mail for prenhall.com, first the host mail1.prenhall.com is tried. In the event that this attempt fails, the host mail2.prenhall.com is tried next, and if this attempt fails as well, the host mail.isp.net is finally contacted. The order used is based on the value of the preference field in the MX records: 10 for mail1.prenhall.com, 15 for mail2.prenhall.com, and 20 for mail.isp.net. Note that several MX records with the same preference value may be defined for the same host. This indicates that the mail administrator for this domain believes that these hosts have equal preference, and attempts to contact them may be tried in any order.

Notice that the weights given in the MX records leave room for future changes. For example, assume that a new SMTP server is added for prenhall.com, and that we'd like to try and use it first before mail1.prenhall.com. A weight of 5 can be assigned for the new server. If weights of 1, 2, and 3 had been assigned to the MX records in Table 3.13

then all of the weights would have to be changed in order to add this new SMTP server.

It is obvious that this eliminates a single point of failure for delivery of electronic mail. In this instance, prenhall.com has three redundant hosts that can be contacted for the delivery of its mail. What is not so obvious is how this scheme prevents the mail servers on these hosts from becoming overloaded. In the above example, it would seem that mail2.prenhall.com would only be contacted in the event that mail1.prenhall.com is not available. This unavailability would normally be due to some failure on the host. But in the case of electronic mail, the SMTP server may be configured with a connection limit. In this situation, once mail1.prenhall.com is serving a certain number of connections simultaneously, it will refuse all subsequent attempts to connect until one of its current connections is finished. In this event, the client whose connection is refused would then attempt to contact mail2.prenhall.com. Whichever host accepts delivery of a message for the user phil@prenhall.com, it will still be stored in the same place for ultimate retrieval by Phil. Thus, there are several paths that a message sent to Phil might take, but it will always end up at the right place. If this were not the case, Phil would have to check in multiple locations in order to read his mail. The precise definition of mail routing and the DNS is defined in RFC 974.

As in the PTR record, the MX record illustrates interaction between resource records in DNS. Not only does it do this, but the MX record also shows how DNS may be used by an application service in a way that is more complex than simply looking up the IP address of a known host. It defines a new property of Internet hosts and domains that is available for retrieval, namely, some other host that can be contacted in order to have electronic mail delivered to users of this host or domain.

SRV Records

MX records are very useful and provide a necessary service in the routing of electronic mail. Service type records (SRV) were defined as an attempt to provide this same service in a more general way in order that other applications (e.g., web servers, ldap servers, etc.) could take advantage of the features that this level of indirection provides. The SRV record specifies the location of the server(s) for a specific protocol and domain, and its RDATA section has the format shown in Figure 3.20.

An interesting point about the SRV record is that the owner field given in the resource record does not specify a particular host name or domain name. It has a specially defined format that gives the name of a

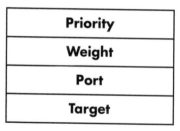

Fig. 3.20 SRV resource record RDATA format.

protocol, the transport layer that is used, as well as the name of a host. The owner name looks like: Service.Proto.Name. The Service portion of the owner name holds the symbolic name of some service (like "ldap" or "http"). The Proto portion of the owner name indicates whether the specified service is available of TCP, UDP, or perhaps some other yet to be defined transport layer. The Name portion of the owner name indicates the domain to which this resource record refers.

In the RDATA section of the SRV record, the two-byte Priority field performs the same function as the Preference section in the MX record. Hosts with the same weight are to be contacted in a "pseudo-random" order, as specified by weighting, given in the Weight section. The two-byte weight field indicates the load balancing mechanism. RFC 2052 (which defines the SRV record) indicates that "When selecting a target host among those that have the same priority, the chance of trying this one first SHOULD be proportional to its weight."

The Port field specifies the port number on which the indicated application server is listening for incoming connections. Even if this port number is the same as the IANA registered port number for this service, it must still be specified. The Target field of the SRV record performs the same function as the Exchange field of the MX record. It specifies the host to contact for the particular application service specified in the owner name. Examples of SRV records (as given in RFC 2052) for the fictional domain asdf.com are given in Table 3.14.

Table 3.14 Sample SRV Resource Records

Owner	Type	Priority	Weight	Port	Target
ftp.tcp.asdf.com	SRV	0	0	21	Server.asdf.com.
Finger.tcp.asdf.com	SRV	1	1	79	Server.asdf.com.
	SRV	1	1	79	Finger.asdf.com.
Telnet.tcp.asdf.com	SRV	0	1	23	Old-slow-box.asdf.com.
	SRV	0	3	23	New-fast-box.asdf.com.
	SRV	1	0	23	Sysadmins-box.asdf.com.
	SRV	1	0	23	Server.asdf.com.
http.tcp.asdf.com	SRV	0	0	80	Server.asdf.com.
	SRV	1	0	8000	New-fast-box.asdf.com.
http.tcp.www.asdf.com	SRV	0	0	80	Server.asdf.com.
	SRV	10	0	8000	New-fast-box.asdf.com.

For telnet, old-slow-box or new-fast-box can be used if either is available. The weighting indicates that three quarters of the telnet connections go to new-fast-box. This allows the load to be shared between both telnet servers. Weights of equal order can be assigned to allow the load to be shared equally among the hosts. This is the case for the two finger servers that are listed in the Table 3.14.

If neither of these hosts is available, switch to use the sysadmins-box and the server. A weight of zero for these records is an indication that these hosts will be contacted only in the event that no host with a positive weight was available. For http, server is the main server and new-fast-box is the backup (on new-fast-box the HTTP demon runs on port 8000). Since both www.asdf.com and asdf.com are supported for web browsers, there are two sets of resource records, one for each web domain that is supported.

SRV record cognizant application clients should do a lookup for QNAME=service.protocol.target, QCLASS=IN, QTYPE=SRV. RFC 2052 specifies that if only the root domain is returned in the response, then no SRV records are available. However, if some SRV records are returned, they should be sorted in the order of the Priority field, and then contacted in that order. Ties are broken among records with the same priority using the algorithm specified by the Weight field of the records.

DNS AND SECURITY

So far there has been no mention of how DNS provides for some level of security of its information. DNS security uses public key cryptography as described in Chapter 2. DNS security provides for integrity protection of the resource records in order to prevent malicious intruders from modifying information in the DNS database. If there were no integrity protection of the resource records, an intruder could modify resource records, and there would be no way to detect this unauthorized change to the data. For example, an intruder could change the MX records for a host and cause all outgoing electronic mail to be relayed to the incorrect mail host. This would allow the intruder to capture all of the organization's outgoing mail.

By providing the capability to digitally sign resource records, DNS allows the resolver to verify the correctness of the resource records. This is the assurance of data integrity. DNS allows the name server to guarantee that the resource records being retrieved are accurate. If there were no such assurances, it might be possible for rogue information to make its way into DNS and point resolvers to the wrong locations on the Internet. DNS security is provided through extensions defined in RFC 2065. RFC 2065 defines mechanisms that allow public key information to be stored in DNS, and also allow resource records to be signed by cryptographic mechanisms.

RFC 2065 describes how these cryptographic mechanisms are used in DNS to create a secure infrastructure. DNS realizes these mechanisms through two resource records, the KEY record and the SIG record. The KEY resource record is used to store public keys in DNS. The public keys that are stored in DNS are typically those that are associated with a specific host or some zone of DNS. The SIG resource record contains a digital signature of some other resource record. The format of the KEY record's RDATA section is illustrated in Figure 3.21.

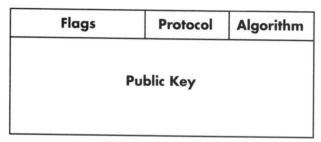

Fig. 3.21 KEY resource record RDATA format.

The Public Key field contains the public key of the owner as described by the domain name described in the owner field of the resource record. The Flags field is a 16-bit field, and it indicates a variety of things. The most important of these is how the owner name of the resource record should be interpreted. The first two bits of the Flags field indicate the "type" of owner. This type is a zone, an individual host, or a specific user on a host. In this last situation, the owner name can be translated to an electronic mail address by changing the first period into an @ (i.e., dee.cybercash.com becomes *dee@cybercash.com*). If both bits in the type field are one, then this is the special indication that there is no public key information in the resource record. The other bits of the Flags field are not particularly important to the discussion here, and are omitted from this text.

DNS assumes that the public key in the record can be used in protocols outside of DNS. The 8-bit Protocol field indicates in which other protocols the public key can be used. The IANA maintains a registry of the registered protocols for this field. Thus, DNS can be used as a repository of public keys for applications other than DNS. The 8-bit Algorithm field indicates which signature algorithm is used to sign records with this key. In order to promote interoperability, RFC 2065 recommends the RSA MD5 algorithm, as described in RFC 1321. If this algorithm is used, then the Algorithm field has the value 1. Other values of this field have not been defined, but could be defined by the IETF should such a need become available. RFC 2065 notes that "the designation of a new algorithm could have a major impact on interoperability and requires an IETF standards action."

The principal purpose of the Key record is for the creation of SIG records, whose RDATA sections are shown in Figure 3.22.

Consider the following example resource record (shown in Table 3.15) slightly modified from an example in RFC 2065.

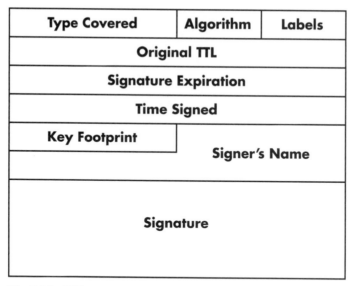

Fig. 3.22 SIG resource record RDATA format.

Table 3.15 Example SIG Resource Record

SIG RDATA Field	Value	Comment
Owner	Big.foo.tld	Not actually in RDATA
Record Type	SIG	SIG resource record
Type Covered	A	Signature of an "A" resource record
Algorithm	1	Use RSA MD5
Labels	3	There are three labels in big.foo.tld.
Signature Expiration	19960102030405	Expires on October 20, 1996
Time Signed	19951211100908	Record signed on December 11, 1995
Key Footprint	21435	16-bit key identifier
Signer's Name	Foo.tld	Signed by the host
Signature	Actual signature goes here	640 bits

This example contains the signature of the host big.foo.tld's "A" resource record, as indicated by the Owner and Type Covered fields. The Key Footprint is used to help identify which KEY record holds the key used to verify the SIG record. This is helpful in the scenario where the signer, foo.tld, has more than one KEY record. Even though the KEY record does not have a Footprint field, this value is easily calculated from the public key. The Signature field contains the actual computer signature of the other resource records that are indicated by the combination of the Owner field and the Type Covered field. RFC 2065 indicates that there is always a SIG record corresponding to a KEY record.

In order to verify the signature that is contained in the Signature field, the following standard mechanism for digital signature verification is used:

1. The KEY record that belongs to the identity contained in the Signer's Name field must be retrieved.
2. The signature of that KEY record should be verified as well. Retrieve the SIG record corresponding to the KEY record from step 1.
3. Compute MD5 digest of the resource record that has been signed.
4. Decrypt the signature contained in the SIG record being verified.
5. If the digest from step 3 matches the decrypted signature from step 4, then the signature is verified.

Note that DNS security is primarily aimed at verifying the integrity of the data in DNS, and not necessarily authenticating the users of DNS. The notion is that as long as the data is guaranteed to be accurate, it doesn't really matter where it came from. However, there is an obvious facility that can be used in the situation in which the resolver and name server wish to authenticate each other. They can use the mutual authentication features in TLS, and run their DNS client/server interaction over a TLS connection rather than an unauthenticated TCP or UDP connection.

CHAPTER SUMMARY

There will be some that will argue that DNS is not really a directory. But the question of whether DNS is a directory can be decided based on the requirements that were defined in the previous chapter. Recalling that the foremost requirement of an Internet directory service is to allow for property-based information retrieval, it is clear that DNS meets this requirement fully. Note also that DNS stores its information in such a way that it clearly fits in well with the rest of the Internet. All of the information in DNS revolves around IP addresses and host names, which make up the infrastructure of the Internet. As this infrastructure expands past the hosts and into named objects and services, new DNS record types are defined to support this infrastructure. In this chapter, most of the DNS record types were defined, and examples were given in many cases.

Also note that DNS operates natively over the defined Internet transport layer protocols (TCP and UDP), and is defined to be operated in a distributed manner. No name server by itself can provide the services of DNS. Name servers cooperate to provide the directory service that comes together as DNS.

Most modern operating systems already include a DNS resolver, name server, or both. For example, Windows NT, NetWare, and virtually every flavor of Unix all include name server software. The reference version of the DNS name server is BIND. BIND's source code can be freely obtained from the Internet Software Consortium at: *http://www.isc.org/products/BIND*. This site also includes compiled binaries for a wide number of operating systems.

LDAP

$\mathbf{T}$he Lightweight Directory Access Protocol (LDAP) is an attempt by the IETF to create a standard protocol for accessing directories that are designed in the manner of the X.500 series or recommendations of the International Telecommunications Union (ITU).[1] The ITU, a standards body that is a division of the United Nations, concentrates on standardizing communications that are to take place between and among various public telecommunications administrations and government postal authorities. The ITU standards are not based on the TCP/IP stack as the IETF standards are; instead, they rely upon the Open Systems Interconnection (OSI) protocol stack, which is defined in the X.200 series of ITU recommendations. The OSI protocol stack has several more layers on top of the transport layer, which adds additional complexity to OSI network clients and servers. The services provided by the OSI transport layers are analogous to those provided by the TCP layer of the Internet stack. However, in the OSI model, network applications do not interface directly to the transport layer, but instead rely upon services that are provided by the session, presentation, and application layers. ITU standards are typically not free, but may be purchased from the ITU (see *http://www.itu.ch*).

The X.500 series of recommendations was originally defined in the period from 1985–1988. Its original requirements were to provide fea-

---

[1] ITU documents are known as Recommendations. They are normally named with a letter and a number. An entire series of related recommendations are numbered closely together to form a series. The recommendations X.400, X.401, X.402, etc. are all related to electronic mail, and are known collectively as the X.400 series. Similarly, X.500, X.501, X.509, etc. are all related to directories, and are known collectively as the X.500 series.

tures to better enable the ITU's X.400 series of recommendations for electronic mail. Among other items, X.500 provided the strong authentication features for communications between clients and servers, as well as the ability for location-independent addressing of electronic mail. Prior to the availability of X.500, one had to be aware of the name of the recipient's service provider, and in what country the recipient was located, in order to address electronic mail in the X.400 system. An example of an X.400 address follows:

C=US; ADMD=ATT; PRMD=Prentice-Hall; O=Prentice-Hall; OU=Authors; SN=Greenblatt; GN=Bruce[2]

This complex addressing was seen as one of the reasons that the X.400 messaging system failed to gain a significant market share. Addressing based on X.500 directory names was an attempt to address this dilemma. Unfortunately, the naming provided by the X.500 information model is not significantly simpler than that provided by X.400. Since its original definition in 1988, the X.500 series has been revised and extended several times to fix implementation errors and to provide additional features. X.500-based directory services never gained significant presence in the market for a variety of reasons, not the least of which was its reliance upon the existence of an OSI protocol stack at a time when most network operating systems did not offer such a service natively.

In order to make the X.500 style of directories more available, the IETF began standardization efforts that led to the development of LDAP. LDAP derives its name from the X.500 client server protocol named Directory Access Protocol (DAP). The first version of LDAP was defined in RFC 1487. A second version was defined in RFC 1777. LDAP version 2 was the first version that was widely implemented. The third version of LDAP was defined in RFC 2251. The definition of LDAP in RFC 2251 improves upon the previous version by adding better support for international character sets, additional security measures, allowing for distributed operations, and providing for extensions to the protocol. LDAP tries to remove some of the complexities of implementing DAP by:

☞ Mapping directly onto the transport layer of the TCP/IP stack

☞ Encoding many elements of the protocol as strings

☞ Using a more lightweight version of the OSI "basic encoding rules"

---

[2] The fields in the X.400 address have the following meanings: C: Country, ADMD: Administrative Management Domain, PRMD: Private Management Domain, O: Organization, OU: Organizational Unit, SN: Surname, GN: Given Name. See X.400 for details on their meaning.

Thus, LDAP makes use of the TCP/IP stack rather than the OSI stack. Since LDAP does not use the OSI stack, the OSI stack won't be discussed in much detail here.

One concept that is borrowed from the OSI world by LDAP involves the OSI basic encoding rules which are part of a feature of the presentation layer of the OSI model known as Abstract Syntax Notation One (ASN.1). ASN.1 is the ITU's mechanism of defining the language that its peer entities use to communicate across a data communications network. ASN.1 defines not only the type of data that is used in communications, but also the mapping of the data layouts into the binary network order. Recalling the discussion of the previous chapter, if a DNS resolver wished to send a 32-bit integer across a socket to a DNS server, then it would just send the four bytes that made up the integer (e.g., 00 00 00 02 for the integer two). If ASN.1 were used, no such simplicity would be available. ASN.1 encodes each piece of data in binary as a type-length-value triple. For example, to encode the integer 100 in ASN.1, the following hexadecimal value might be transmitted:

```
02 0001 64
```

The first byte above indicates that the type is an integer (type = 2). The second pair of bytes indicates the length of the value field is one byte. The final byte is the value field, which in this case is the single byte representation of the desired value to be transmitted. Longer data items, and other types of data, can add significant complexity to the parsing and building of ASN.1 protocol data units. ASN.1 allows for the definition of complex data items.

LDAP PROTOCOL DEFINITION

Just as the protocol that is exchanged between DNS peer entities (i.e., the resolver and the server) is known as a DNS message, the protocol that is exchanged between LDAP peer entities is known as an *LDAPMessage*. RFC 2251 defines the ASN.1 syntax for an LDAPMessage as:

```
LDAPMessage ::= SEQUENCE {
    messageID  MessageID,
    protocolOp  CHOICE {
        bindRequest  BindRequest,
        bindResponse  BindResponse,
        unbindRequest  UnbindRequest,
        searchRequest  SearchRequest,
        searchResEntry  SearchResultEntry,
```

```
            searchResDone   SearchResultDone,
            searchResRef    SearchResultReference,
            modifyRequest   ModifyRequest,
            modifyResponse  ModifyResponse,
            addRequest   AddRequest,
            addResponse  AddResponse,
            delRequest   DelRequest,
            delResponse  DelResponse,
            modDNRequest  ModifyDNRequest,
            modDNResponse  ModifyDNResponse,
            compareRequest  CompareRequest,
            compareResponse  CompareResponse,
            abandonRequest  AbandonRequest,
            extendedReq  ExtendedRequest,
            extendedResp  ExtendedResponse },
      controls [0]  Controls OPTIONAL }
```

This notation indicates that whenever an LDAPMessage is passed between an LDAP client and an LDAP server, it is composed of either two or three pieces of information. The first piece of information that is always included in an LDAPMessage is a sequence number, which is contained in the field named *messageID*. The LDAP messageID performs that same function as the ID field in the DNS message header. It allows the LDAP client to correlate a server response with a previously submitted request. This is due to the fact that the LDAP protocol requires the server to copy the messageID from the client's request into any response that it returns. The type of the messageID field of the LDAPMessage is a messageID. In ASN.1, each field in the sequence is given as a name identifying the field, followed by the type of the field. A messageID is actually defined in LDAP as an Integer type, which in ASN.1 is the following:

```
    MessageID ::= INTEGER (0 .. maxInt)
```

MaxInt is defined as the largest 32-bit integer (2147483647). So, as long as the LDAP client keeps incrementing the value of the messageIDs that it uses in the protocol, it can always correlate the response back with the original request that it submitted. After the LDAP client submits its two billionth (or so) request, it should "roll over" the messageIDs, and start them again at number 0. The second field that always appears in the LDAPMessage contains the protocol operation itself, which is in the field named *protocolOp*. The fact that the protocolOp field is an ASN.1 CHOICE indicates that it may contain only one of the fields that are contained within the curly braces that follow. The protocolOp field in an LDAPMessage submitted by a client will normally contain one of the defined LDAP operation requests. The operations that are defined by LDAP are:

☞ Bind
☞ Unbind
☞ Search
☞ Compare
☞ Add
☞ Modify
☞ ModifyRDN
☞ Delete
☞ Abandon

Each of the LDAP defined operations has a different syntax. This is a mild departure from DNS, where each DNS operation had an identical syntax, independent of the value of the OPCODE field in the DNS header. However, the response to each LDAP operation is still an LDAPMessage. As might be imagined, an LDAP search operation is contained in an LDAPMessage which has a `protocolOp` field with the value *searchRequest*.

The final field that may appear in the structure is the Control field. Unlike the `messageID` field and the `protocolOp` field, the Control field may or may not be present in the LDAPMessage. If present, it indicates some additional request or response information above and beyond what is normally placed in the protocol. For example, pretend that an LDAP client is preparing an LDAPMessage to retrieve information about people that match some criteria, e.g., that live in a particular city. The base LDAP protocol allows the server to return the matching entries in whatever order it wants. If the LDAP client wants the data sorted in some manner, then it would attach a Sorting Control field with the LDAPMessage. A more detailed example of this control will be supplied later.

Notice that LDAP defines nine different operations, and their corresponding responses. However, in the protocol itself there is an extra operation and its defined response called the Extended Request and Response. The Extended Request is new to LDAP in version 3, and provides for future extensibility. It allows future versions of LDAP to define new operations. It also allows for vendors of LDAP products to supply new features in a standardized manner. One example of an LDAP extension is the mass import of data. The LDAP Add operation only allows for the addition of one object at a time to the directory. If the LDAP client wants to initiate the addition of several thousand objects, it would have to send a separate LDAPMessage for each object to be added to the directory. This is quite onerous, as is the subsequent requirement to correlate each response that is returned with the original request in order to generate a report on the various successes and failures. So, in order to facilitate this new feature, an extension could be defined that would allow the LDAP client to create just one LDAPMessage that would contain all of the objects to be added to the directory. Of course, a second extension would have to be defined so that the server could return all of the results in a single LDAPMessage as well. More details on this extended operation will be given later.

LDAP INFORMATION MODEL

Just as in DNS, the information that is available via LDAP is organized in a hierarchical manner. In DNS, each object in the directory is named by a host name. In LDAP, each object in the directory is given a special name, known as the distinguished name (or simply the object's DN). An example of the hierarchy used in LDAP is illustrated in Figure 4.1.

In DNS, in order to form the host name, one starts from the bottom of the hierarchy and works toward the top, and each name component is separated by a period. A similar approach is taken in LDAP, except that a comma separates the name components. So, the sales organizational unit at the bottom of Figure 4.1 would have the distinguished name:

```
OU=Sales, O=Acme, C=US
```

This string representation in LDAP is a major departure from the X.500 syntax. X.500 uses distinguished names as well, but in X.500 this information is represented in ASN.1 syntax as a sequence of three name components. The actual ASN.1 syntax used in X.500 distinguished names is:

```
DistinguishedName ::= RDNSequence

RDNSequence ::= SEQUENCE OF RelativeDistinguishedName

RelativeDistinguishedName ::= SET SIZE (1..MAX) OF
    AttributeTypeAndValue

AttributeTypeAndValue ::= SEQUENCE {
    type AttributeType,
    value AttributeValue }
```

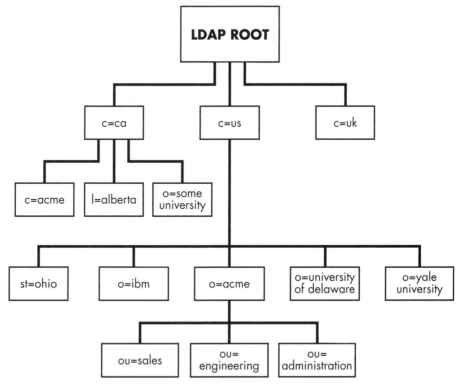

Fig. 4.1 Example LDAP information hierarchy.

ASN.1 Digression

Distinguished names are represented as simple strings in LDAP, but they yield the following information (see Figure 4.2) when encoded in the ASN.1 BER according to the definitions in X.500:

```
0011  0000  0010  1000
      0011  0001  0010  0110
            0011  0000  0000  1100
                  0000  0110  0000  0011  OID for OU
                  0001  0011  0000  0101  "Sales"
            0011  0000  0000  1011
                  0000  0110  0000  0011  OID for O
                  0001  0011  0000  0101  "Acme"
            0011  0000  0000  1001
                  0000  0110  0000  0011  OID for C
                  0001  0011  0000  0010  "US"
```

Fig. 4.2 ASN.1 representation of a distinguished name.

This representation in Figure 4.2 is known as an object identifier, or OID for short. OIDs are numeric identifiers that are defined in ASN.1, and have an especially unusual encoding in OSI protocols that will be left to the reader to discover. In the above ASN.1 example, the encoding of the OIDs has been omitted, as this technique presents unnecessary complexity for our purposes, and a length of three has been assumed for each of the attribute type OIDs. So how is this ASN.1 encoding to be interpreted? Each line in the above example represents one ASN.1 piece of information. Starting at the top, we have the hexadecimal digits, 30 28. In ASN.1, each piece of information is composed of an identifier, a length, and a value. The ASN.1 identifier is also made of three pieces of information: a class, a primitive/constructed (P/C) bit, and a type. The two class bits are almost always both set to zero, which indicates that one of the "universal" ASN.1 types has been used. The other class values aren't normally used in LDAP ASN.1. The P/C bit indicates whether the value field holds an actual low level value (primitive, indicated by a zero), or contains another ASN.1 piece of information (constructed, indicated by a one). The last five bits of the identifier field give the type of the data. In this case, the type is set to hexadecimal 10, which indicates a sequence type. Thus, a universal (00), constructed (1), sequence identifier is indicated by the hexadecimal value 30. The next byte indicates the length of the value field, which in this case is the hexadecimal value 2B. ASN.1 has a special way of writing the length for information that is longer than 127 bytes. In this form, bit 8 of the first bit is set to 1, and the other seven bits encode the number of subsequent bytes that actually hold the length. Some encodings of ASN.1 always use this long form of the length and set the first byte to 1000 0100, which indicates that the length is placed in the next four bytes, which can easily be decoded into a 32-bit unsigned integer.

Because the distinguished name is constructed, the value field contains another ASN.1 structure. In this case, it is the sequence of relative distinguished names (RDN). Notice that the identifier byte is again a 30, which indicates a sequence type, while the length of the value is 29. Inside of this sequence is each of the three RDNs. In X.500, each RDN is a combination of a type and a value. The type field is an OID that indicates the type. For example, the OID for the "c" attribute that denotes the country name portion of the DN is 2.5.4.6. ASN.1 encodes this in a way that combines the first two subidentifiers into one. This special encoding saves one byte in the encoding of most OIDs, at the price of obscuring the value of the OID from human viewers. The first subidentifier is multiplied by 40 and added to the second subidentifier. Each subsequent subidentifier is left unmolested. So, the encoding of the OID 2.5.4.6 is the following hexadecimal:

```
06 03 55 04 06
```

The first byte is the ASN.1 type for an OID (i.e., 6). The second byte indicates that the length is 03. The final three bytes are the actual encoding of the OID. An OID sub-identifier with a value greater than 127 is given a special encoding that takes up several bytes. In this encoding, the first bit of each byte is an indication of whether it is the last byte of the subidentifier. So, to encode the subidentifier 180, the two bytes 81 34 are needed. The first bit of each byte is discarded, and the remaining seven bits are concatenated to form the value of the actual subidentifier. In this case, we have 000 0001 011 0100. When pieced together, this 14-bit number is indeed 180 in decimal form. You'll need to polish up on your seven-bit arithmetic if you're going to get good at deciphering ASN.1 OIDs.

In the LDAP protocol, this encoding of the OID is discarded in favor of the string encoding, which encodes the OID 2.5.4.6 as the ASCII string "2.5.4.6." So, the actual ASN.1 encoding of this OID is 04 07 "2.5.4.6." The type 04 indicates the ASN.1 octet string type, which is ASN.1 catchall type for arbitrary binary data. Similarly, the example DN is encoded in LDAP as 04 14 "OU=Sales, O=Acme, C=US." In these examples, the quoted data indicates that the actual ASCII codes are used in the protocol.

This is a major simplification that LDAP makes: The distinguished name has been changed from a sequence of bytes that is nearly incomprehensible by the human observer to a simple string that is immediately decipherable without any auxiliary parsing program. This type of simplification is used in many areas of LDAP, where previous binary representations of data used in the X.500 protocols are replaced with string representations in LDAP. Note in the above example, that in the LDAP encoding of the distinguished name that the OIDs are not used, and that in their place, the textual descriptions of the attribute types are used.

Schema Construction and the LDAP Name Space

Each LDAP server has information about some set of distinguished names that are organized in a hierarchical manner. LDAP assumes that the combination of the host name and distinguished name uniquely identifies an object in the directory. Thus, two different directory servers might maintain two different objects with the same distinguished name. This can cause problems if the two LDAP servers are connected and attempt to synchronize their information. However, no problems need arise as long as the LDAP servers are allowed to maintain their own information. Note the difference between the assumption here and the assumption in DNS. In DNS, objects in the directory are named uniquely by a host name. Because the DNS directory service is universally connected via the Internet, one will never encounter two different DNS objects with the same host name. This is because each DNS server is designated to administer some portion of the DNS namespace, and host name to IP address resolution will be broken if there are two different hosts that have been assigned the same name.

It is common practice in LDAP for administrators to set up the top of the namespace themselves, and they have substantial freedom to do so. For example, most LDAP trees in the United States, will be rooted with the single object named by the distinguished name "C=US." In this name, the "C" is the abbreviation for the attribute: countryName. The object identified by a countryName attribute is a country Object. This object has other attributes besides its name. For example, it is allowed to have a description. There is no universal guarantee that the description that is present in the "C=US" object on one directory server will also be present on some other directory server. In this instance, nothing bad happens just because my "C=US" object is not the same as your "C=US" object.

In order to illustrate the information structure of LDAP, let's again consider the example of a directory that contains information about breeds of dogs. Presume that this directory is maintained by the Society of Internet Dog Kennels, or SIDK as it is commonly known. The administrator has chosen to use the "O=Internet" object as the root of its directory tree. It would be inappropriate to place the object representing the SIDK organization underneath any particular country object, since the dog breeds and breeders are located throughout the world. This points out one of the shortcomings of the LDAP information model. Each object has only one "parent object" in the directory hierarchy. So even though some members of SIDK are located in France, and some in the United States, there is no way to logically represent this information in the LDAP hierarchy. This is because the object named by "O=SIDK, C=US," and the object named by "O=SIDK, C=FR" are presumed to be two different objects, and there is no way of indicating in LDAP that they represent the same underlying object. What would be preferred is that the French members of SIDK are located under the "O=SIDK, C=FR" object, while the American members of SIDK are located under the "O=SIDK, C=US" object. Unfortunately, such a representation is not allowed in LDAP. In order to represent an international organization, the SIDK administrators have chosen to place their object underneath the "O=Internet" object in the directory.

In LDAP, each object is allowed to logically contain other objects. Placing one object beneath another in the hierarchy represents this containment notion. So far we've seen two different kinds of objects: the country object and the organization object, although admittedly in very little detail. Now, a few LDAP objects will be examined in more detail.

An *object class* identifies each kind of object that is stored in LDAP. An object class definition is made up of several items:

☞ the name of the object class
☞ the name of the super class
☞ the list of mandatory attributes of this object class
☞ the list of optional attributes of this object class
☞ the type of object class: ABSTRACT, STRUCTURAL, or AUXILIARY

The attributes of an object class are divided into those that must be in every object (the mandatory ones), and those that are in some objects of that class but are missing from other objects of that class (the optional ones). The most basic LDAP object class is the one named "top." The `top` object class is the only LDAP object class that does not have a super class. All other LDAP object classes are descended from "top." The `top` object class has the following definition (as taken from RFC 2256):

```
(2.5.6.0 NAME 'top' ABSTRACT MUST objectClass)
```

This LDAP object class definition indicates that the object class named "top" has exactly one mandatory attribute named *objectClass*. Since it is not mentioned here, the object class `top` does not have any optional attributes. Since it is also absent, the object class `top` does not have a super class. The keyword ABSTRACT in the definition of "top" indicates that no additional objects of that type may be created. The `top` object class may only be used in the definition of other object classes. Since no additional top objects can be created, it does not matter how they are named, but the components of an object's distinguished name are normally composed from the mandatory attributes.

The dotted numeric identifier at the beginning of the object class definition is another way of representing the name of the object class. In this case, the name "top" and the numeric identifier "2.5.6.0" both refer to the same thing, i.e., the object class named "top." In LDAP, OIDs are encoded as the character string representation, and that is how they appear in the protocol. Each OID is universally unique. Thus, no matter where the OID "2.5.6.0" appears, it always refers to the object class named `top`.

Normally in LDAP the numeric identifier for the object class name is not used, and the textual name is used. This is due to the fact that in LDAP an OID is defined as either the descriptive form or the numeric form. Since people greatly prefer to see the descriptive form, that is what is commonly used.

Top's sole attribute, `objectClass` attribute, is defined as:

```
( 2.5.4.0 NAME 'objectClass' EQUALITY objectIdentifierMatch
SYNTAX 1.3.6.1.4.1.1466.115.121.1.38 )
```

The OID for the `objectClass` attribute is "2.5.4.0." The next part of the attribute definition identifies the type of matching rules that can be used in LDAP searches. In this case, LDAP searches can only be performed for exact equality against `objectClass` attributes. So, an LDAP search could be performed in order to retrieve all objects that were of the type "person." But, an LDAP search to retrieve all objects that had an `objectClass` attribute greater than "person" would be illegal, since only the EQUALITY matching rule is allowed. The last portion of the attribute definition describes the syntax of the attribute values. This numeric identifier is another OID, as defined in RFC 2252, which in this case indicates that the syntax is of type "OID." Remember that in LDAP the OID syntax refers to either the numeric identifier form or the textual description form, and that in the case of the `objectClass` attribute, the textual format is nearly always used.

The next object classes that will be examined are the `organization` object class and the `organizationalUnit` object class. These two similar object classes will be used to define the top level containers in the example directory tree (of the SIDK organization). These two object classes have virtually identical definitions in RFC 2256 as follows:

```
(2.5.6.4 NAME 'organization' SUP top STRUCTURAL MUST o
  MAY (userPassword $ searchGuide $ seeAlso $ businessCategory $
  x121Address $ registeredAddress $ destinationIndicator $
  preferredDeliveryMethod $ telexNumber $ teletexTerminalIdentifier $
  telephoneNumber $ internationaliSDNNumber $
  facsimileTelephoneNumber $ street $ postOfficeBox $ postalCode $
  postalAddress $ physicalDeliveryOfficeName $ st $ l $ description))

( 2.5.6.5 NAME 'organizationalUnit' SUP top STRUCTURAL MUST ou
  MAY ( userPassword $ searchGuide $ seeAlso $ businessCategory $
  x121Address $ registeredAddress $ destinationIndicator $
  preferredDeliveryMethod $ telexNumber $ teletexTerminalIdentifier $
  telephoneNumber $ internationaliSDNNumber $
  facsimileTelephoneNumber $ street $ postOfficeBox $ postalCode $
  postalAddress $ physicalDeliveryOfficeName $ st $ l $ description))
```

These two object class definitions are significantly longer than the definition of the "top" abstract class. Notice that the only difference in the two definitions is that the `organization` object class has a mandatory attribute named "o," and the `organizationalUnit` object class has a mandatory attribute named "ou." In these object class definitions, the super class field is present, and this field indicates that they are both derived from the class, "top." When one object class is a super class of another class (the subclass), this means that the subclass has all of the mandatory and optional attributes of the super class. So, in addition to all of the attributes mentioned, all `organization` and `organizationalUnit` objects in the directory will also have an `objectClass` attribute. One final object class from RFC 2256 that will be used to populate objects in the sample directory is the one that is used to represent people objects in the directory. This is the `person` object class:

```
( 2.5.6.6 NAME 'person' SUP top STRUCTURAL MUST (sn $ cn)
  MAY (userPassword $ telephoneNumber $ seeAlso $ description))
```

In this object class, both the `surname` attribute (`sn`) and the `common name` attribute (`cn`) must be present, in addition to the `objectClass` attribute that is inherited from the top object class. The LDAP protocol expects the `cn` attribute to be used in the formation of the DN of the directory object representing that person. In organizational directories, the `cn` is often used to hold an employee identification number. Note also that LDAP allows an object to have more than one `cn` attribute, and not all of them need to be unique identifiers in the directory context. For example, the `cn` attribute can hold a user identifier that is employed by the user to authenticate to the network.

This notion of multivalued attributes is common throughout LDAP. For example, any person object that appears in the directory will have two values of the `objectClass` attribute: person and top. This is very analogous to the situation in DNS in which the same Internet host may have several valid names. In other words, it is possible for the two host names, mail.acme.com and news.acme.com, to refer to the same IP address. In LDAP it is possible for two common names to refer to the same underlying directory object. With these object class definitions, enough is in place in order to set up the structure of the example directory (see Figure 4.3).

In this figure the boxes with the light shading represent `organizationalUnit` objects; the boxes with the dark shading represent person objects; and the unshaded box represents the top level Internet organization object. In this example, the directory content consists of 10 objects: four `organizationalUnits`, five `person` objects, and one organization. In

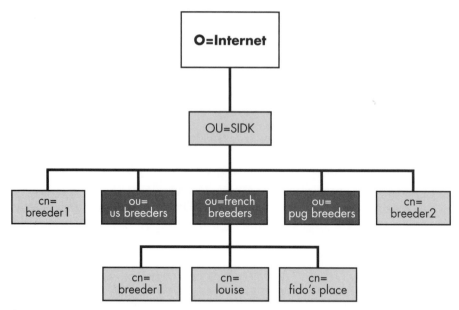

Fig. 4.3 Sample Directory Information Tree (DIT).

LDAP terminology the content of the directory is called the Directory Information Tree (DIT). The objects in the figure are represented only by their RDNs, but they may have other attributes associated with that object. Consider the "US breeders" `organizationalUnit` in Table 4.1.

Table 4.1 Sample OU Definition

Attribute Type	Attribute Value(s)
OU	"US Breeders", "United States Breeders"
ObjectClass	"top," "organizationalUnit"
Description	"Dog breeders that are located in the United States of America"
SeeAlso	"ou=American Breeders, o=Internet"

In this object, both values for the mandatory attributes of the object class are present. In this case, they are given in bold. The object inherits the mandatory nature of the `objectClass` attribute from its super class, "top." In addition, it has the mandatory attribute "ou" from the definition of the `organizationalUnit` object class. Notice that for each of these two mandatory object classes there are two values. In this instance, it indicates that the two DNs, "ou=us breeders, o=Internet" and "ou=United States Breeders, o=Internet," refer to precisely the same object in the DIT. Notice also that of the numerous available optional attributes for the `organizationalUnit` object class, two are present in this object. The object has a description attribute present, as well as a seeAlso attribute. The description attribute contains a short textual overview of the purpose of the object. In this case, the description attribute indicates that the object contains information about dog breeders located in the U.S. The seeAlso attribute indicates that a somewhat-related object is the object denoted by the DN "ou=American Breeders, o=Internet." Unfortunately, the `seeAlso` attribute doesn't indicate the nature of the relationship between the objects, only that there is one. Consider the "fido's place" person object in Table 4.2.

Table 4.2 Sample `Person` Object

Attribute Type	Attribute Value(s)
CN	"fido's place" "acme dog breeding, inc." "SN: 032861"
ObjectClass	"top," "person"
TelephoneNumber	"1234-12-12," "fax: 0912203993"
Description	"World renowned breeders of canine type animals," "We also breed cats, but don't tell anyone"

Note the similar nature of the attributes between this object and the previous example, "ou=us breeders, o=Internet." An important item to note is that even though the object class is person, the object obviously does not represent a person. It clearly represents a company of some sort that breeds dogs and (judging from the second value of the description attribute) cats.

One obvious flaw in the design of the information structure for this directory is that none of the available object classes or attributes have much to do with breeding dogs. This is not surprising, as it is the intent of the definitions RFC 2256 to provide the starting point for definitions, and that numerous other object classes and attributes will likely be defined in the future by various special interest groups. Indeed, the IETF itself has already defined a schema for the support of an Internet White Pages Services (IWPS). The IWPS schema is intended to provide most of the information about people that would likely be used in searches. This schema, defined in RFC 2218, indicates that an object class that is defined to hold information about Internet users should have the following information:

☞ Field Name

☞ E-mail

☞ Cert

☞ Home Page

☞ Common Name

☞ Given Name

☞ Surname

☞ Organization

☞ Locality

☞ Country

☞ Language Spoken

☞ Personal Phone

☞ Personal Fax

☞ Personal Mobile

☞ Personal Pager Number

☞ Personal Postal Address

☞ Description

☞ Title

☞ Office Phone

☞ Office Fax

☞ Office Mobile Phone

☞ Office Pager

☞ Office Postal Address

RFC 2218 doesn't define an LDAP object class, it just mentions the kinds of information that an LDAP object class should hold. In addition to the above IWPS style information, the example directory needs to hold the kind of information that is specific to the breeders of dogs that populate the SIDK organization's DIT. In order to allow for this type of information to be present in the directory, two additional object classes will be defined: *breeder* and *breedingOrganization*. In defining these additional object classes, a significant decision must be made. They can either be defined as structural subclasses of object classes that are already defined, or they can be defined as auxiliary object classes. An auxiliary object class is one that can be added to an existing object in the directory in such a way that the additional attributes defined in the auxiliary object class are added to the object. This is very similar to the use of the subclass, except that an object's auxiliary object classes can change over time. LDAP allows an object to just have one base structural object class; if this needs to change, then the object must be deleted from the directory and subsequently added to the directory again with a new object class. This is a dangerous thing to do, since all references to the old object may be damaged (or even deleted) when the object is destroyed. So, it is safer for the SIDK organization to define private information as auxiliary object classes.

For our goals here, the OID serves no real purpose, so it won't be defined. The breeder object class has the following definition:

```
(NAME 'breeder' SUP top AUXILIARY MUST (breed $ emailAddress)
  MAY (homePage $ givenName $ postalAddress $ breedersOrganization))
```

In this definition, some of the attributes from RFC 2218 have been selected. Additionally, several attribute definitions that are unique to the SIDK organization have been defined. Since there is no IETF standardized definition for them, we'll supply it for breed and breedersOrganization:

```
(NAME 'breed' EQUALITY caseIgnoreMatch
    SUBSTR caseIgnoreSubstringsMatch
    SYNTAX 1.3.6.1.4.1.1466.115.121.1.15{64} )
```

```
(NAME 'breedersOrganization' EQUALITY distinguishedNameMatch
    SYNTAX 1.3.6.1.4.1.1466.115.121.1.12 SINGLE-VALUE )
```

These definitions require a little explanation. When a client performs LDAP searches, the breed attribute may be found by supplying either the entire string (an EQUALITY match) or only part of the string (a SUBSTR, i.e., substring match). The OID that is given after the SYNTAX keyword is defined in RFC 2252 indicates that breed attributes are defined using the directoryString syntax. An attribute that is encoded using the directoryString syntax is a character string that is encoded in the UTF-8 representation of the Unicode character set. Unicode is a special character set in which virtually any character that is used in human communication can be represented by either two bytes or four bytes. The UTF-8 representation (defined in RFC 2279) is a special transformation of Unicode in which some characters are represented using only a single byte, while other characters may be represented by as many as six bytes. Unicode characters that also appear in the seven-bit ASCII character set are represented by one byte in the UTF-8 transformation. Other Unicode characters are represented in UTF-8 depending upon their Unicode representation. RFC 2253, which defines the UTF-8 string representation of distinguished names, shows an example in Table 4.3.

Table 4.3 Sample UTF-8 String

Unicode Letter Description	10646 code	UTF-8	Quoted
LATIN CAPITAL LETTER L	U0000004C	0x4C	L
LATIN SMALL LETTER U	U00000075	0x75	U
LATIN SMALL LETTER C WITH CARON	U0000010D	0xC48D	\C4\8D
LATIN SMALL LETTER I	U00000069	0x69	I
LATIN SMALL LETTER C WITH ACUTE	U00000107	0xC487	\C4\87

These five characters could be written in printable ASCII (useful for debugging purposes) as follows:

```
Lu\C4\8Di\C4\87
```

Notice that the ASCII characters L, u, and i have the same representation in UTF-8 as they do in standard ASCII representation. The other two characters that don't appear in ASCII, but are in Unicode, require two bytes per character. Thus, the five-character string above requires seven bytes to represent. This definition of the breed attribute allows it to hold dog breed names that contain characters outside of ASCII. The breedersOrganization attribute allows the breeder object to contain the distinguished name of an organization that has sanctioned this breeder. Notice that the breedersOrganization attribute has the keyword SINGLE-VALUE present. This indicates that there may only be one value of this attribute present in the object. So, while each breeder may have several breed values present in the directory object, it may only have one breedersOrganization attribute value present. Note that if this restriction didn't make sense since in the real world representation of the data to be contained in the directory, then the SINGLE-VALUE restriction should be dropped from the attribute definition.

Now that the breed object class has been defined, the breedingOrganization must be specified as well:

```
(NAME 'breedingOrganization' SUP top AUXILIARY MUST (breed $
emailAddress) MAY (homePage $ contactUser $ postalAddress))
```

This requires the additional definition of the contactUser:

```
(NAME 'contactUser' EQUALITY distinguishedNameMatch
    SYNTAX 1.3.6.1.4.1.1466.115.121.1.12)
```

The contactUser attribute of the breedingOrganization gives the distinguished names of some users that can be contacted as representatives of the organization. Notice that while the breedingOrganization object class has the `breed` attribute, just as the `breeder` object class does, they have slightly different semantics in each definition. When used in the `breeder` object class, the `breed` attribute is intended to represent the types of dogs the breeder breeds. When used in the `breedingOrganization` object class, the `breed` attribute is intended to represent the types of dogs that can be in the dog shows that this organization officially sanctions.

With these object class and attribute definitions, the example DIT entries can now be updated (see Tables 4.4 and 4.5).

Table 4.4 Sample OU Entry Updated

Attribute Type	Attribute Value(s)
OU	"US Breeders," "United States Breeders"
ObjectClass	"top," "organizationalUnit," "breedingOrganization"
Description	"Dog breeders that are located in the United States of America"
SeeAlso	"ou=American Breeders, o=Internet"
Breed	"pug," "poodle," "beagle," "irish setter"
EmailAddress	*"info@usbreeders.org"*
Homepage	*"http://www.usbreeders.org"*
ContactUser	"cn=alice, ou=us breeders, o=Internet"

Table 4.5 Sample Person Entry Updated

Attribute Type	Attribute Value(s)
CN	"fido's place" "acme dog breeding, inc." "SN: 032861"
ObjectClass	"top," "person," "breeder"
TelephoneNumber	"1234-12-12," "fax: 0912203993"
Description	"World renowned breeders of canine type animals" "We also breed cats, but don't tell anyone"
Breed	"pug"
EmailAddress	*"Fido@fidosplace.fr"*
Homepage	*"http://www.fidosplace.fr"*

Notice how these objects have been filled out with more information that is appropriate to the SIDK organization's directory instead of the simple generic person and organizational attributes that are supplied by the base LDAP object class definitions. In the above objects, there is no way for the LDAP client to determine whether the breeder object class is auxiliary or structural. If the breeder object class were defined as a structural sub-class of the person object class, there would be no difference in the defini-tion of the attributes of the above objects. Thus, there is no real reason that the LDAP client implementation needs to know whether any particular object class is structural or auxiliary when reading objects from the direc-tory. However, as was mentioned before, the only values of the objectClass attribute that can be changed are the auxiliary ones. The base structural attribute value of an object in the directory can never be changed.

LDAP FUNCTIONAL COMPONENTS

Just as in DNS, there are only two functional components in LDAP: the LDAP client and the LDAP server. They communicate with each other by exchanging the previously mentioned construct. LDAP allows the client and server to communicate over a TCP connection, a TLS connection, or even the connectionless UDP protocol. However, the version of LDAP that operates over UDP (which is known as Connectionless LDAP (CLDAP)) does not allow any LDAP operations other than the search and abandon operations. This is due to the fact that UDP does not allow for long-term connections to be established. UDP allows for a single request and a single reply to be generated before the UDP socket is gone. Also, only results that can fit into a single UDP packet can be returned with-out truncation. For these reasons, the principal implementation of LDAP is over the connection-oriented transport, TCP, rather than the connec-tionless transport, UDP. Given that, this discussion of LDAP will not be concerned with CLDAP (as defined in RFC 1798), and instead will con-centrate solely on the connection-oriented version of LDAP as defined in RFC 2251.

The LDAP client initiates all LDAPMessages that represent requests which cause a response to be returned by an LDAP server. The LDAP client requests and the possible responses are shown in Table 4.6.

Table 4.6 LDAP Requests and Corresponding Responses

LDAP Client Request	LDAP Server Response
BindRequest	BindResponse
UnbindRequest	
SearchRequest	SearchResultEntry, SearchResultDone, SearchResultReference
ModifyRequest	ModifyResponse
AddRequest	AddResponse
DelRequest	DelResponse
ModDNRequest	ModDNResponse
CompareRequest	CompareResponse
AbandonRequest	
ExtendedRequest	ExtendedResponse

Notice that some client requests don't require a server response, while the LDAP search requests have more than one possible response from the server defined. Thus, the functional components have a very simple interaction, as shown in Figure 4.4.

Even though the LDAP specification only defines the two functional components, it does define the referral interaction between the client and server in a manner that is similar to the definition in the DNS protocol. With the addition of the referral concept, the functional interaction between the LDAP components can be more complex, as illustrated in Figure 4.5.

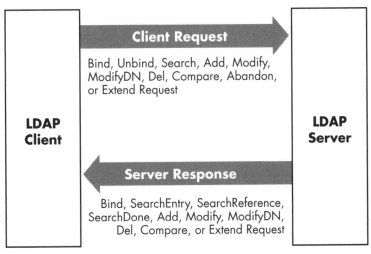

Fig. 4.4 LDAP requests and responses in a client/server operation.

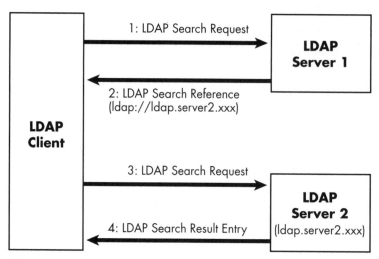

Fig. 4.5 LDAP referrals.

Thus, LDAP allows for a search that is submitted to one directory server to be referred to some other directory server. Notice that LDAP defines only the interaction between an LDAP client and an LDAP server. This question then arises: how does LDAP Server 1 in the above figure know that it is to refer a client search request to some other server if LDAP servers don't interact? The notion that LDAP servers don't interact is a common misconception. LDAP only defines the client-server interaction; it certainly does not restrict LDAP servers from using other protocols for their interaction. For example, LDAP servers can use the Common Indexing Protocol (CIP) to exchange a wide variety of information. CIP is an IETF protocol that will be discussed in some detail in a later chapter. In reality, the interaction among LDAP functional components is more likely to resemble that shown in Figure 4.6.

Note also that LDAP can be used as a front-end to an X.500 directory server. In this X.500 scenario, IETF protocols wouldn't be used for server-to-server interaction. Instead, X.500 has defined several special protocols for use in several different types of server-to-server communication. For more information on these protocols, the reader is referred to the X.500 series of recommendations, as they won't be discussed here (see, a referral can be done even without using a directory server).

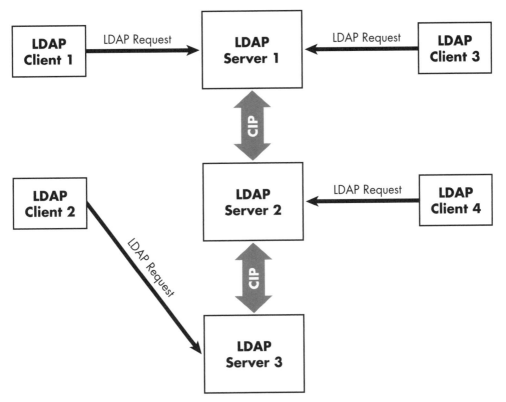

Fig. 4.6 Complex interaction among LDAP components.

PROTOCOL DETAILS

In LDAP, the LDAP client initiates all operations. The client sends an LDAPMessage structure that contains some requests. If appropriate for the operation, the server will reply with an LDAPMessage structure that contains a response to the request. Note that the client may send multiple request messages to the server without waiting for a response for each request. This mode of operation is known as *asynchronous client-server communication*. This is due to the fact that the requests and response are not synchronized between the client and the server. It is permissible for the client to wait for a response to each request prior to submitting a subsequent request. If the client is operating in this mode, then it is using what is known as *synchronous client-server communication*.

Bind and Unbind Operations

The first operation that usually occurs in an LDAP session is the `bind` operation. The LDAP `Bind` is used to allow the client to identify itself to the server. This notion of client identification is normally termed authentication. Depending upon the form of the `Bind`, it also allows the server to authenticate itself to the client. In LDAP v3, there are three types of `Bind` operations that have been defined:

- ☞ Anonymous Bind
- ☞ Simple Bind
- ☞ SASL Bind[3]

Previous versions of LDAP defined additional `bind` types, but these have been deprecated in version 3 and are no longer used. The `anonymous bind` is an indication that the client either does not have an account with the LDAP server, or is not willing to identify itself. If the `anonymous bind` is successful, then the client will normally have limited rights on the server. It is unlikely that an LDAP server would allow an unknown server to make modifications to the DIT; thus, anonymous users typically have access to read the directory only, and cannot make changes to any entries. If the first operation in an LDAP session is not a `bind`, then the server should treat that operation as if it had been preceded by an `anonymous bind`. Thus, it would be redundant for the first operation in a session to be an `anonymous bind`.

The second form of the `bind` is the `simple bind`. In this form, the client supplies a name and a password. If the password is omitted from the `simple bind`, then it is treated as anonymous. Since it is considered insecure to allow the transmission of a password across the Internet, use of the `simple bind` should only be allowed over an encrypted TLS session. It might also be appropriate in situations where both the client and server are situated on the same side of a very secure firewall, and the network connections are secured from eavesdropping. All things considered, `simple binds` over TCP connections should not occur. The `bind` operation has the following ASN.1:

---

[3] SASL is the Simple Authentication and Security Layer and is defined in RFC 2222. SASL is a general-purpose authentication protocol that is used in a wide variety of Internet applications in addition to LDAP (e.g., POP, IMAP, and SMTP).

```
BindRequest ::= [APPLICATION 0] SEQUENCE {
        version              INTEGER (1 .. 127),
        name                 LDAPDN,
        authentication       AuthenticationChoice }

    AuthenticationChoice ::= CHOICE {
        simple  [0] OCTET STRING,
            -- 1 and 2 reserved
        sasl    [3] SaslCredentials }
```

Notice that there is no choice specified for the anonymous bind. This is due to the fact that the simple bind choice is overloaded. If the name field has a zero length or the simple choice is used, but a zero length value is provided, then an anonymous bind is used. If a name is provided, the simple choice is used and some value (other than the null value) is provided, it is considered a simple bind. The version field in the bind operation indicates the version of LDAP that the client wants to use. This field allows the client and the server to agree on an LDAP version prior to initiating a session. When translated into binary, a typical anonymous bind is encoded as shown in Table 4.7.

Table 4.7 Encoding of the Anonymous Bind Request

Binary Format	Hexadecimal	Meaning
0110 0000 0000 0111	6007	Application 0, length 7
0000 0010 0000 0001 0000 0011	020103	Version is 3
0000 0100 0000 0000	0400	Name is null
0000 0000 0000 0000	0000	Choice is 0, credentials are null.

Thus, the LDAP anonymous bind requires nine bytes to encode. Note that the bind is placed inside the construct described earlier. Notice that the first pair of bits is '01' in the identifier octet of the operation. This is the ASN.1 indication that the encoding is not of the universal sort, but is instead using the application variety. By using the ASN.1 application notation, LDAP encodes the opcode in the tag. In this case, the tag is 0, so the lower five bits of the identifier octet are set to zero to indicate the opcode. Each LDAP operation has been assigned a different application tag, in order that the opcode of the construct may be easily deciphered. Notice that the third bit of the identifier octet is set to one. This indicates that the value portion of the encoding contains another structure. This constructed indication is always present in an ASN.1

sequence. Notice also that both the name field is length zero, as is the password field. A typical simple bind with a user named "bruce" and a password of "secret" would be encoded as shown in Table 4.8.

Table 4.8 Encoding of the `Simple Bind`

Binary Format	Hexadecimal	Meaning
0110 0000 0001 0010	6012	Application 0, length 18
0000 0010 0000 0001 0000 0011	020103	Version is 3
0000 0100 0000 0005 0110 0010 0111 0010 0111 0101 0110 0011 0110 0101	04056272756365	Name is "bruce"
0000 0000 0000 0110 0111 0011 0110 0101 0110 0011 0111 0010 0110 0101 0111 0100	0006736563726574	Choice is 0, credentials are "secret"

The `simple bind` that includes a name and a password requires 20 bytes to encode. Notice again that the application tag is zero, which is indicative of the `bind` operation. Note that in the `simple bind`, LDAP does not indicate that the octet string can only contain a static password, i.e., one that is always the same from one session to another. One possible alternative to the static password is a token-based scheme in which a token is issued to a user that displays a secret code which updates itself at periodic intervals according to some devilishly clever algorithm (known to the server). Thus, the LDAP client could include the currently displayed secret code on its token in the `simple bind`. Then the server could verify whether the code that is supplied is the one that should be displayed on the token according to the secret algorithm. If the client-supplied octet string agrees with the one that the server computes, then the `bind` is considered successful. Note that if the `bind` fails, the server will normally not close the underlying connection, and the client can try again. The result of the `bind` operation has the following syntax:

```
BindResponse ::= [APPLICATION 1] SEQUENCE {
     COMPONENTS OF LDAPResult,
     serverSaslCreds [7] OCTET STRING OPTIONAL }

LDAPResult ::= SEQUENCE {
     resultCode ENUMERATED {
          success    (0),
          operationsError (1),
          protocolError (2),
          . . .
```

```
                    invalidCredentials (49),
                    ...}
            matchedDN LDAPDN,
            errorMessage LDAPString,
            referral [3] Referral OPTIONAL }
```

Notice that the application tag of the BindResponse is one. The ASN.1 "COMPONENTS OF" notation indicates that all of the elements of the LDAPResult structure are placed in the BindResponse. In the case of the BindResult, there will not be a matchedDN field or a referral field, so the matchedDN field will always be length zero, and the referral field will be omitted entirely. A typical successful BindResponse would only have the resultCode field present, and would be longer than zero. This would yield an encoding as shown in Table 4.9.

Table 4.9 Encoding of a Successful Bind Response

Binary Format	Hexadecimal	Meaning
0110 0001 0000 0111	6107	Application 1, length 7
0000 0010 0000 0001 0000 0000	020103	ResultCode is success (0)
0100 0000	0400	No matchedDN
0100 0000	0400	No errorMessage

Notice that the ENUMERATED field in the syntax code is just encoded as an integer. LDAP defines many resultCodes other than the three listed above in the definition of LDAPResult, but the list of codes has been truncated for the purpose of readability. If the client supplied an incorrect password, then the server would return the invalidCredentials resultCode, which is 49 decimal, which yields the following encoding (see Table 4.10).

Table 4.10 Encoding of an Unsuccessful Bind Response

Binary Format	Hexadecimal	Meaning
0110 0001 0000 0011	6103	Application 1, length 3
0000 0010 0000 0001 0011 0001	020131	ResultCode is invalidCredentials (49)
0100 0000	0400	No matchedDN
0100 0000	0400	No errorMessage

In either case, the messageID in the surrounding LDAPMessage would be the same in the client request and in the server response. Assuming that the messageID in this case is the integer one, and that no controls are present, the entire bind request message would be encoded as shown in Table 4.11.

Table 4.11 Complete LDAPMessage Holding a `Bind` Request

Binary Format	Hexadecimal	Meaning
0011 0000 0001 0111	3017	Sequence construct, length 23
0000 0010 0000 0001 0000 0001	020101	MessageID is 1
0110 0000 0001 0010	6012	Application 0, length 18
0000 0010 0000 0001 0000 0011	020103	Version is 3
0000 0100 0000 0005 0110 0010 0111 0010 0111 0101 0110 0011 0110 0101	04056272756365	Name is "bruce"
0000 0000 0000 0110 0111 0011 0110 0101 0110 0011 0111 0010 0110 0101 0111 0100	0006736563726574	Choice is 0, credentials are "secret"

The successful bind response message would be encoded as shown in Table 4.12.

Table 4.12 Complete LDAPMessage Holding a `Bind` Response

Binary Format	Hexadecimal	Meaning
0011 0000 0000 1100	300C	Sequence construct, length 12
0000 0010 0000 0001 0000 0001	020101	MessageID is 1
0110 0001 0000 0111	6107	Application 1, length 7
0000 0010 0000 0001 0000 0000	020103	ResultCode is success (0)
0100 0000	0400	No matchedDN
0100 0000	0400	No errorMessage

Notice in these LDAPMessage structures that there is nothing that uniquely identifies them as being LDAP protocol data units (PDU). The reason that this works is due to the fact that the LDAP server listening on TCP port 389 (or whatever port it is configured to listen on) will only be expecting to receive LDAPMessage PDUs. When data starts arriving on the configured port, the LDAP server will expect only an LDAPMessage. If the LDAP server is unable to parse to data as an LDAPMessage, then it will normally drop the TCP connection. This is because the absence of LDAP PDUs is an indication that the client is not speaking a version of LDAP that the server understands. Prior to dropping the connection, the server sends a special type of message known as a disconnection notification.

The third form of the LDAP Bind is the SASL Bind. If the SASL authentication choice is made in the bind Request, then the following ASN.1 is used to provide the authentication data:

```
SaslCredentials ::= SEQUENCE {
    mechanism          LDAPString,
    credentials        OCTET STRING OPTIONAL }
```

The mechanism specified above must be IANA registered SASL authenticated. The most interesting SASL mechanism for LDAP is the "EXTERNAL" mechanism. If the SASL EXTERNAL mechanism is used, then this is an indication that the client has requested the server to use authentication information from a lower layer protocol by using the SASL EXTERNAL mechanism. This lower layer protocol in the case of LDAP is likely to be TLS. In this situation, the credentials can be omitted. If TLS authentication is used, then a successful setup of the underlying TLS connection will result in the exchange of X.509 certificate information. The certificate information as specified in X.509 is based upon public-key cryptography. As was discussed earlier, public-key cryptography is a system in which each user has two data items (known as keys) that are used in encrypting data. One of the keys must be kept secret (i.e., the secret key or sometimes called the private key); the other key can be freely published (i.e., the public key). Any data that is encrypted with one of the keys can only be decrypted using the other key. Several encryption algorithms have been devised that make use of public-key cryptographic principles (e.g., RSA Encryption, as specified in RFC 2313). The two keys have a special mathematical relationship; they must be generated as a pair together. Once the keys have been generated, a special agent, known as a certificate authority (CA), formats the public key as an X.509 certificate.

An X.509 certificate contains the public keys of a user, together with some other information, rendered unforgeable by encryption with the private key of the CA that issued the certificate. The validity of the user's certificate can be verified by retrieving the public key of the CA and decrypting the portion of the certificate that was encrypted. If the certificate information decrypts successfully with the CA's public key, then it must have been originally encrypted with the CA's secret key. The part of the certificate that has been encrypted by the CA contains attributes about the owner of the certificate that have theoretically been authenticated by the CA prior to the issuance of the certificate. Among these "authenticated attributes" is the DN of the owner of the certificate. Thus, when the SASL EXTERNAL mechanism is used, the certificates that have been exchanged at the TLS layer can be retrieved by the LDAP entities.

The LDAP server can use the client's certificate, and can be assured that the certificate really does belong to the TLS client on the other side of the TLS connection. The LDAP client can have similar assurance about the server's certificate. The LDAP server can match the TLS client with some user in the directory by retrieving the DN from the certificate and it with the DN of some object in the directory. The exact set of pairing rules by which an LDAP server matches the DN from an X.509 certificate with the DN of some user in the directory are not specified by LDAP. However, it can be assumed that the LDAP server will keep a table in some secure location that maps the certificates that have been issued with the users that are allowed to authenticate to the LDAP server. Since there was a mutual exchange of certificate information at the TLS layer, the LDAP client can also verify that it is talking to the correct LDAP server.

The use of other SASL mechanisms is possible in LDAP, but they will not be covered here. Of particular note is the fact that some SASL mechanisms may require multiple exchanges of data before the security layer has been successfully negotiated. In this scenario, the LDAP client must submit multiple BindRequests, and appropriate BindResults must be returned by the LDAP server in order to complete the negotiation successfully.

Note that bind operations may be sent at any time that an LDAP connection is open so as to modify the identity of the client. When a connection to the LDAP server is first established, the anonymous identity is used. Each subsequent bind operation that is submitted by the LDAP client changes its identity. This behavior is especially useful in situations where an LDAP client application is shared among several users. It is also useful in situations where a user has several different accounts that are used to access different LDAP services.

The companion operation to the bind is the unbind. Whatever LDAP connection was previously established is terminated by the unbind operation. Thus, when an LDAP server receives an unbind operation, the protocol session is considered terminated. The unbind operation as follows has the simplest syntax of any of the operations:

```
UnbindRequest ::= [APPLICATION 2] NULL
```

Any unbind operation is encoded the same way (see Table 4.13).

Table 4.13 Encoding of the `Unbind` Request

Binary Format	Hexadecimal	Meaning
0110 0010 0000 0111	6202	Application 2, length 2
0000 0101 0000 0000	0500	ASN.1 NULL Value

Notice that the NULL value has the ASN.1 universal class number 5, and is always encoded with a zero length value. There is no response defined for the unbind operation. The LDAP server will normally drop the underlying transport connection. An unbind operation can also be used to abort a partially established multistage SASL Bind.

`Search` Operation

The most used LDAP operation is the `search` operation. This is the only standard LDAP operation that is available for LDAP clients to use in the retrieval of information from the directory. The `search` operation is LDAP's solution to the principal function of a Directory service (i.e., property-based information retrieval). The LDAP `search` operation has the following ASN.1 syntax:

```
SearchRequest ::= [APPLICATION 3] SEQUENCE {
    baseObject  LDAPDN,
    scope  ENUMERATED {
        baseObject  (0),
        singleLevel  (1),
        wholeSubtree  (2) },
    derefAliases  ENUMERATED {
        neverDerefAliases  (0),
        derefInSearching  (1),
        derefFindingBaseObj  (2),
        derefAlways  (3) },
    sizeLimit  INTEGER (0 .. maxInt),
    timeLimit  INTEGER (0 .. maxInt),
    typesOnly  BOOLEAN,
    filter  Filter,
    attributes  AttributeDescriptionList }
```

The `baseObject` field indicates where in the DIT the server should begin its search. The search always begins at this object and possibly continues downward into the objects that it contains. The scope field indicates which of the contained objects (if any) should be used in the search. In the sample DIT shown in Figure 4.3, if the `baseObject` field is "O=Internet," then the different values of the scope field have the following effect on the search:

☞ `BaseObject`—only the directory entry "O=Internet" is included in the search

☞ `SingleLevel`—only the directory entries, "OU=SIDK, O=Internet," and "O=Internet," are included in the search

☞ `WholeSubtree`—all of the directory entries in the DIT are included in the search

The `derefAliases` field describes how the client wants alias objects to be handled. An alias is a special LDAP object class whose sole purpose is to "point" to some other LDAP object. It has the following ASN.1 definition:

(2.5.6.1 NAME 'alias' SUP top STRUCTURAL MUST aliasedObjectName)

Where the `aliasedObjectName` attribute is defined as:

(2.5.4.1 NAME 'aliasedObjectName' EQUALITY distinguishedNameMatch
SYNTAX 1.3.6.1.4.1.1466.115.121.1.12 SINGLE-VALUE)

If a server de-references an alias object, then, when an alias is encountered in a search result, the object or objects named by the alias's `aliasedObjectName` attribute are substituted in the search result in place of the alias object. The `sizeLimit` field specifies an upper bound on the amount of data that is returned as a result of any search. This upper bound is specified in terms of the number of matching entries that the server is to return. If a value of 0 is specified, then that is an indication that the client wants all matching entries to be returned in the search result. The `timeLimit` field specifies an upper bound on the amount of time (in seconds) that the server is permitted to spend in executing the client's search request. If a value of 0 is specified, then that is an indication that the client wants the server to spend as much time as is necessary in order to complete the search. In normal situations, LDAP servers can determine the results of a search very quickly. However, in situations where the data that the originating LDAP server requires in order to implement the search is spread across multiple other LDAP servers around the Internet, the amount of time required can be significantly higher.

The `typesOnly` field indicates whether the client wants the server to return the underlying data for objects that will be returned in the search results. If `typesOnly` is set to the BOOLEAN value TRUE, then only the names of the attributes are present in the search results. If it is set to FALSE, then both the names of the attributes and the corresponding values are present in the search results. The filter field is the most important field in the `searchRequest`. It specifies which objects in the DIT are to be returned in the search results. LDAP uses the following ASN.1 specification for a filter:

```
Filter ::= CHOICE {
    and                 [0] SET OF Filter,
    or                  [1] SET OF Filter,
    not                 [2] Filter,
    equalityMatch       [3] AttributeValueAssertion,
    substrings          [4] SubstringFilter,
    greaterOrEqual      [5] AttributeValueAssertion,
    lessOrEqual         [6] AttributeValueAssertion,
    present             [7] AttributeDescription,
    approxMatch         [8] AttributeValueAssertion,
    extensibleMatch     [9] MatchingRuleAssertion }
```

Notice that the defintion of filter is recursive in that the "logical" filter choices include the filter type as their types. The attributeValueAssertion specifies the following attribute type and attribute value:

```
AttributeValueAssertion ::= SEQUENCE {
        attributeDesc AttributeDescription,
        assertionValue AssertionValue }


AssertionValue ::= OCTET STRING
```

In the case of the equalityMatch, entries in the DIT match the search filter if they have at least one value of the specified attribute that is exactly the same as the given `assertionValue`. The attribute type is given as an attribute description. In normal situations, the attribute description is just an attribute type, but LDAP allows the description to contain tags that further qualify the attribute. For example, the surname attribute typically uses the string "`sn`." However, if the clients wants to perform a search using only the French value of the surname, it could use the string "sn;fr" in the attribute description. The use of language codes in LDAP is specified in an Internet Draft that has not yet been finalized. Normally, attribute values are specified as strings in LDAP. LDAP allows the client to request that the values be returned in their native binary format. RFC 2251 defines this option to allow the client to override the normal string representation. If the binary option is specified, then the attribute is returned using the ASN.1 BER encoding.

One example of an LDAP defined attribute that is usually returned using the binary format is the user's X.509 certificate. The binary option for this attribute would be specified as: "userCertificate;binary." `LessOrEqual` and `greaterOrEqual` filters use the same syntax as the equality filter. Notice that in order to perform a search for an attribute that has a value that is strictly less than some specified `assertionValue`, a "not" filter is used that includes the `greaterOrEqual` filter. This is due to the fact that anything that isn't greater or equal to some value must, by definition, be less than that same value.

LDAP doesn't define what it means for an attribute value to satisfy an approxMatch. This filter type is defined in order to allow an attribute value to match the filter if it somehow approximately matches the value stored in the DIT. How two values "approximately" match is not defined, and is left to the interpretation of the server implementation. Thus, the results of an approxMatch are unpredictable, and may vary from one server implementation to another. The following substrings filter type is the most complex of the filter types:

```
SubstringFilter ::= SEQUENCE {
    type AttributeDescription,
    — at least one must be present
    substrings SEQUENCE OF CHOICE {
        initial [0] LDAPString,
        any [1] LDAPString,
        final [2] LDAPString } }
```

The `substrings` filter allows a search to be performed that matches all or part of some string. A discussion of the extensible match will be deferred until later. The present filter is especially useful, even though it is the simplest of all the filter types. It allows a search to be performed that will succeed whenever the supplied attribute type is present in the entry. For example, if one wanted to find users with electronic mail accounts, a present filter could be included in the search that supplied an `attributeDescription` with the string "mail."

The final field of the search operation is the attributes field. This field indicates which attributes from the matching entries in the DIT will be returned. A special case is used for this field when no attributes are listed. This special case is an indication that all available attributes from each matching entry are to be returned. A second special case for this field will be mentioned later when LDAP operational attributes are discussed.

The sample DIT from Figure 4.3 will be used as the target for the example search operations. The first example will be a search to find all of the people in the directory. There are two ways to implement this search. The first would be to use a present filter for the attribute "`cn`." The second, and better way, would be to use an equality filter testing for "objectClass=person." The reason that the equality filter is a better choice in this instance is that the `cn` attribute is used in several different object classes, and this filter might match objects in the directory other than people. In this instance, "O=Internet" can be used as the base object. In many instances, an LDAP server is configured with a default search base, and the search operation can use the null string for this field. We want to search the whole subtree, but don't want to de-reference any aliases. Aliases wouldn't turn up in the search results anyway, since their `objectClass` attribute wouldn't match the supplied person value. Setting the `timeLimit` and `sizeLimit` to zero (indicating no limits) completes the parameters for the search operation. This search operation would be encoded as shown in Table 4.14.

Table 4.14 Encoding the `Search` Request

Binary Format	Hexadecimal	Meaning
0011 0000 0001 0111	3017	Sequence construct, length 23
0000 0010 0000 0001 0000 0001	020101	MessageID is 1
0110 0011 0001 0010	6312	Application 3, length 18
0000 0100 0000 1010 0100 1111 0011 1101 0100 1001 0110 1110 0111 0100 0110 0101 0111 0010 0110 1101 0110 0101 0111 0100	040A4F3D496 E7465726D6574	Search base is "O=Internet"
0000 0010 0000 0001 0000 0000	020100	Scope is 0 (whole subtree)
0000 0010 0000 0001 0000 0000	020100	DerefAliases is 0 (don't do it)
0000 0010 0000 0001 0000 0000	020100	SizeLimit is 0
0000 0010 0000 0001 0000 0000	020100	TimeLimit is 0
0010 0011 0001 0111	2317	Choice is 3,
0011 0000 0001 0101	3015	equality filter
0000 0100 0000 1011 0110 1111 0110 0010 0110 1010 0110 0101 0110 0011 0111 0100 0100 0011 0110 1100 0110 0001 0111 0011 0111 0011	040B6F626A6 56374436C617 373 040670657273 6F6E	"objectClass = person"
0000 0100 0000 0110 0111 0000 0110 0101 0111 0010 0111 0011 0110 1111 0110 1110		
0011 0000 0000 0000	3000	Empty attributes list, return everything

Notice that the application tag is three, which indicates a search operation. Notice that the choice of filter types is three, which indicates that an equality filter is used. Now that the search has been submitted, the client will normally wait patiently for a response from the server, but it could just as well formulate another request and submit that one. LDAP does not impose any upper limit on the number of requests that a client can submit while waiting for responses to be returned. Recall the DIT shown in Figure 4.3, as the server will use it to create the response. There are five objects in the search scope (i.e., entire subtree) that match the search filter:

☞ Cn=breeder1, OU=SIDK, O=Internet

☞ Cn=breeder2, OU=SIDK, O=Internet

☞ Cn=breeder1, OU=french breeders, OU=SIDK, O=Internet

☞ Cn=louise, OU=french breeders, OU=SIDK, O=Internet

☞ Cn=fido's place, OU=french breeders, OU=SIDK, O=Internet

Even though the `objectClass` attribute values aren't shown in Figure 4.3, they can be inferred from the presence of the `cn` attribute. This isn't always a guarantee though, since the `cn` attribute is used as an RDN in many object classes. The following three separate types can appear in response to a `SearchRequest` message:

☞ `SearchResultEntry`

☞ `SearchResultReference`

☞ `SearchResultDone`

All of the DIT entries the server sends back to the client that satisfy the filter in the request are sent back in the `SearchResultEntry` message. If the server has not explored a portion of the DIT indicated by the search base in the request, and wants to indicate that to the client, then it sends that indication in a `SearchResultReference` message. `SearchResultReference` messages normally contain an indication that the client should explore the indicated portion of the DIT on some other (named) LDAP server. At the end of all of the `SearchResultEntry` and `SearchResultReference` messages, the server finishes with a `SearchResultDone` message. Any error messages that the server needs to pass to the client are sent in the `SearchResultDone` message.

Thus, the response to this `SearchRequest` message will actually be contained in two separate LDAPMessages. Each of the five DIT entries that match will be placed into their own `SearchResultEntry` message. These five `SearchResultEntry` messages will be followed by one `SearchResultDone` message. Note that the sequencing of the messages is guaranteed by LDAP's use of connection-oriented transport, such as TCP.

Such sequencing would not be guaranteed over UDP. Hence, in the definition of CLDAP (which operates over UDP), there is no `SearchResultDone` messages, and all matching entries are placed in one server response message. The syntax for the `SearchResultEntry` message follows:

```
SearchResultEntry ::= [APPLICATION 4] SEQUENCE {
    objectName LDAPDN,
    attributes PartialAttributeList }

PartialAttributeList ::= SEQUENCE OF SEQUENCE {
    type AttributeDescription,
    vals SET OF AttributeValue }
```

For purposes of conciseness, assume that each of the DIT entries has only the mandatory attributes from the person and breeder object classes. These mandatory attributes are:

☞ ObjectClass

☞ Cn

☞ Sn

☞ Breed

☞ emailAddress

The server's first `SearchResultEntry` message should appear as that seen in Table 4.15.

Table 4.15 Encoding the `SearchResultEntry`

Binary Format	Hexadecimal	Meaning
0011 0000 1010 1100	30AC	Sequence construct, length 172
0000 0010 0000 0001 0000 0001	020101	MessageID is 2
0110 0100 1010 0111	64A7	Application 4, length 167
0000 0100 0010 0000 0100 0011 0110 1110 0011 1101 0110 0010 0111 0010 0110 0101 0110 0101 0110 0100 0110 0101 0111 0010 0011 0001 0010 1100 0010 0000 0100 0011 0100 1011 0010 1100 0010 0000 0100 1111 0011 1101 0100 1001 0110 1110 0111 0100 0110 0101 0111 0010 0110 1110 0110 0101 0111 0100	0420 436E3D627265 65646572312C 204F553D5349 434B2C204F3 D496E7465572 6 E6574	Matching DN is "Cn=breeder1, OU=SIDK, O=Internet"

Table 4.15 Encoding the SearchResultEntry (continued)

Binary Format	Hexadecimal	Meaning
0011 0000 1000 0011	3083	Sequence construct, length is 131 (5 attributes are inside)
0011 0000 0010 0101	3025	Sequence Construct (1st attribute), size is 37
0000 0100 0000 1011 0110 1111 0110 0010 0110 1010 0110 0101 0110 0011 0111 0100 0100 0011 0110 1100 0110 0001 0111 0011 0111 0011	040B6F626A6 56372436C617 373	Attribute type is objectClass, size is 11
0010 1111 0001 0110	2F16	Set Construct (here are the object classes), length is 22
0000 0100 0000 0110 0111 0000 0110 0101 0111 0010 0111 0011 0110 1111 0110 1110	040670657273 6F6E	Values are: "person", "top," and "breeder." Note that the values may appear in any order.
0000 0100 0000 0011 0111 0100 0110 1111 0111 0000	0403746F70	
0000 0100 0000 0111 0110 0010 0111 0010 0110 0101 0110 0101 0110 0100 0110 0101 0111 0010	040762726565 646572	
0011 0000 0001 0000	3010	Sequence Construct (2nd attribute), size is 16
0000 0100 0000 1011 0110 0111 0110 1110	0402636E	Attribute type is cn, size is 2
0010 1111 0000 1010	2F0A	Set Construct (here's the cn), length is 10
0000 0100 0000 1000 0110 0010 0111 0010 0110 0101 0110 0101 0110 0100 0110 0101 0111 0010 0011 0001	040862726565 64657231	Attribute Value is "breeder1"
0011 0000 0000 1101	300D	Sequence Construct (3rd attribute), size is 13
0000 0100 0000 0010 0111 0011 0110 1110	0402736E	Attribute type is sn, size is 2
0010 1111 0000 0111	2F07	Set Construct (here's the sn), length is 7
0000 0100 0000 0101 0111 0011 0110 1101 0110 1001 0111 0100 0110 1000	0405736D6974 68	Attribute Value is "smith"

Table 4.15 Encoding the SearchResultEntry (continued)

Binary Format	Hexadecimal	Meaning
0011 0000 0001 0100	3014	Sequence Construct (4th attribute), size is 20
0000 0100 0000 0101 0110 0010 0111 0010 0110 0101 0110 0101 0110 0100	040562726565 64	Attribute type is breed, size is 5
0010 1111 0000 1011	2F0B	Set Construct (here's the breeds), length is 11
0000 0100 0000 0011 0111 0000 0111 0000 0111 0101 0110 0111	0403707567	Attribute Value is "pug"
0000 0100 0000 0011 0111 0000 0110 1111 0110 1111 0110 0100 0110 1100 0110 0101	0406706F6F64 6C65	Attribute Value is "poodle"
0011 0000 0010 0011	3023	Sequence Construct (5th attribute), size is 35
0000 0100 0000 1100 0110 0101 0110 1101 0110 0001 0110 1001 0110 1100 0100 0001 0110 0100 0110 0100 0111 0010 0110 0101 0111 0011 0111 0011	040C656D6169 6C4164647265 7373	Attribute type is emailAddress, size is 12
0010 1111 0001 0011	2F13	Set Construct (here's the address), length is 19
0000 0100 0001 0001 0110 0010 0111 0010 0110 0101 0110 0101 0110 0100 0110 0101 0111 0010 0011 0001 0100 0000 0111 0011 0110 1001 0110 0011 0110 1011 0010 1110 0110 1111 0111 0010 0110 0111	041162726565 646572314073 69636B2E6F72 67	Attribute Value is "breeder1@sidk.org"

This is the ASN.1 encoding of the first `SearchResultEntry` message sent by the LDAP server in response to the original `SearchRequest`. This message would be followed by four more `SearchResultEntry` messages that would each contain one of the matching entries. After all five `SearchResultEntry` messages have been sent over the TCP (or TLS) connection by the server, it would send a final SearchResultDone message to indicate that there are no more matching entries in the DIT. Notice that there is no indication of how many matching entries there are in any of the results that the server returns. The SearchResultDone message has the following format:

```
SearchResultDone ::= [APPLICATION 5] LDAPResult
```

The encoding of the successful completion of the search is given in Table 4.16.

Table 4.16 Encoding the `SearchResultDone` Message

Binary Format	Hexadecimal	Meaning
0110 0101 0000 0111	6507	Application 5, length 7
0000 0010 0000 0001 0000 0000	020103	ResultCode is success (0)
0100 0000	0400	No matchedDN
0100 0000	0400	No errorMessage

Notice that this message is nearly identical to the `BindResponse` message, except that the application tags are different. Notice that all of the data in the `SearchResultEntry` message is really character string data. The ASN.1 tag 04 that normally indicates an octet string type is used vigorously by LDAP to encode character string data that is in UTF-8 format. Every attribute type and value is given in this encoding. In this example, all of the data is from the ASCII character set, but there is no reason that the attribute values could not use characters outside of this character set.

In situations where the DIT is actually spread across multiple LDAP servers, `SearchResultReference` messages can be used. Imagine that the information shown in the sample DIT shown in Figure 4.3 can be accessed on the LDAP server with the hostname *ldap1.sidk.org.* Assume that there is an additional LDAP server that is maintained by the U.S. breeders, namely *ldap.us.sidk.org.* This LDAP server maintains all information in the DIT in the container, OU=US Breeders, OU=SIDK, O=Internet. Thus, the response to the above `SearchRequest` message in this scenario would contain a `SearchResultReference` message with an indication that the LDAP client should contact the other LDAP server. The `SearchResultReference` message has this syntax:

```
SearchResultReference ::= [APPLICATION 19] SEQUENCE OF LDAPURL

LDAPURL ::= LDAPString
```

The format of an LDAP URL is defined in RFC 2255. The basic format uses the string "ldap" as the protocol identifier, and the hostname is followed by the appropriate directory context to use for a search. The LDAP URL for the US Breeders OU on this second LDAP server would be:

```
ldap://ldap.us.sidk.org/OU=US%20Breeders, OU=SIDK, O=Internet
```

Notice that spaces in name components are encoded using the UTF-8 escape mechanism as the sequence "%20." Thus, this `SearchResult-Reference` would be encoded as shown in Table 4.17.

Table 4.17 Encoding the `SearchResultReference`

Binary Format	Hexadecimal	Meaning
0111 0011 0011 1111	733F	Application 19, length 63
0000 0100 0011 1101 0110 1100 0110 0100 0110 0001 ...	043D6C6461...	LDAP URL, length is 61

Since it was already shown earlier in this section, most of the encoding of the URL was omitted. Also, the initial sequence structure of the LDAPMessage and the `MessageID` have been left out, since it has already been shown a few times. The LDAP client may use the URL returned in a subsequent search operation that it would submit to the LDAP server that is named in the URL. Note that if there were no matching entries in the DIT which correspond to the submitted search filter, then the LDAP URL would not be returned in the `SearchResultReference`. Instead, it would be returned to the URL in a special type of error message known as an *LDAP referral*. The LDAP referral mechanism and the similar `SearchResultReference` message are very similar to the DNS referral mechanism. The LDAP referral is contained in the `SearchResultDone` message with a resultCode of referral (10), and the referral field of the `LDAPResult` is present. Such a `SearchResultDone` message would be encoded like shown in Table 4.18.

Table 4.18 Encoding a `SearchResultDone` with a Referral

Binary Format	Hexadecimal	Meaning
0110 0101 0000 0111	6107	Application 5, length 7
0000 0010 0000 0001 0000 1010	02010A	ResultCode is referral (10)
0100 0000	0400	No matchedDN
0100 0000	0400	No errorMessage
0000 0011 0110 1100 0110 0100 0110 0001 ...	043D6C6461...	LDAP URL, length is 61

Other errors can be returned in response to a search. These would also appear in the SearchResultDone message. Some of the most common errors to be returned are:

☞ `timeLimitExceeded` (3)—The amount of time specified in the search request has passed without the LDAP server being able to complete the search. The client should resubmit the search with a larger `timeLimit`, or with a more refined filter.

☞ `sizeLimitExceeded` (4)—The number of entries that the server found that match the specified server filter was more than the number of entries specified in the `sizeLimit` field of the search request. The number of entries returned is equal to the value specified in the `sizeLimit` field.

☞ `NoSuchAttribute` (16)—This is an indication that one of the attributes requested in the `SearchRequest` is not available for this object (or object class).

☞ `NoSuchObject` (32)—This is normally an indication that the specified search base is unknown to this LDAP server.

Making Changes (`Add`, `Modify`, and `Delete` Operations)

Unlike DNS, LDAP defines operations that can actually change the content of the DIT. The three main operations that are defined are: `Add`, `Modify`, and `Delete`. The `add` operation creates a new entry and places it in a specified location in the DIT. The `modify` operation makes changes to an existing DIT entry, while the `delete` operation removes an object from the DIT. Each of these operations targets one entry per request. Thus, mass changes to the DIT require numerous LDAP operations. The `add` request is defined as:

```
AddRequest ::= [APPLICATION 8] SEQUENCE {
    entry LDAPDN,
    attributes AttributeList }

AttributeList ::= SEQUENCE OF SEQUENCE {
    type AttributeDescription,
    vals SET OF AttributeValue }
```

The format of the `AddRequest` message is virtually identical to the format of the `SearchResultEntry` message. The only difference is in the application tag. Thus, the protocol that is submitted in the creation of the DIT entry is the same as the protocol that is returned when viewing the DIT entry. Of course, the read operation may not see all of the available attributes in the DIT entry (especially if not all of the attributes were requested). Note that the DN named in the entry field must not already exist in the DIT. This will cause an error to be returned.

The modify request is defined as:

```
ModifyRequest ::= [APPLICATION 6] SEQUENCE {
    object LDAPDN,
    modification SEQUENCE OF SEQUENCE {
    operation ENUMERATED {
            add (0),
            delete (1),
            replace (2) },
    modification AttributeTypeAndValues } }

AttributeTypeAndValues ::= SEQUENCE {
    type AttributeDescription,
    vals SET OF AttributeValue }
```

Notice again the similarity between the ModifyRequest message and the SearchResultEntry message. In this case there is an additional field present in the request. The operation field is an indication of what the server should do with the modification field that is also present in the message. The behavior is as follows:

☞ Add (0)—add the values given in the modification field to the indicated attribute type.

☞ Delete (1)—remove the values given the modification field from the indicated attribute type. If no values are given in the modification field, then the entire attribute is removed from the entry.

☞ Replace (2)—remove all values of the given type from the specified DIT entry and replace them with the new values that are specified in the modification field. Just as in the case of the previous modification type, if no values are given in the modification field, then the entire attribute is removed from the entry or is ignored if the entry does not currently have an attribute of this type.

Note that the modify operation may not remove mandatory attributes from an object. The cn attribute therefore could never be removed from a person object. The delete operation is the final major LDAP operation that makes changes to the DIT. Its syntax is simply the name of the entry in the DIT to delete:

```
DelRequest ::= [APPLICATION 10] LDAPDN
```

The responses to each of these operations is the familiar LDAPResult message:

```
ModifyResponse ::= [APPLICATION 7] LDAPResult
AddResponse ::= [APPLICATION 9] LDAPResult
DelResponse ::= [APPLICATION 11] LDAPResult
```

In the normal course of events, the responses to these operations look exactly like the successful response to the search operation. However, there are different error conditions with these operations that commonly occur. They are as follows:

☞ InsufficientAccessRights (50)—This error is returned if the identity specified in the bind does not have the necessary privileges to perform the specified change to the DIT. Not all users are allowed to make changes to entries in the DIT. In some situations, users are allowed to make minor changes to their own entries, but no further changes are allowed. Other users, like the LDAP administrator, are allowed nearly unrestricted access to make changes to the DIT.

☞ ObjectClassViolation (65)—This error is returned when a change to an entry has been attempted that would result in missing mandatory attributes. It may also be returned when an attribute for addition is specified to an entry that is not available for that object class. For example, the attempt to add a breed attribute to a person object without also adding the breeder object class would result in this error being returned, since breed is not specified as an attribute of the person object class.

☞ EntryAlreadyExists (68)—This error is returned when an add operation specifies an entry's DN that is already present in the DIT.

☞ NoSuchObject (32)—This error is returned when a modify or delete operation specifies an entry's DN that can't be found in the DIT.

Lesser Used Operations (Modify DN, Compare, and Abandon)

The previous sections have specified the operations that are most commonly used in LDAP. There are three additional operations (Modify DN, Compare, and Abandon) that have been carried over in LDAP from X.500 that are not widely used. But just because they aren't widely used doesn't mean that they don't perform functions that are considered useful in some scenarios. The modify DN operation is used to change the distinguished name of an entry in the DIT. This operation is occasionally use-

ful when an entry in the DIT needs to be moved to some other portion of
the DIT. If the object were deleted and re-added to the other portion of
the DIT, then any Aliases and privileges that referenced the entry would
no longer apply to the newly added entry, whereas the intention of this
operation is to allow the renamed operation to retain its previous identity. This operation is defined as:

```
ModifyDNRequest ::= [APPLICATION 12] SEQUENCE {
    entry LDAPDN,
    newrdn RelativeLDAPDN,
    deleteoldrdn BOOLEAN,
    newSuperior [0] LDAPDN OPTIONAL }
```

The entry field specifies the current DIT entry to be renamed. The
combination of the newrdn field and the newSuperior field specify the
new name of the entry. If the newSuperior field is not present in the
request message, then the newrdn field replaces the last DN component
of the current DIT entry. The deleteoldrdn field specifies whether the
current DIT entry is allowed to remain present in the DIT. This field normally has the value true, which indicates that the DN named in the entry
is no longer available.

The compare operation allows the LDAP client to specify a single
attribute type and value and have it compared to the same attribute of an
existing entry in the DIT. X.500 originally defined this operation to allow
directory-enabled applications to check the password that was given to
them by their users with the password that was stored in the directory.
The compare operation has this syntax:

```
CompareRequest ::= [APPLICATION 14] SEQUENCE {
    entry LDAPDN,
    ava AttributeValueAssertion }

AttributeValueAssertion ::= SEQUENCE {
    attributeDesc AttributeDescription,
    assertionValue AssertionValue }
```

The AVA field contains the attribute type and value that the server
should compare to the attributes stored in the specified DIT entry. If any
of the attributes of that entry have a value that is exactly equal to the
specifed assertionValue, then the server returns true, otherwise, the
server returns false.

The abandon operation is normally used in accompaniment with a
search operation when it seems to be taking too long. This operation is
useful in situations where the LDAP server is acting in tandem with

other LDAP servers to perform an operation. For example, a server may need to collect data from several different sources to accumulate the complete search response, and occasionally the wait to collect the data may be very long due to the vagaries of Internet communication. Thus, the client may indicate to the server that it is unwilling to wait for completion of the operation. There is no response defined or needed for the abandon operation. The LDAP server must immediately stop working on the specified operation. The abandon operation simply specifies the MessageID of the previous operation that should be abandoned as follows:

```
AbandonRequest ::= [APPLICATION 16] MessageID
```

Note that this MessageID must have been used in a request message that was initiated in this LDAP session. So, if the client wanted to abandon the search request submitted above, it would use the MessageID number 2 in its abandon request, as shown in Table 4.19.

Table 4.19 Encoding the Abandon Request

Binary Format	Hexadecimal	Meaning
0111 0000 0000 0111	7003	Application 16, length 3
0000 0010 0000 0001 0000 0010	020102	The MessageID to Abandon is 2.

Extended Operations and Controls

One of the new features that is provided by LDAP v3 versus previous versions of LDAP is the ability to define extensions to the protocol using the constructs of the protocol itself. The designers of LDAP foresaw the need to provide an extensible protocol so that there would be no fourth version of LDAP. The extension operations allow additional operations to be defined for services not available elsewhere in LDAP. Thus an extension operation would be defined for a new type of search. However, one might define an extension operation to turn on and off TLS without losing the LDAP connection. Such an operation would be beneficial in allowing an LDAP server listening on the same port to support both TLS sessions as well as TCP sessions. In order to define such an operation, the first thing that must be defined is an OID that represents the request to start using TLS, and a second OID that represents the request to stop using TLS. Since legal OIDs can only start with the digit zero, one or two, the sample OID that will be allocated for these LDAP extended operations will start with three (which is definitely *not* legal). Assume that the OID 3.0

is the root of the OIDs that will be used. Thus, the OIDs for these extended operations are:

☞ 3.0.0—Start using TLS Request

☞ 3.0.1—Start using TLS Response

☞ 3.0.2—Stop using TLS Request

☞ 3.0.3—Stop using TLS Response

The actual syntax that is used in any LDAP extended request is:

```
ExtendedRequest ::= [APPLICATION 23] SEQUENCE {
    requestName [0] LDAPOID,
    requestValue [1] OCTET STRING OPTIONAL }
```

The corresponding response syntax is:

```
ExtendedResponse ::= [APPLICATION 24] SEQUENCE {
    COMPONENTS OF LDAPResult,
    responseName [10] LDAPOID OPTIONAL,
    response [11] OCTET STRING OPTIONAL }
```

LDAP allows any arbitrary sequence of bytes to be included in the requestValue field of the `ExtendedRequest` operation. Similarly, any byte sequence can be used as the value of the response field of the ExtendedResponse. In the case of TLS operations the LDAP client could include information that would aid the LDAP server in retrieving the TLS authentication information from the underlying TLS layer. Similarly, the LDAP server could include in the response field the identity that it is assuming for the LDAP client. Given these example extended operations, the LDAP client would send this request to switch from the standard LDAP over TCP mode to the more secure LDAP over TLS mode; (see Table 4.20).

Table 4.20 Encoding an `Extended` Request to Begin TLS

Binary Format	Hexadecimal	Meaning
0111 0111 0000 1001	7709	Application 23, length 3
0000 0100 0000 0101 0011 0011 0010 1110 0011 0000 0010 1110 0011 0000	0405332E302E 30	OID is 3.0.0, Start using TLS request
0000 0100 0000 0000	0400	No parameters (use TLS defaults?)

In this example, the client indicates an extended request by setting the application tag of the LDAPMessage to 23. The exact type of extended request is indicated by the first parameter of the request, which in this case is the OID 3.0.0, that is indicative of the start using TLS request. Assuming that the request is successful, the LDAP server would respond with an extended response LDAPMessage with the OID 3.0.1. Such a message would be encoded like that shown in Table 4.21.

Table 4.21 Encoding the `Extended` Response

Binary Format	Hexadecimal	Meaning
0111 1000 0000 0011	6103	Application 24, length 3
0000 0010 0000 0001 0000 0000	020100	ResultCode is success (0)
0100 0000	0400	No matchedDN
0100 0000	0400	No errorMessage
0000 0100 0000 0101 0011 0011 0010 1110 0011 0000 0010 1110 0011 0001	0405332E302E 31	OID is 3.0.1, Start using TLS response

Notice that the LDAP server did not include a matched DN. The matched DN field is normally only included in LDAP responses to add requests. If the LDAP server wanted to include the DN of the directory object that it has assumed for the client, it would have to include it in the optional response field (which in this example has been omitted). If for some reason the LDAP server did not understand the OID in the `extendedRequest` message from the client, it would still respond with an `ExtendedResponse` message, but would use a `ResultCode` of `protocol-Error` (2). Once the server has responded with a successful `resultCode`, the client is obligated to attempt to initiate a TLS session over the currently connected TCP socket. A similar client-server exchange would appear when the LDAP client was finished using TLS and wanted to return to a native mapping of LDAP onto the TCP data stream. In this case, however, the client would issue a request using the OID 3.0.2, and the server would (hopefully) respond with the OID 3.0.3. Note again that the OIDs used in these examples are completely illegal, and could never be used in the construction of actual LDAP extended operations.

The other form of protocol extensions that are provided for in LDAP is the control. LDAP controls are additional optional parameters that can be included in any LDAPMessage. While the extended operation is designed to provide for new kinds of requests and responses, the control is used to extend existing operations. The format of the control is:

```
Controls ::= SEQUENCE OF Control

Control ::= SEQUENCE {
    controlType LDAPOID,
    criticality BOOLEAN DEFAULT FALSE,
    controlValue OCTET STRING OPTIONAL }
```

This definition of the control allows more than one control to be included in the same LDAP operation. The controlType field contains the OID that identifies the control. The criticality field indicates what the server should do with a control that it does not recognize. If the criticality field has the Boolean value FALSE, then the LDAP server can perform the operation (search or whatever) and safely ignore the control, if it does not recognize the control. If the criticality field has the Boolean value TRUE, then the server *must not* perform the operation and *must* instead return the resultCode unavailableCriticalExtension (12), if it does not recognize the control. RFC 2251 does not define any controls, but definition of several controls began immediately after the approval of LDAP v3 as a proposed standard.

One of these controls defines an LDAP v3-based mechanism for signing directory operations in order to create a secure journal of changes that have been made to each directory entry. The initial draft specification of this control uses the OID = 1.2.840.113549.6.0.0, and is defined by following ASN.1 syntax:

```
SignedOperation ::= CHOICE {
    SignbyServer [0] BOOLEAN
    SignatureIncluded [1] OCTET STRING }
```

This control has two choices, one of which is a client indication that the server should cryptographically sign the operation, while the other choice allows the client to include a cryptographic signature of the operation. This control makes use of the signature formats defined in the S/MIME specification (RFC 2311). Signed operations are presumed to be LDAP operations that modify the DIT (e.g., add, modify, or delete). It allows the client to choose the criticality of the signedOperation. If it is marked critical, and the server understands the control, then the server is obligated to attach the signature included by the client to the object being modified. Thus, later on, LDAP clients can view the history of changes that have been applied to a directory entry.

Use of LDAP to Support a Public Key Infrastructure

One of the interesting applications of LDAP is its use in support of a Public Key Infrastructure (PKI). A PKI is used to provide a tool to support public-key encryption. Public-key encryption is a form of encryption in which each user has two keys, a key being an input parameter to the encryption or decryption operation. Normally, the two keys of a user are named d (the decryption key) and e (the encryption key). So, in using the public-key encryption algorithm, R, the encryption of the document X with key e is represented as $R(X, e)$. Similarly, $R(Y, d)$ represents the decryption of the document Y with key d. The interesting characteristic of public-key encryption is that the two keys used in the algorithms are related in a special mathematical way such that knowing one of the keys is of virtually no help in deriving the other key. Therefore, it is possible to publish the encryption keys for the users in LDAP so that they are publicly available, and there is no perceived risk at the compromise of the users' private keys. One of the more popular algorithms for public-key cryptography is RSA encryption, as defined in RFC 2313.

If a user, Alice, wished to encrypt a document X for private transmission to a user, Bob, then she would only need to access Bob's LDAP entry and retrieve his public key. Once in possession of Bob's public key, Alice could encrypt the document as $Y = R(X, e_{Bob})$. Alice could then safely transmit the document Y over the public data network, secure in the knowledge that only someone in possession of Bob's private key can decrypt Y. With any luck, Bob has kept his private key secure, and only he will be able to decrypt Y. Thus, when he receives the document, he will be able to retrieve the original document by performing the decryption step: $X = R(Y, d_{Bob})$. Notice that whatever action was performed with one key is undone with the other key. Therefore, in public-key cryptography, the application of the encryption key followed by the application of the decryption results in the original document being returned (i.e., $R(R(X, e_{Bob}), d_{Bob})$ always equals X).

As was discussed in the earlier section on security, digital signatures are another important use of public-key cryptography. RFC 1321 conjectures that it is computationally infeasible to produce two messages having the same message digest, or to produce any message having a given specified target message digest. This means that given two different documents, the likelihood of them having the same MD5 digest is only one in approximately 1.7×10^{38}, which is quite an unlikely event. Similarly, since there is no obvious way to create a document with a specific digest, one would have to try, on average, 1.7×10^{38} different documents before finding one with the desired message digest. In terms of time, if one was able to compute 100 MD5 message digests per second, it would take, on average, 539 septillion centuries to find a document with a specific digest. This computational difficulty is crucial in the use of digital signatures. Note that MD5 is not an encryption algorithm, and it does not take any keys as parameters.

The second step in the production of a digital signature is the encryption of the digest. In this case, the digest is encrypted with the private key, d. Thus, if Alice wants to sign a document X for distribution, she digests the message and then encrypts it as: $S_X = R(MD(X), d_{Alice})$. When Bob receives document X along with a signature S_X, he can verify the signature by digesting X, decrypting the signature S_X, and comparing the two results. Thus, if the equation $R(S_X, e_{Alice}) = MD(X)$, then Bob has been able to successfully verify Alice's signature on the document X. This verification proves two things:

☞ X was not modified in transit

☞ X was really sent by Alice, since no one else could have known her private key

In order to verify the signature, Bob can retrieve Alice's public key from her directory entry via LDAP. Public keys are normally stored in directories in the form of *certificates*. One popular certificate format is defined in the ITU document X.509, though there are others (notably, PGP defined in RFC 1991). An X.509 certificate has the following important fields (among many others):

1. The DN of the owner of the certificate

2. The DN of the issuer of the certificate

3. The time period during which the certificate is valid

4. An alternative name for the owner (e.g., the e-mail address)

It is often the case that items 1 and 2 above are the same, which results in what is known as a *self-signed* certificate. Sometimes item 1 above is empty in the certificate, and only the alternative name format is available. This is acceptable since LDAP allows searches to be performed using any available attribute (including common name or e-mail address). The issuer of the certificate is normally called a Certificate Authority (CA). A CA is important because the CA guarantees the authenticity of a certificate, and also signs the data in the certificate. Since a CA signs the certificates that it issues (using its private key), it should also have a certificate available in the directory in order that the information in the certificates that it issues can be verified. Note that the DN in the certificate need not match the DN in the directory entry. This may be due to several factors:

☞ The user's directory entry has been renamed since the certificate was issued.

☞ The DN in the certificate is in the DIT of the CA, and not in the DIT of the certificate owner.

☞ The user doesn't have a directory entry.

In this last case, LDAP isn't much use in looking up a non-existent entry, but perhaps future research will reveal a clever solution to this problem of finding things that don't exist. The entry for the CA not only contains its certificate, but also contains another attribute known as a Certificate Revocation List (CRL). A CRL contains the list of certificates that were issued by the CA that would normally be valid according to the time interval contained in the certificate, but are considered *revoked* by the CA. The CA that issued it no longer considers a revoked certificate to be valid, and users should act with caution when dealing with a revoked certificate. The principal reason that an issuing CA would revoke a certificate is that the private key corresponding to the public key in the certificate has been compromised. RFC 2256 defines these two object classes in order to support a PKI:

```
( 2.5.6.15 NAME 'strongAuthenticationUser' SUP top AUXILIARY
    MUST userCertificate )
```

```
( 2.5.6.16 NAME 'certificationAuthority' SUP top AUXILIARY
    MUST ( authorityRevocationList $ certificateRevocationList $
    cACertificate ) MAY crossCertificatePair )
```

These object classes are of the auxiliary form, and can be attached to any object in the directory. Normally, organization or organizationalUnit objects in the directory represent certificationAuthority entries. If the CA will only issue a certificate to an end user, and not to another CA, then the authorityRevocationList attribute will be empty. This attribute (called the ARL) contains the list of certificates that were issued to other CAs that have been revoked. The certificate of the CA is stored in the cACertificate field. The optional crossCertificatePair attribute is a special way that a CA entry can list the certificates of other CAs that it trusts, so that the certificate of each trusted CA is signed. Given that background information, the sequence of operations that should be issued in order for Alice to encrypt a document for Bob (assuming that Alice knows that Bob's e-mail address is *bob@someplace.com*) is:

1. Use DNS to retrieve the SRV records for *ldap.someplace.com* so that the appropriate LDAP server can be found. Assume that the LDAP server that is found is *ldap.someplace.com*.

2. Submit an LDAP `SearchRequest` message to LDAP with a search filter of *mail=bob@someplace.com*, an empty search base (since SRV records unfortunately don't indicate what search base should be used), a subtree search scope, and an attribute list that includes the userCertificate;binary attribute.

3. Extract Bob's certificate from the `SearchResult` message. If it isn't in the SearchResult message, then LDAP can't be used to get the certificate, and it will send Bob a message asking for his certificate. When it is received, proceed to the next step. A referral message might be received at this step, in which case another LDAP `SearchRequest` message should be submitted to the referred-to LDAP server.

4. Extract the issuer's DN from Bob's certificate. Submit another LDAP `SearchRequest` message to the server from which Bob's certificate was retrieved. This time use the DN of the CA as the search base, set the search scope to base object, and ask for the cACertificate;binary and the certificateRevocationList;binary attributes.

5. If for some reason this CA is unknown to Alice, she should extract the issuer's DN from the certificate of this CA, and repeat step 4 using this DN instead of Bob's DN until a known (and trusted) CA is found. This time, the authorityRevocationList;binary attribute should be retrieved instead of the certificateRevocationList;binary attribute.

6. The CRL retrieved in step 4 is scanned to see if Bob's certificate is present. The public key in the CA's certificate is used to verify Bob's certificate. Any ARLs retrieved in step 5 are scanned to see if the CA certificate has been revoked. The public keys in any certificates retrieved in step 5 are used in the validation of the retrieved CA certificates.

7. Once all CRLs, ARLs, and CA certificates have been validated, Alice can proceed in the knowledge that Bob's key can still be used, and that only Bob can decrypt the message that Alice encrypts. If any of these steps fail, no such assurance can be made, since Bob's certificate or one of the certificates along the chain of issuing CAs may have been compromised.

Some of the information retrieved in these steps may be cached and not looked up each time a certificate is used. However, the older the information in the cache is, the more likely the case that an invalid or compromised key may be used, and information that is thought to be secure is actually quite vulnerable.

CHAPTER SUMMARY

In this chapter we discussed the many LDAP operations, and how the base set of LDAP operations can be enhanced through extensions and controls. We also discussed how the information that is stored in LDAP can be structured through the schema. We also went into detail about how LDAP can be used to support a Public Key Infrastructure. All of these features are readily available in many modern operating systems that already include an LDAP server. Most web browsers are capable of limited LDAP client capabilities. For example, Windows 2000 Server includes Active Directory, which implements LDAP. NetWare includes Novell Directory Services (NDS), which also implements LDAP. NDS is also available on other platforms including Windows NT and many flavors of Unix. Netscape Directory Server also implements LDAP, and is available on many platforms as well. A reference version of the LDAP server is OpenLDAP. OpenLDAP's source code can be freely obtained from the OpenLDAP Group at: *http://www.openldap.org/software.*

## CHAPTER 5

Text-Based Internet Directory Services

So far the only real directory services that have been discussed in any detail are DNS and LDAP. This chapter will add several more directory services to the landscape by analyzing: Finger, Whois, and Whois++ services. These directory Services all share the distinction of being *text-based* directory services. A text-based directory service is specially designed so that all parts of the communication between the client and the server are implemented in text. In this scenario, text has the meaning of sequences of character strings. The characters in the protocol were historically drawn from the ASCII character set, but have more recently been implemented in the UTF-8 transformation of the Unicode character set. These text-based directory services are in contrast to LDAP, which defines a binary protocol making use of ASN.1. Even though it is similar to DNS, which uses text-based messages that are exchanged between the client and server, DNS is not text-based. Much of the DNS protocol is textual in nature (e.g., host names and IP addresses), but the protocol makes use of many features that are encoded as bit strings and other binary data formats. For example, the TTL (Time to Live) field that appears in each DNS resource record is an encoded 32-bit integer.

The main advantage of the text-based directory services is that the client can be very simple, and, in fact, can be implemented as a simple terminal interface (e.g., telnet), in which the end user is expected to directly type the elements of the protocol. Another advantage is that protocol analyzer tools that listen in on the exchange between the client and the server can very easily display the network communication to the end user. Non text-based protocols require complex decoding tools in order to be able to display the information effectively to the end user of the protocol analyzer. A fourth text-based directory service has also been defined by the IETF. It is Referral Whois (RWhois). RWhois won't be discussed in this chapter, since it has much in common with Whois++ but uses a slightly different protocol.

These text-based directory services are defined in RFCs as shown in Table 5.1.

Table 5.1 RFCs for Text-Based Directories

Directory Service	RFC
Finger	RFC 1288
Whois	RFC 954
Whois++	RFC 1913, RFC 1914
Rwhois	RFC 2167

Finger and Whois were actually defined much earlier, and are examples of the earliest implementations of Internet directory services that were specifically designed for the search and retrieval of user-based information (i.e., White Pages Services).

FINGER

In the Finger protocol, the server is known as a remote user information program (RUIP). The Finger client sends text-based queries to an RUIP, which processes the query and returns a string of unformatted text that contains information about the desired user. The Finger protocol is defined using the Augmented Backus-Naur Form (ABNF) grammar. The ABNF used in IETF documents is defined in RFC 2234. Each line in an ABNF grammar is a rule. A rule is defined by the following sequence:

```
name = elements crlf
```

where <name> is the name of the rule, <elements> is one or more rule names or terminal specifications, and <crlf> is the end-of-line indicator, than a carriage return followed by a line feed. The <elements> part of the rule indicates what can be substituted for the rule name. Elements are a sequence of one or more rule names or terminal values. Terminal values are just integers. Characters in ABNF are just non-negative integers. ABNF permits specifying literal text string directly, enclosed in quotation-marks. For example:

```
command    = "command string"
```

Vertical bars in ABNF represent choices: For example:

```
InternetProtocol = "LDAP" | "DNS" | "Finger"
```

This rule indicates that an InternetProtocol is represented by one of the three character strings given in the <elements> section of the rule. Rule names can also be given in the <elements> section. For example:

```
Protocol = "X.500" | InternetProtocol
```

This rule indicates that a Protocol is represented by one of the three InternetProtocol possibilities or the string "X.500." If two elements are placed next to each other in a rule, then they are to be concatenated. For example:

```
VersionNumber = "v1" | "v2" | "v3"
VersionedProtocol = InternetProtocol VersionNumber
```

These two rules indicate that a VersionedProtocol is one of the three InternetProtocol possibilities followed by one of the three VersionNumber possibilities. So a valid result of the rules is: "LDAPv3." The ABNF representation of the Finger protocol as defined by RFC 1288 is shown in Figure 5.1.

In this grammar, the rule names are enclosed in curly brackets. If an element is optional, it is enclosed in square brackets. From the Finger grammar, it can be seen that there are two types of queries. A Q1 query is a request for user information, and a Q2 query is a request for the RUIP to forward the query to another RUIP host. Either type of query is terminated with a carriage return, linefeed character sequence. In the BNF specification, the square brackets (i.e., [and]) enclose optionally

```
{Q1}   ::= [{W}|{W}{S}{U}]{C}
{Q2}   ::= [{W}{S}][{U}]{H}{C}
{U}    ::= username
{H}    ::= @hostname | @hostname{H}
{W}    ::= /W
{S}    ::= <SP> | <SP>{S}
{C}    ::= <CRLF>
```

Fig. 5.1 Grammar for the Finger protocol.

present elements. In the Finger protocol, the "/W" token is a request for a more verbose response from the RUIP. Support for this token is optional, so the RUIP may ignore it. So, in the Q1 query, the query takes one of the following two formats:

```
Null command line - {C}
User name specified - {U} {C}
```

The null command line format in the Finger protocol is a request for a list of all connected users. If the user name is specified, then the request is for information about the specified user. The user name is normally specified in the format of a login ID on the specified Internet host. Recalling that all data in the Finger protocol is presumed to be textual, if the RUIP received the command line: "bruce<CRLF>", it might produce the response as shown in Figure 5.2.

In a situation where the RUIP receives only the command line: "<CRLF>", it might produce the response as shown in Table 5.2.

Table 5.2 Another Typical Finger Response from the RUIP

Login	Name	TTY	Idle	When	Office
Bruce	Bruce Greenblatt	10	1:11	Sat 20:47	Home x1234
green	Joe Green	11	24	Mon 15:46	Work x3074

Notice that the Finger protocol has no provision for the modification of directory information. Thus, it is a *read-only* directory service. The data that is used by the Finger service is created and updated by some means other than the Finger protocol. On Unix systems, the data accessed by the RUIP is the same data that is used by the system administrator in creating and changing the user information. Alternatively, it is natural to imagine a scenario in which the information that the RUIP uses to formulate its queries is actually administered by an LDAP server. This scenario is represented in Figure 5.3.

```
Login name: bruce              In real life: Bruce Greenblatt
Directory: /usr/local/bruce    Shell: /bin/csh
Last login: Sat Oct 24 20:47 on tty10 from home
No unread mail
Project:
Plan:
```

Fig. 5.2 Typical Finger response from the RUIP.

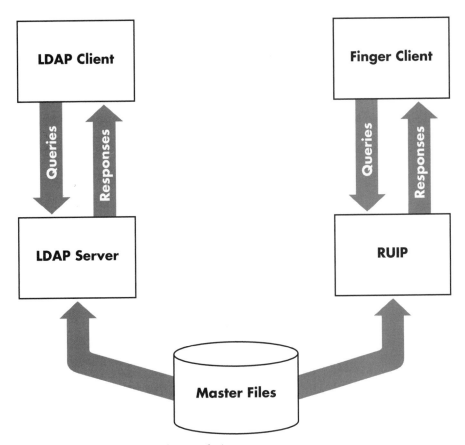

Fig. 5.3 Finger and LDAP sharing data.

In this scenario both the LDAP server and the RUIP need to access the same data. In this environment, there must be some mechanism that locks the RUIP from accessing various pieces of information in the master files when they are in the process of being updated. In order to avoid this and other complications, one can imagine a scenario in which the RUIP retrieves information from the master files by using LDAP. This alternative is shown in Figure 5.4.

In this scenario, the RUIP is written in such a way that the Finger queries it receives are answered by retrieving data from LDAP. In effect, the RUIP acts as an LDAP client. Since the Finger client doesn't authenticate to the RUIP, there is no need for the RUIP to authenticate to the LDAP server. The RUIP doesn't need to implement the LDAP bind operation since LDAP v3 servers treat operations that aren't preceded by a bind as an anonymous bind. In LDAP v2, the client needed to send a bind

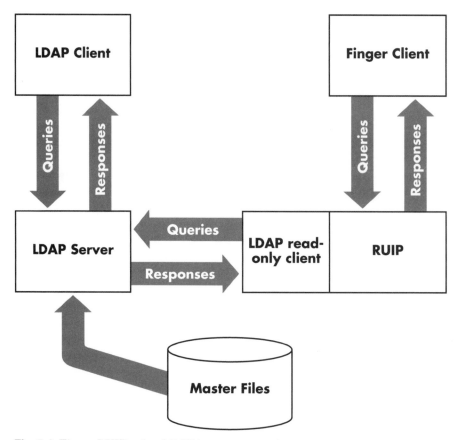

Fig. 5.4 Finger RUIP using LDAP to answer queries.

request in the first Protocol Data Unit (PDU) of the connection. Thus, the RUIP only needs to implement the Search operation.

In the case of the null command line, the RUIP needs to get the appropriate attributes for all users that are currently logged in. Unfortunately, there is no standard LDAP definition for the term *logged in*. In some directories, like Novell's NDS, the standard LDAP schema has been extended. NDS defines an attribute *Login Time* for its *User* object class that can be queried to determine if a user is currently connected.[1] The RUIP just needs to perform a subtree search for users that have a *Login Time* attribute value, and presume that these users are the ones that are connected.

---

[1] This information is published in the NDS Schema Specification that is part of Novell's NDS SDK.

If the RUIP receives a command line with a user name on it, then it needs only return information about the one user. In this case, the RUIP needs to perform a subtree search for users that have a *cn* attribute value equal to the value that the RUIP received on the command line. In either situation, the command line received by the RUIP is turned into a single LDAP operation. Note that the RUIP may receive a referral from the LDAP server in some instances. Since the Finger protocol doesn't support the notion of a referral, it cannot return such an indication to the Finger client.

WHOIS

The Whois directory service provides an implementation that allows for more structured information than does the Finger protocol. Whois has a few more query types, but it is still a read-only directory service. As described in RFC 954, the original Whois implementation provided a way to look-up information in the DDN Network Information Center (NIC) at SRI International on behalf of the Defense Communications Agency (DCA). The Whois client would generally access the Whois server that was running on one of the SRI-NIC machines. RFC 954 even gives the IP addresses to use in order to contact these machines over TCP. Note that even though Whois was originally specified as a mechanism to contact Whois servers that were running on the SRI-NIC machines, there is nothing in the protocol that prohibits a Whois server from running on any other Internet host. Thus, Whois servers have quickly become widespread, as an additional means for making information available about registered users.

The intention of Whois is to provide a way to access information about people that is collected through the DNS registration process. Whenever a new host name is registered on the Internet, a set of information is collected about various technical and administrative contacts. Some of this information can be made available via DNS through its records. However, with DNS, one needs to know the host name in order to be able to find out information about any of the users that are listed in the DNS. With Whois, this information is made available using the properties of the people rather than the properties of the host. Whois servers are expected to operate by listening for client connections on the well-known TCP (or UDP) port numbered 43. Just as in the Finger protocol, client commands that are sent to the Whois server are a single textual string that is terminated by a carriage return, line feed (CRLF) pair. The records in Whois each have a unique identifier associated with them known as a *handle*. The Whois handle is analogous to the distinguished name concept in LDAP and the host name in DNS. Notice that in the Finger protocol there was no specifically allocated field in any record that contained a unique identifier for the record.

Once the Whois server returns an appropriate response to the client command, the connection is closed. Whois commands are always searches, as the Whois protocol does not permit clients to make changes to the Whois database. The Whois client requests normally consist of a name specification, which indicates the matching names for which the client is searching. The name specification is the Whois analog for the LDAP search filter. While RFC 954 doesn't include the BNF for a name specification, it can be presented as shown in Figure 5.5.

Thus, a name specification may begin with one of the two Whois name specification commands, or it may be a request for help. If the Whois command line consists of the question mark character followed by a carriage return line feed pair, then it is a request by the Whois client to get a list of the current name specification formats that are supported by the Whois server. This is an interesting departure from all of the other directory protocols previously discussed. The Whois protocol was intended to be used directly by a human user at a terminal. This help command allowed the Whois user to find out how to use the currently installed version of the Whois service. In a more advanced world, this type of command allows the Whois client application to adapt to new command types. A similar feature in LDAP allows the LDAP client to query the LDAP server's rootDSE object in order to determine all of the available LDAP object classes and attribute types.

If the name specification begins with the exclamation point character ("!"), then the search is used to match Whois handles only. If the name specification begins with the period character ("."), then the search is used to match names only. If neither of the special characters are present, then the search is used to match both names and handles. If the name specification ends with an ellipsis ("..."), then the server will patch anything in the command line argument up to the point of the ellipsis. If the ellipsis is absent, then only records that are an exact match for the name specification are returned to the Whois client.

```
{ command-line } ::= { Help } | { NameSpecification }
{ Help } ::= "?" <CRLF>
{ NameSpecification } ::= [ "!" | "." ] username <CRLF>
```

Fig. 5.5 Grammar for the Whois name specification.

The Whois protocol also allows the search for e-mail addresses. If the name specification includes the at sign ("@"), then the search is used to match e-mail addresses. Thus, the Whois protocol allows for searches against three distinct fields in the Whois records, as follows:

☞ Handles
☞ Names
☞ E-mail addresses

Notice the advancement of Whois over Finger in the progression towards a *property-based information retrieval* service. The Finger protocol only supports searches against the name field of the record. The e-mail address search can itself take the following three different forms:

☞ Smith@ [looks for mailboxes with username SMITH]
☞ @Host [looks for mailboxes on HOST]
☞ Smith@Host [Looks for mailboxes with username SMITH on HOST]

Remember that whatever form of the e-mail address search is used, the name specification will always contain an "@" character. While Whois provides a richer search protocol than its predecessor Finger does, all Whois searches will still only return people objects. Just as a Finger server can be designed to run on top of LDAP, a Whois server can also make use of LDAP for its information retrieval service, as displayed in Figure 5.6.

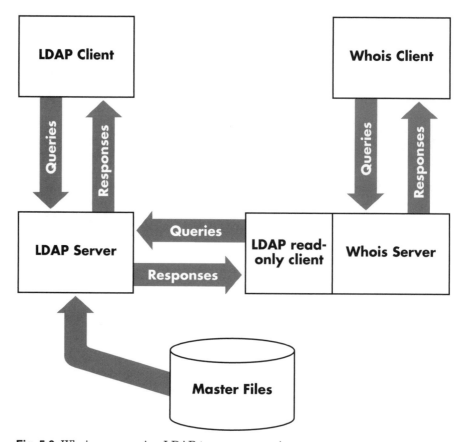

Fig. 5.6 Whois server using LDAP to answer queries.

Now consider how this Whois server might be implemented by making use of the LDAP read-only client. Based on the format of the name specification, the Whois server would perform as follows:

☞ First character is "?"—Return the standard help message.
☞ First character is "!"—Equate Whois handle to LDAP CN attribute.
  • If the name specification ends in ". . ."—Use the initial form of the substring filter choice.
  • Otherwise—Use the equality form of the search filter.
☞ First character is "."—Equate Whois name to LDAP given name (givenName) and surname (sn). If the Whois name has a comma, use it to get the surname that appears prior to the comma and the given name that appears after the comma. Use both of these attributes as equality matches in the search filter.

☞ First character is something else—Use a combination of the above two mechanisms so that the search uses sn, givenName, and cn attribute types in the search filter.

☞ Name specification contains an "@" character—Use the mail attribute instead of the other attributes listed above. Depending on whether the "@" is the first character, the last character, or appears somewhere in the middle, use the following filter forms:

- Final form of substring search filter
- Initial form of substring search filter
- Equality form of search filter

Thus, it is straightforward to translate the received Whois name specifications into LDAP searches. It is simply a matter of parsing the string received for the various Whois special characters.

WHOIS++

Whois++ is the third generation of text-based directory services. As discussed in the previous sections, Finger is the first generation, and Whois is the second generation. Finger provides a simple mechanism of retrieving user records when the client provides the name of the user. Whois provides a richer search mechanism than Finger, by allowing for searches based on several different user properties (name, handle, and e-mail address), as well as a simple form of substring search. Whois++ provides several new features as enhancements to the basic service that Whois provides. They are listed as follows:

☞ Data within each record is organized as a set of attribute-value pairs.

☞ The records in the database have a specific type. Each record is based on one of a set of templates that have been defined. Whois++ templates are analogous to the LDAP object classes.

☞ Whois++ databases that are accessible on the Internet have unique handles that are registered with IANA.

☞ Whois++ client queries can be routed to another Whois++ server.

☞ Whois++ servers support a set of "help" commands.

☞ Basic authentication support has been added.

☞ Connections are not always terminated after a single client command.

Whois++ is still only an information retrieval service, and does not support any facilities for clients to make changes to entries in the Whois++ database. Whois++ servers support two different operating modes: base level or indexing. A base level server contains only filled templates. An indexing server contains forward knowledge about the information contained in other base level or indexing servers. A single server can operate in either mode, or simultaneously support both modes. The forward knowledge that is housed in indexing servers contains pointers to the information in other Whois++ servers. Thus, when an indexing server is queried, the results that it returns to the Whois++ client can include referrals to other Whois++ servers. The forward knowledge is normally generated when an indexing server polls another server in order to retrieve the forward knowledge. Two types of forward knowledge are the *centroid* and the *tagged index object*. These will be defined later in the book during the discussion of the Common Indexing Protocol (CIP) in Chapter 6. The architecture of the indexing system is illustrated in Figure 5.7.

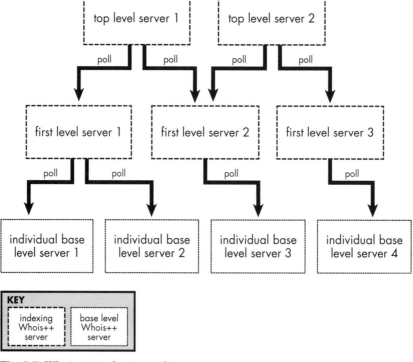

Fig. 5.7 Whois++ indexing architecture.

Figure 5.7 shows that the top-level servers poll the first level servers for their forward knowledge. In turn, the first level servers poll the individual base-level servers for their forward knowledge. Thus, top-level server 1 has forward knowledge from base-level servers 1, 2, and 3. Top-level server 2 has forward knowledge from base-level servers 3 and 4. Note that all of the servers in the figure support Whois++ client queries. So, when it receives a query, top-level server 1 would route the client to one of the first level servers, which in turn would route the query to the appropriate base-level server.

Structure of Whois++ Information

Unlike DNS and LDAP, the information in the Whois++ directory is not organized in a hierarchical fashion. Recall that in DNS the host names are organized hierarchically so that the host *acme.com* is considered the parent of the host *www.acme.com*. Similarly, the LDAP distinguished name concept logically organizes the data in a hierarchical fashion. Thus, the entry *o=acme, c=us* is considered the parent of the entry *cn=bruce, o=acme, c=us*. In Whois++, no such hierarchical arrangement is required. Whois++ assumes that any logical organization is maintained by the data itself.

For example, one type of object that can be maintained in Whois++ is the domain concept of DNS. Thus, every domain entry in Whois++ would be logically arranged by its very nature into a hierarchy. Another type of object that can be maintained in Whois++ is a person. The goal here would be to maintain the people so as to implement a White Pages or Yellow Pages service. The information associated with each person would logically create a hierarchy. One obvious way to support this notion would be to use some property of people that naturally arranges itself into a hierarchy. It is possible to use the address information of each person to do this. Some of the address properties that can be used for the hierarchical organization are:

☞ Country
☞ State or Province
☞ Locality (City or Town)
☞ Street

Using these properties would require Whois++ entries for the various countries, states, cities, and streets. Once these are in place, even though Whois++ has done nothing to enforce any structure on the information, the data has logically organized itself into a hierarchical form. This form is illustrated in Figure 5.8, a portion of a sample Whois++ database.

Even though the information in the entries is arranged in a hierarchical fashion above, it is not because Whois++ entries have names that somehow are hierarchical, like the DNS host name or the LDAP distinguished name. It is the information in the entries that creates the hierarchy. For example, Royal Street is a road in New Orleans, which is a city in Louisiana, which in turn is a state in the U.S. In Whois++, each record in the database has a unique handle. In addition to the handle field, each record has a specific set of attributes, determined by the template type used for the entry. Within each entry, every value associated with an attribute can be any ASCII (or UTF-8 encoded) string up to a

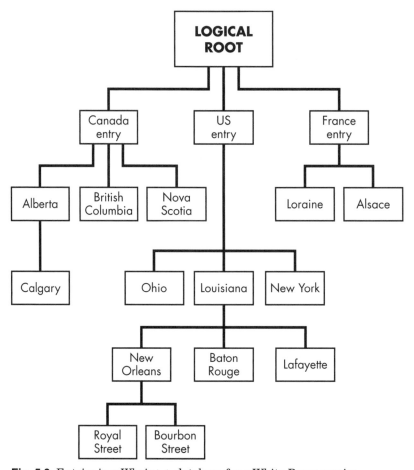

Fig. 5.8 Entries in a Whois++ database for a White Pages service.

specified length. This length is specified within the Whois++ template definition. The entries in Figure 5.8 fall into four different types of template use:

☞ Country: Canada, US, France
☞ State/Province: Alberta, British Columbia, Nova Scotia, Ohio, Louisiana, etc.
☞ City: Calgary, New Orleans, Baton Rouge, Lafayette
☞ Street: Bourbon Street, Royal Street

Whois++ templates are not yet standardized, but as of the writing of this book, an IETF draft document proposes a set of templates that may be standardized. Attributes and clusters define each template. Attributes and clusters in turn also define each cluster. This clustering principle is only used in the Whois++ specification to make it easier to describe what attributes should be grouped together, and what attributes are required in a template. As examples, consider the following cluster and template definitions as shown in Table 5.3.

Table 5.3 Whois++ Organization Cluster

Field Name	Required	Description
(ADDRESS*)		Address of the Organization
(E-MAIL*)		E-mail address(es) of the Organization
Name:	R	Name of the Organization
(PHONE*)		Telephone numbers of the Organization
Type:		Type of Organization (University, Commercial, etc.)
URI:		Uniform Resource Identifier for the Organization

Notice that in this cluster definition references are made to other clusters. This is indicated by the field names in parentheses. The notation (Address*) indicates that the Organization cluster includes by reference any field from the Address cluster. The Address cluster is defined as that shown in Table 5.4.

Table 5.4 Whois++ Address Cluster

Field Name	Required	Description
Address:	R	Full Address
Address Type		Type of Address (e.g., work or home)
Address City	R	Address City
Address Country	R	Address Country
Address Room		Address Room
Address State		Address State, County, or Province
Address Street		Address Street
Address Zip Code		Zip Code
Address Locality		Geographic Region

Table 5.5 Whois++ Person Cluster

Field Name	Required	Description
(E-MAIL*)		Electronic mail address(es) of the person
(ADDRESS*)		Address of the person
(PHONE*)		Telephone number of the person
(NAME*)	R	Name of the person
(ORG-PERSON*)	R	Organization related contact for this person
Homepage-URI		Uniform resource identifier for the person's homepage
Picture-URI		Uniform resource identifier for the person's picture
Language-Pref		Person's language of preference

Similar clusters are defined for E-mail, Name, Org-Person, and Phone. The clusters in Table 5.5 can be used in any template definitions. Table 5.6 shows some examples of template definitions.

Table 5.6 Whois++ Organization Template

Field Name	Required	Description
Keywords		Any keywords that might facilitate finding this record
Internet-Domain		Organization's Internet domain name
Domain-Contact-(PERSON*)		Admin contact for this organization
(ORGANIZATION*)		Actual organization information
(RECORD*)		Record information

Table 5.7 Whois++ User Template

Field Name	Required	Description
Keywords		Any keywords that might facilitate finding this record
(PERSON*)	R	Actual user information
(PGP-PUBLIC-KEY*)		Their PGP public key values
X509-CERT-URI		URI for the user's X.509 certificate (perhaps an LDAP or HTTP url)
(RECORD*) Record information		

The Whois++ user template (Table 5.7) is intended to be compatible with the abstract Internet White Pages Service schema as published in RFC 2218. Each Whois++ template is expected to include fields from the record cluster. The record cluster contains creation and modification information that is comparable to the LDAP operational attributes. The fields in the record cluster are shown in Table 5.8.

Table 5.8 Whois++ Record Cluster

Field Name	Required	Description
Record-Creation-Contact-(PERSON*)		Contact information for the person who created this record
Record-Creation-Date		Date that this record was created
Record-Last-Modified-Contact-(PERSON*)		Contact information for the person who last modified this record
Record-Last-Modified-Date		Date that this record was last modified
Record-Last-Verified-Contact-(PERSON*)		Contact information for the person who last verified the information in this record
Record-Last-Verified-Date		Date that the information in this record was last verified

So, a record with the template type of user can have fields that are taken from the record cluster, the person cluster, and the PGP-public-key cluster. In turn, the person cluster allows the user records to include fields from several other clusters.

Example Whois++ Directory

Let's reconsider the example directory information that was used to build the LDAP directory for the SIDK (Society of Internet Dog Kennels). That directory tree is reproduced in Figure 5.9.

A comparable Whois++ database would have the same 10 objects. An interesting item to note is that Whois++ does not define a template for the Organizational Unit concept. So, in order to represent the OU objects in the SIDK organization's directory, the Whois++ organization template will be used. The Organization template will also be used to model the Internet organization. For the other objects in the directory, the person template will be used. Now, examine some of the Whois++ entry definitions in more detail, as shown in Table 5.9.

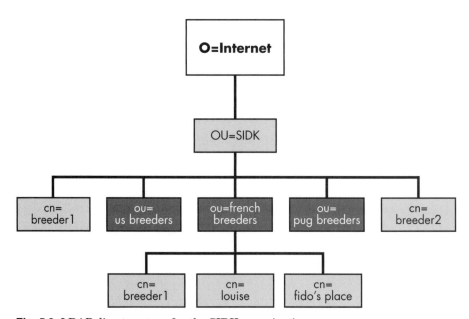

Fig. 5.9 LDAP directory tree for the SIDK organization.

Table 5.9   Whois++ Entry for the Internet Organization

Attribute Name	Value
Handle	1
Template	Organization
Keywords Internet-Domain	Internet, IETF ietf.org
Domain-Contact-Homepage-URI	*http://www.ietf.org*
Domain-Contact-Email	*ietf-info@ietf.org*
Name	Internet Engineering Task Force
Type	Open Community Educational
Address	IETF Secretariat c/o Corporation for National Research Initiatives 1895 Preston White Drive, Suite 100 Reston, VA 20191-5434 USA

Notice that the attributes that begin with domain contact are taken from the person cluster. In actuality, the domain-contact-e-mail attribute is taken from the e-mail cluster, since that cluster is incorporated by reference into the person cluster. The name, type, and address fields are taken from the organization cluster (Table 5.10).

Table 5.10   Whois++ Entry for the SIDK Organization

Attribute Name	Value
Handle	2
Template	Organization
Keywords	Dog Breeders
Internet-Domain	SIDK.org
Domain-Contact-Homepage-URI	*http://www.sidk.org*
Domain-Contact-Email	*Dog-info@sidk.org*
Name	Society of Internet Dog Kennels SIDK
Type	Educational
Address	Society of Internet Dog Kennels 1234 Canine Ct. Someplace, TX 77777
Record-Creation-Date	12 September 1996
Record-Creation-Contact-Name	Bruce Greenblatt

Notice that there is nothing in the entry for the SIDK organization that indicates that it is an organizational unit of the Internet. Is this good or bad? The answer depends on perspective. In the real world, the SIDK organization is not actually part of the Internet organization. They are two completely separate organizations, each having their own employees and members. It is modeled that way in LDAP because the X.500 model creates some restrictions on the objects that can appear directly beneath the root. In the case of Whois++, the management of the root container is not a problem, since there is no Whois++ root. Also, the entry for the SIDK organization also includes fields from the record cluster that indicate the creation date for the record, and who created the record.

Table 5.11 Whois++ Entry for the U.S. Group Within the SIDK Organization

Attribute Name	Value
Handle	3
Template	Organization
Keywords	Dog Breeders US Subgroup SIDK
Internet-Domain	US.SIDK.org
Domain-Contact-Homepage-URI	http://www.us.SIDK.org
Domain-Contact-E-mail	US-dog-info@SIDK.org
Name	Society of Internet Canine Kennels, US Subgroup
Type	Educational
Address	Society of Internet Canine Kennels US Subgroup 1234 Canine Ct. Someplace, TX 77777
Record-Creation-Date:	28 March 1997
Record-Creation-Contact-Name:	Bruce Greenblatt

Notice in Table 5.11 that there is nothing structural within the U.S. subgroup's entry to identify it is hierarchically subordinate to the SIDK organization's entry. The values of the Keywords field is a hint, but is not a definitive indication like the distinguished names that are used in the LDAP directory tree. The definitions of the other dog breeding subgroups (i.e., French Breeders and Pug Breeders) would be similar to the U.S. breeders.

Table 5.12 Whois++ Entry for the User Entry for Louise

Attribute Name	Value
Handle	4
Template	User
Keywords	Dog Breeders
Internet-Domain	SIDK.org
Homepage-URI	http://www.SIDK.org/~louise
E-mail	Louise@SIDK.org
Name	Louise Lebreedeur
Address	1234 Kennel Ave. Noplace, CA 99999
Organization-Name	SIDK
Organization-URI	http://www.SIDK.org
Record-Creation-Date	12 September 1996
Record-Creation-Contact-Name	Bruce Greenblatt

Notice in Table 5.12, the hint in Louise's entry that points to an organization named SIDK in her entry. This is present to indicate that Louise (the person) is actually a member of the SIDK organization, and is not necessarily an indication of any hierarchical relationship that is to be maintained by the Whois++ database. Notice that in each of the entries that all of the attribute values consist of words that are separated by *white space*. This is a general characteristic of entries in Whois++ databases, and is designed to facilitate the fast implementation of searches. Because searches in Whois++ are always string-based, the entire database can leverage well-known string search mechanisms that have been refined over many years of research. This allows the Whois++ search engine to be well indexed and, therefore, normally very fast.

Whois++ Searches

The most common command that is sent from the Whois++ client to the Whois++ server is the search command. A typical search consists of one or more search terms. Each search term is comparable to the LDAP attribute value assertion. An example of a search term is *"name=Greenblatt"*. Each search term can be combined with another by making use of the logical operators AND, OR, and NOT. Whois++ always uses an implied AND between search terms that are listed sequentially. At the end of all of the search terms, global constraints for the search operation

may be specified. The colon (":") character separates the search terms
and the constraints. Each individual search term may have local constraints applied only to it by appending a semi-colon (";") character and
the constraints to the search term. Thus, there are four formats of the
search term:

☞ A search string followed by an optional semicolon and set of semicolon-separated local constraints.
☞ A search term specifier (as listed in Table 5.12) followed by a "=",
  then by a search string, an optional semicolon, and a set of semicolon-separated local constraints.
☞ An abbreviated search term specifier, followed by a search string,
  then by an optional semicolon, and a set of semicolon-separated
  local constraints.
☞ A combination of attribute name, followed by "=", then by a search
  string, an optional semicolon, and a set of semicolon-separated local
  constraints.

The different specifiers are given in Table 5.13.

Table 5.13 Whois++ Specifiers

Specifier	Meaning
ATTRIBUTE-VALUE	Allows for the combination of attributes and values in a single search term
HANDLE	Confine searches to handles
SEARCH-ALL	Search everything
TEMPLATE	Confine searches to template names
VALUE	Confine searches to attribute values (this is the default)

The search specifier is combined with the search terms to create a
valid search string that can be interpreted by a Whois++ server. Any
search proceeds by somehow matching the supplied search string against
the words that are contained in each entry in the Whois++ database. As
has been mentioned, constraints can be applied to individual search
terms, or they can be applied globally to the search string as a whole. The
most useful constraint is the *search* constraint. It is used to specify the
matching rule that is to be used in the search. The default method that is
to be used is *exact* matching. The matching rules that are available in
Whois++ are:

☞ *Exact:* The search will succeed for a word that exactly matches the search string.

☞ *Substring:* The search will succeed where the search string matches part of a word.

☞ *Regex:* The search will succeed for a word when the search string is treated as a regular expression and it matches the searched data. Regular expressions are built up by using constructions of '*', '.', '^', '$', and '[]'.

☞ *Fuzzy:* The search will succeed for words that match the search using an algorithm for matching closely related words. Which approximate matching algorithm is used is dependent upon the choice of the Whois++ server.

☞ *Lstring:* The search will succeed for words that begin with the search string.

Some examples of searches are:

☞ *Template=organization and name=SIDK*—This search string matches any entry that uses the organization template, and contains the word *SIDK* in the value of the name attribute. Notice that the VALUE specifier is assumed, as is the exact matching rule.

☞ *Bruce and Greenblatt*—This search string matches any entry that contains the words Bruce and Greenblatt anywhere in any attribute values. Note that the words need not appear in the same attribute value. Further, notice that the attribute names are not required. This is very different from the LDAP search mechanism that requires an attribute to be named.

☞ *Value=phone; search=substring*—This search string matches any entry having an attribute value matching the string **phone.** For example, the value Acme Telephone Company would be matched. However, this will not match the attribute name phone. This is due to the fact that the VALUE specifier is used here.

☞ *Search-all=Bruce; search=lstring; case=consider*—This search string matches any entry that has an attribute name, a template name, or an attribute value that begins with the string Bruce. The additional specifier, case=consider, indicates that the capitalization of the string Bruce should exactly match the words in the Whois++ database. Normally, case is ignored in Whois++ matching rules.

☞ *Internet; search=substring and (peter or paul): include name, e-mail*—This search string matches any entry that contains the words peter or paul somewhere within the record, and has the string Internet somewhere within a word in the record. The include constraint at the end is an indication that the results should only include the name and e-mail fields.

Search Results

There are several different response formats that can be used by the Whois++ server. The client has control over which format is used by specifying a *format* global specifier in the search string. The valid response formats are:

- ☞ *Full:* This format provides the full contents of the template that matches the supplied search string. This includes the template type, the server handle, and the optional record handle.
- ☞ *Abridged:* This format provides a brief summary, including the server handle, the corresponding record handle, and relevant information from that template.
- ☞ *Handle:* In this format, only the server handle and the record handles from the matched entries are returned.
- ☞ *Summary:* In this format, only the number of matching entries and the list of templates from the matching entries are returned.
- ☞ *Server-To-Ask:* In this format, the server only returns pointers to other servers who might be able to answer the specified query. This is used in situations where index information has been exchanged among the Whois++ servers. This format is analogous to the LDAP referral construct.

Each response from the server consists of a system-generated message, followed by the formatted server response, and a second system-generated message. The system-generated messages always contain a numeric identification code. The generic format is:

```
'%' <system messages> <nl>
[ <formatted response> ]
'%' <system messages> <nl>
```

Normally the client only needs to parse the numeric reply code identifier to understand the meaning of the system-generated message. Some of the more commonly used reply codes are found in Table 5.14.

Table 5.14 Commonly Used Whois++ Reply Codes

Reply Code	Meaning
110	Too many hits
111	The requested constraint isn't supported on this server
200	Command OK
201	Command completed successfully
203	Server is about to close the connection
430	Authentication to the server is required to proceed
500	Syntax error
530	Authentication failed

The complete list of reply codes is given in RFC 1835. If there are no matches to the client's query, the server need not generate a formatted response, but it must still provide the two system-generated messages. Each formatted response has a specified START line, and a specified TERMINATION line. Each line in the formatted response can be no longer than 81 characters. If the response would normally contain a line that has more than 81 characters, it is broken into multiple lines of no more than 81 characters each. Each CONTINUATION line is to begin with the "+" character in the first column instead of the normal leading character. The TERMINATION line is always the character "#", followed by one white space character (SPACE or TAB), the special string "END", and zero or more characters followed by a newline. This is an example of a server's FULL response format.

```
# FULL USER SERVERHANDLE1 LL1
Name: Louise Lebreedeur
e-mail: louise@SIDK.org
Internet-domain: SIDK.org
Organization-name: SIDK
# END
# FULL USER SERVERHANDLE1 BR1
Name: Breeder1
e-mail: breeder1@SIDK.org
Internet-domain: SIDK.org
Organization-name: SIDK
#END2
```

---

[2] Note that the system-generated messages that would actually appear in the protocol have been omitted here for clarity.

This is an example of a server's ABRIDGED response format:

```
# ABRIDGED USER SERVERHANDLE1 LL1
Louise Lebreedeur louise@SIDK.org
# END
# ABRIDGED USER SERVERHANDLE1 BR1
Breeder1 breeder1@SIDK.org
#END
```

This is an example of a server's HANDLE response format:

```
# HANDLE USER SERVERHANDLE1 LL1
# HANDLE USER SERVERHANDLE1 BR1
```

This is an example of a server's SUMMARY response format:

```
# SUMMARY SERVERHANDLE1

Matches:     20
Templates:   User
             Organization
# END
```

Whois++ System Commands

In addition to its rich information search facility, Whois++ supports a wide variety of commands that are intended to help the client learn about how the service operates. The server answers Whois++ commands that are always issued by clients. These commands are summarized in Table 5.15.

Table 5.15 Whois++ Help Commands

Whois++ command	Meaning
Describe	The server responds with a brief description of the server. The description is issued by making use of the *Services* template.
Help	The server responds with a short help message. The command takes an optional argument. If present, the server responds with help on the information specified by the client.
List	The server responds with the names of all of the available templates on the server.
Show	The server responds with information about a specific template that has been given as the argument to the Show command.
Version	The server responds with the highest version of the Whois++ protocol that is supported. The version specified in RFC 1835 is "1.0."

For example, the List command might have this response:

```
# FULL LIST SERVERHANDLE1
Templates: USER
-ORGANIZATION
-SERVICES
-HELP
# END
```

The hyphen character in the first column of the response is an indication that there is a line break in the attribute value. Similarly, the response to the Show USER command might be:

```
# FULL USER SERVERHANDLE1
Name:
Email:
Work-Phone:
Organization-Name:
City:
Country:
# END
```

In addition to these Help commands, Whois++ also supports commands that allow the client to discover the nature of the *mesh* of index servers in which the server is participating. Mesh is the term used by Whois++ to refer to a collection of servers that exchange index information. These commands are summarized in Table 5.16.

Table 5.16 Whois++ Commands for Mesh Discovery

Whois++ Command	Meaning
Polled-For	This command requests the list of other servers that this server has polled. The response gives the list of templates for the server, and attributes for each template.
Polled-By	This is the inverse to the Polled-For command. This command requests the list of other servers that have polled this server. The response gives that list of templates and attributes that were given out to each of the polling servers.

```
# FULL POLLED-FOR SERVERHANDLE1
Server-Handle: serverhandle5
Template: ALL
Field: Name,Address,Job-Title,Organization-Name,
+Organization-Address,Organization-Name
# END
# FULL POLLED-FOR SERVERHANDLE1
Server-Handle: serverhandle4
Template: USER
Field: ALL
# END
```

Sample Whois++ Conversation

Here is a complete conversation that might take place between the
Whois++ client and server. It is taken from the example given in RFC
1835. The server's replies are preceded by the ">" character, while the
client requests are preceded by the "<" character. These two characters
would not appear in the actual protocol exchange.

```
>% 220-Welcome to
>% 220-the whois++ server
>% 220 at ACME inc.
<name=Nick:hold
>% 200 Command okay
>
># FULL USER ACME.COM NW1
> name: Nick West
> email: nick@acme.com
># END
># SERVER-TO-ASK ACME.COM
> Server-Handle: SUNETSE01
> Host-Name: whois.sunet.se
> Host-Port: 7070
># END
># SERVER-TO-ASK ACME.COM
> Server-Handle: KTHSE01
># END
>% 226 Tranfer complete
<version
>% 200 Command okay
># FULL VERSION ACME.COM
> Version: 1.0
># END
>% 226 Tranfer complete
>% 203 Bye
```

Notice that the server closes the connection after the first client command that does not contain the *hold* constraint. Notice also that the reply to a successful command always begins with reply code 200.

CHAPTER SUMMARY

This chapter has presented some alternative directory access protocols to LDAP. Where LDAP intends to be a general-purpose tool for retrieving and manipulating property-based information, the text-based directory services presented in this chapter have more specific goals. The intention of these directory services is to be optimized for those situations in which the vast majority of data (and, hence, the queries for that data) are textual in nature. The text-based directory services also allow for their clients to run directly over the transport layer as a simple telnet-style client. Normally, in these services an effort has been made to keep the server's responses readable by humans. This ensures low entry costs and significantly eases the debugging effort for the services' implementers.

Back End Directory Protocols

$\mathbf{U}$p to now in this book we have focused primarily on how directory clients communicate with directory servers, and what the clients can do with the services that are provided to them. This chapter will deviate from that discussion in order to focus on some of the ways those directory servers can communicate among themselves. Recall our earlier definition of directory services that states they provide a property-based information retrieval service. This definition describes the client-server interaction in directories. Why do directory servers need to communicate among themselves?

In order to answer this question, we need to revisit some of the earlier discussions on client-server interactions. In some instances, a client will make a request of a server that this server is unable to fulfill, but it will refer the client to some other server, as in Figure 6.1.

In this figure we see that LDAP Server 1 has referred the client to LDAP Server 2 for the correct response to the client's request. But how does LDAP Server 1 know that LDAP Server 2 has the correct response? One way of knowing would be if LDAP Servers 1 and 2 had exchanged some information that allowed LDAP Server 1 to know about the data in LDAP Server 2's repository. So, one of the requirements for the Back End Directory Protocols is to allow servers to be able to refer clients' requests to another appropriate server.

Another requirement that forces directory servers to communicate is the notion that Internet directories are replicated databases. This is illustrated in Figure 6.2.

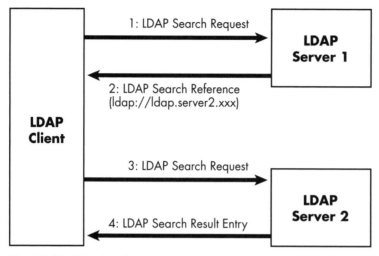

Fig. 6.1 LDAP referrals.

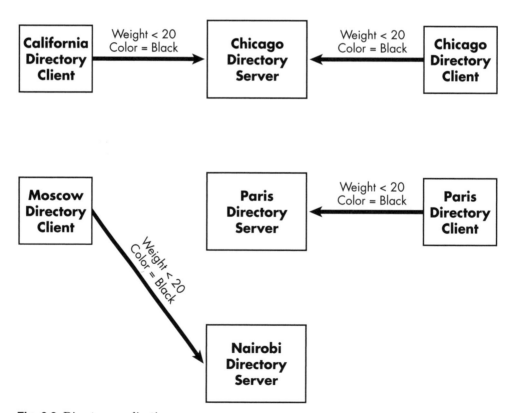

Fig. 6.2 Directory replication.

Here the directory clients are allowed to access any of the three directory servers to obtain the response to their request. As modifications are made to the information in the directory at one server, the changes are replicated to each of the other servers. In this manner, all of the information in the directories is kept synchronized. This directory synchronization allows for uniform responses to the clients' queries, independent of which server is contacted. Note that the synchronization flow among the directory servers is not shown in Figure 6.2.

There is a special case in data synchronization where extra care must be taken. This is the case in which the clients' authentication information is being distributed across the network. By distributing the authentication information among directory servers, a single client can authenticate itself to many directory servers. The authentication information is what allows the client to confirm its identity, if this information is compromised, rogue users could then authenticate themselves to the directory using some real user's identity. Once this happens, the information in the directory is compromised. Furthermore, depending on the level of access that this real user has, the rogue user may be able to modify the information in the directory. If users' passwords are stored in the directory and must be transmitted to multiple directory servers, the passwords could be compromised during transmission across the network.

For this reason, some directory servers choose not to directly store users' credentials in the directory. Instead, stronger forms of authentication based upon public key technology allow clients to prove that they have knowledge of the private key component of the key pair that corresponds to a known public key. In this way, the client has proven its identity to the server, but the server has not kept any secret data about the client. In this scenario, the directory servers need only have knowledge of the user's public key in certificate form, and passwords are not used. Since the directory servers do not have to distribute secret data, there can be a much higher sense of security and less chance that the directory data will be compromised.

If password-based authentication is to be used in a distributed environment, there is another alternative to distributing users' passwords across the network. The users' bind request (in the case of LDAP) could be chained from one directory server to another across a secured connection (e.g., a TLS connection). In this situation, users' passwords are kept in a single location, while the remainder of the directory servers can communicate to that *password server* in order to verify the credentials.

A notion similar to replication is that of *index exchange*. Servers can exchange index information that allows them to know the kinds of information that are held by other servers. For example, a server could create an index that contains the last names of all of the users in its local repository, and exchange this information with another directory server. This exchange allows each of the servers to know about the users' names that are in each other's repositories. One protocol that allows for such an exchange is the Common Indexing Protocol (CIP), the use of which is illustrated in Figure 6.3.

Notice that the LDAP servers are communicating with each other by using CIP. Thus, each LDAP server understands two different protocols: LDAP and CIP. By exchanging the index information, the LDAP servers are able to create referrals appropriately for the LDAP clients.

A final reason that directory servers need to communicate is so that they may implement *request chaining*. In certain situations it may not be appropriate for a server to return a referral to the client. Here, the server may take it upon itself to query other directory servers in order to obtain the result for the client's request. Request chaining is illustrated in Figure 6.4.

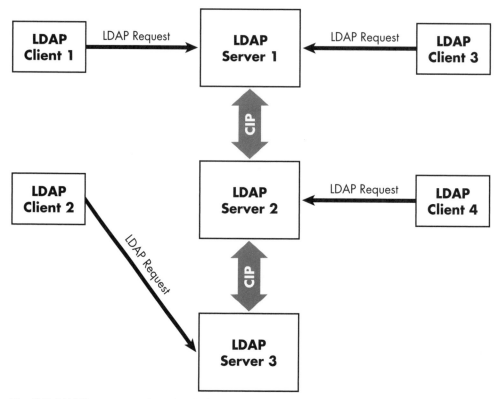

Fig. 6.3 LDAP servers exchanging indices with CIP.

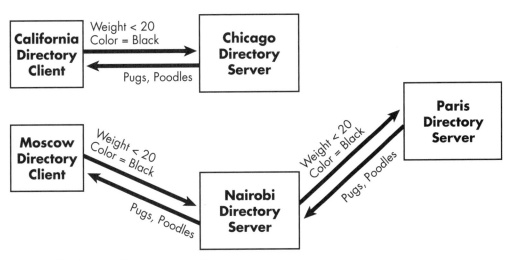

Fig. 6.4 Chaining of directory operations.

In this illustration, the Nairobi directory server does not know the answer to the client's request, but instead of returning a referral to the Moscow Directory Client, it chains the client's request over to the Paris directory server. In this case, the Paris directory server knows the correct answer to the request, and returns it to the Nairobi directory server, which in turn returns the result to the Moscow directory client.

Using LDAP for Directory Synchronization

LDAP is normally used as a client-server protocol, but it can also be used in server-to-server mode as well. In any directory synchronization scenario there is more than a single active directory server. The data that is stored on the servers is being continuously updated. Since the servers are attempting to provide a unified view of the data, any changes to the data must be pushed out to each of the directory servers that stores that entry. In this scenario, it will be assumed that LDAP is the only protocol that the servers are supporting. In such an LDAP environment, the data is organized into *subtrees*. Recall the information that is used in the directory for the SIDK organization. Consider this slightly modified tree shown in Figure 6.5.

Notice that there are three distinct subtrees underneath the main organization. This notion plays an important role in how LDAP servers can replicate and synchronize their data. The typical manner in which LDAP servers are able to synchronize those changes to the directory infor-

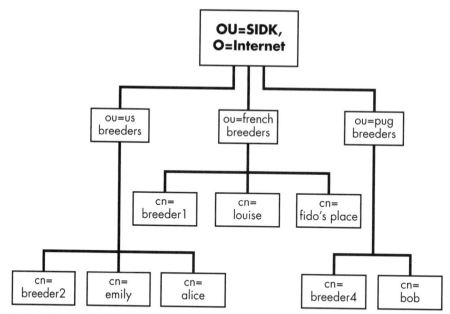

Fig. 6.5 Modified SIDK DIT.

mation is in classifying themselves as masters or slaves.[1] A directory server is said to master data if it is responsible for propagating changes made to its data to all of the other directory servers. These other directory servers are slaves for that portion of the DIT that is mastered by the master directory server. Each directory server in the system can be made to be the master for zero or more subtrees in the DIT. Two directory servers are not normally allowed to master the same subtree in the DIT. Directory servers that support such multimaster scenarios[2] require significantly more complex synchronization mechanisms than are discussed here.

Assume that the SIDK organization maintains four directory servers in its network: DS1, DS2, DS3, and DS4. The SIDK DIT is divided into three partitions based on the subtrees: ou=us breeders, ou=french breeders, and ou=pug breeders. The mastering relationships are indicated in Table 6.1.

---

[1] In some systems, the master-slave relationship is known as a supplier-consumer relationship. Master is equivalent to supplier and slave is equivalent to consumer.

[2] Novell's NDS is one such directory server.

Table 6.1 Replication Agreements for the SIDK Organization's Directory Servers

	Ou = us breeders	Ou = french breeders	Ou = pug breeders
DS1	Master	Master	Read-only slave
DS2	Read-only slave	Read-write slave	Master
DS3	Read-only slave	Read-only slave	Read-only slave
DS4	Read-write slave	Read-only slave	No replica

Notice that changes can be made to some of the slave directory servers for (but not all) subtrees of the DIT. For example, if an LDAP modify operation were applied to the object: cn=emily, ou=us breeders, ou=SIDK, o=Internet on DS2 or DS3, the server would be obligated to reject the request and return an error in the LDAPResult message. An appropriate result code would be the operationsError (1) code. The same modify operation would be successful if it were submitted to DS1 or DS4. Notice that DS3 does not allow any operations that change the DIT. Also, DS4 does not keep a complete copy of the DIT; it is missing the subtree underneath ou = pug breeders. Notice further that changes to the ou = pug breeders subtree may only be made on DS2.

The information in Table 6.1 above is termed a *replication agreement*. The administrator defines this agreement when the directory server is installed. It can be modified subsequently as new directory servers are added to the network, when the portions of the DIT are defined, or when the master (or slave) role of a directory server is changed. Once the replication agreement has been defined, the LDAP servers will communicate their changes on regular intervals. No special extensions to the LDAP protocol are needed to support this replication. This is due to the fact that the identities of the servers are used in the LDAP bind. Assume that the masters initiate the replication process. When the time comes for a replication operation between DS1 and DS2, server DS1 binds to DS2 using the standard LDAP bind and whatever authentication method is appropriate. In replication scenarios, strong authentication-using techniques such as TLS are highly recommended.

Once the LDAP connection is up between the two servers, DS1 need only transmit all of the LDAP operations that changed the DIT to DS2 in exactly the same format as it received them. DS2 will implement these operations just as DS1 did, and will thus end up with an identical DIT. In the case of the read-write slave (such as DS2 for the ou = french breeders portion of the DIT), after DS1 has transmitted all of the changes it has received, DS2 will respond by transmitting all of the changes that it has received.

When the replication agreement allows changes to an entry on more than one server, then there is the possibility (actually, the likelihood) that collisions will eventually occur. Consider the following scenario:

☞ DS1 and DS2 synchronize every day at 1 a.m. GMT.

☞ The directory administrator for DS1 submits a modify operation for cn = louise, ou = french breeders, ... at 6 a.m. that replaces the description attribute with "the best breeder of French Poodles."

☞ The directory administrator for DS2 also submits a modify operation for cn = louise, ou = french breeders, ... at 7 a.m. that replaces the description attribute with "a really good breeder of French Poodles."

At their next scheduled synchronization at 1 a.m. the next day, DS1 will report its change to DS2. DS2 will then respond with its change. Each directory server will notice that the same entry has been affected by multiple modify operations. Since DS1 is the master for this entry, it is up to DS1 to decide what to do about this collision. There is no standard definition for the required behavior for DS1 in its collision resolution algorithm. In the case presented above, a simple algorithm based upon the time at which the modifications were made would be sufficient. Here, since the modify operation at DS2 took place later, it is the one that would take precedence, and the description attribute would have the value: "a really good breeder of French Poodles." This is because directory servers have attempted to *serialize* operations. In distributed systems, serialization is an attempt to place the operations that happened at different locations along a single time line. In this scenario, the serialization results in the time line shown in Figure 6.6.

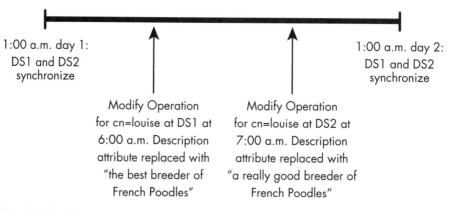

Fig. 6.6 Serialization time line.

In the serialization of these two operations it is obvious that the second modification (from DS2) will overwrite the description attribute that had been modified earlier by the administrator at DS1. Other situations are not as easy to serialize. Consider the following scenario in which the LDAP servers still synchronize each day at 1 a.m.:

1. The directory administrator for DS1 submits a modify operation for cn = louise, ou = french breeders, ... at 6 a.m. that replaces the surname attribute with "Jones" when it had been "Smith."
2. The directory administrator for DS1 submits a modify operation for cn = louise, ou = french breeders, ... at 6:01 a.m. that replaces the givenName attribute with "Louise."
3. The directory administrator for DS2 submits a modify operation for cn = louise, ou = french breeders, ... at 6 a.m. that replaces the givenName attribute with "Eloise."
4. The directory administrator for DS2 submits a modify operation for cn = louise, ou = french breeders, ... at 6:01 a.m. that replaces the surname attribute with "Smith-Jones" when it had been "Smith."

After the completion of the operations, but prior to the next synchronization between DS1 and DS2, the attribute values for the entry are: (see Table 6.2).

Table 6.2   Values for cn=louise Between Synchronization Operations

Attribute	Value on DS1	Value on DS2
GivenName	Louise	Eloise
Surname	Jones	Smith-Jones

If the simple serialization mechanism is used, then the result will be a combination of the changes that were made by the two administrators. The givenName attribute will have the value "Louise," and the surname attribute will have the value "Smith-Jones." Thus, the final result after the next synchronization may be different than what either administrator had expected. This serialization notion of "last change wins" is a widely implemented method of collision resolution. Note that the serialization mechanism is only effective if the directory servers have a mechanism of also synchronizing their clocks. If they don't have such a mechanism, then there will be no way to serialize the operations. Thus, each time the servers synchronize their data, they must also agree on what the current time is.

One can imagine scenarios in which a subtree has many replicas that can be modified, instead of just the two directory servers in the previous examples. As the number of writeable replicas increases, the collision resolution procedures must become increasing complex and more time consuming. It will also be more likely that scenarios will arise when the results of the synchronization will be different than what any of the administrators had intended. Thus, great care must be taken in designing the distribution of the DIT in a multi-master directory infrastructure. In order to simplify the administration, it is often desirable to make all of the replicas other than the master read-only. In this case, the synchronization is much simpler. The master directory server for each replica only needs to forward the LDAP operations to each of its slaves, with no need for any collision resolution procedures.

USING THE COMMON INDEXING PROTOCOL

The Common Indexing Protocol (CIP) is designed to facilitate the routing of queries. Query routing is the process that allows a directory server to return a referral to the directory client, which allows the client to submit the query to a knowledgeable directory server. CIP is a protocol used between servers in a network to pass hints that make data access by clients at a later date more efficient. In the CIP environment, query routing allows queries to be redirected toward the servers holding the actual results via reference to the indexing information that has to be exchanged.

CIP is purely a "back end" protocol. It is implemented in and "spoken" only among network servers. This is in contrast to LDAP, which is designed to be a client-server protocol, but in some situations may be used as a back end protocol. These servers that exchange index information using CIP must also support a data access protocol (e.g., LDAP, Whois++) in order to communicate with clients. For example, in LDAP referral generation, the LDAP server will refer to the indexing information collected via CIP for guidance on how to create the referral. Each directory server that creates indices for use in a CIP index exchange supports one or more *datasets*. The dataset is the CIP term that indicates the set of information from which the index was created. Recall the DIT from Figure 6.5. Instead of the replication setup described in Table 6.1, assume that indices are exchanged according to Table 6.3 below:

Table 6.3 Index Exchange Agreements for the SIDK Organization's Directory Servers

	Ou = us breeders	Ou = french breeders	Ou = pug breeders
DS1	Master	No information	Receive index
DS2	Receive index	Master	No information
DS3	Receive index	Receive index	Master
DS4	Receive index	Receive index	Receive index

Notice that in this scenario there is no replication among the directory servers. All changes to the data must be made directly to the master LDAP server. The servers instead will exchange indices among themselves to return referrals for the LDAP client requests to the appropriate LDAP server. Notice that server DS4 has only the index information to go by for responding to client requests. This allows DS4 to function as a central clearinghouse for index information that can be forwarded to any other LDAP server. The connections between the servers participating in the CIP index exchange is called a mesh. There are no restrictions on how the directory administrators can connect the servers that participate in the mesh. For example, the four directory servers might be connected as shown in Figure 6.7.

In this scenario, each of the subtrees in the DIT identifies a single dataset. DS1 is responsible for creating the index for the dataset that represents the "OU = us breeders" subtree. Similarly, DS2 is responsible for creating the index for the dataset that represents the "OU = french breeders" subtree. In the above mesh, DS1 will pass the index that it creates to DS4 only. DS4 will pass to DS1 the index for the dataset that was indexed by DS3 for the "OU = pug breeders" subtree. Since DS1 received the index for the "OU = pug breeders" dataset from DS4, any referrals

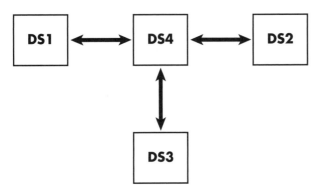

Fig. 6.7 CIP index-exchange mesh.

that DS1 generates based on the information in this index will point to DS4, and not DS3. When the LDAP client makes its subsequent request to DS4, it will then be referred to DS3. Thus, the client will make its request three times in this scenario before a successful result is returned. Each CIP dataset is described by two parameters:

☞ Dataset Identifier (DSI)—The DSI is a string which globally and uniquely identifies the dataset from which the index was created.
☞ Base-URI—The URI (or URIs) that forms the base for any referrals that are to be generated based on the index object for this dataset.

For example, the Base-URI for the "ou = us breeders" dataset would be: ldap://DS1/ou = us breeders, ou = SIDK, o=Internet, in the case that an LDAP URL is used as the Base-URI. The DSI is an object identifier (as in the LDAP OID notation) that uniquely identifies this dataset. It is up to the directory administrator to assign a unique DSI for each of the datasets being indexed.

CIP Index Objects

CIP is always used in tandem with an index object since CIP defines a protocol for exchanging index objects. The servers create these index objects from an underlying dataset. Directory servers establish a communication and identify each other using CIP, and then exchange index information. The directory server that initiates the CIP connection is referred to as the *sender*. The directory server that accepts a sender's incoming connection and responds to the sender's requests is called a *receiver*. The sender and receiver exchange messages over a TCP connection using a simple text protocol. Unlike DNS, LDAP, and Whois++, there is no well-known port that has been assigned for CIP. Since it is expected that only directory servers will communicate using CIP, the directory servers will be required to configure themselves with a host name and a port for their CIP peer. The CIP protocol is very simple, as defined using this BNF (see Figure 6.8).

Notice that CIP uses MIME for encoding its commands and other protocol elements. This allows the protocol to stay textual, and yet allows international characters and other binary data to be included in the protocol (e.g., in index objects). This also enables CIP commands and index objects to be exchanged via electronic mail in addition to a connection-oriented protocol (i.e., TCP or TLS). Each CIP request begins with the request header. This request header is simply a MIME content type. For example, the request header *application/index.cmd.poll* is used in CIP to

```
      Cip-Req = Req-Hdrs CRLF Req-Body
     Req-Hdrs = *( Version-Hdr | Req-Cntnt-Hdr )
     Req-Body = Body { format of request body as in [CIP-MIME³] }
         Body = Data CRLF "." CRLF
         Data = { data with CRLF "." CRLF replaced by CRLF ".." CRLF }
  Version-Hdr = "Mime-Version:" "1.0" CRLF
Req-Cntnt-Hdr = "Content-Type:" Req-Content CRLF
  Req-Content = { format is specified in [CIP-MIME] }
      Cip-Rsp = Rsp-Code CRLF [ Rsp-Hdrs CRLF Rsp-Body ]
                [ Indx-Cntnt-Hdr CRLF Index-Body ]
     Rsp-Code = DIGIT DIGIT DIGIT Comment
      Comment = { any chars except CR and LF }
     Rsp-Hdrs = *( Version-Hdr | Rsp-Cntnt-Hdr )
Rsp-Cntnt-Hdr = "Content-Type:" Rsp-Content CRLF
  Req-Content = { format is specified in [CIP-MIME] }
     Rsp-Body = Body { format of response body as in [CIP-MIME] }
Indx-Cntnt-Hdr = "Content-Type:" Indx-Obj-Type CRLF
 Indx-Obj-Type = { any registered index object's MIME-type }
   Index-Body = Body
```

Fig. 6.8 CIP protocol specification.

request the transfer of an index object. CIP uses response codes in the same manner that Whois++ does. The two CIP request types that are most widely used are:

☞ application/index.cmd.noop—This is just a request that the sender can use to see if the other end of the connection is responding correctly. The appropriate response has a code of 200, which indicates that the command was received, and no further response is forthcoming.

☞ application/index.cmd.poll—This command requires the type of index object and the DSI to be used as parameters, and is a request to get an update of the index object specified in the DSI.

Thus, CIP is a very simple protocol that allows servers to request index objects from other servers (and virtually nothing else). In response to the poll command, an index server may reply with one or more index objects. The response is always a MIME multipart object, with each part

---

[3] [CIP-MIME] is the Internet draft that defines the encoding in MIME of the CIP contents. Each index object specification will conform to this specification.

of the object being of the type `application/index.obj._type_` (where `type` is replaced by the actual type of the index object). A typical CIP conversation is given in Figure 6.9. The sender's data is preceded by "`>>>`" and the receiver's data is preceded by "`<<<`."

The response codes used in CIP are similar to those used in Whois++. Each index object that is specified will give the DSI and Base-URI as parameters. Normally, the response will include only a single index object. Only one index object specification will be described here, but CIP allows for any number of index object specifications to be defined.

```
{ sender-CIP connects to receiver-CIP }
<<< % 220 Example CIP server ready<cr><lf>
>>> # CIP-Version: 3<cr><lf>
<<< % 300 CIPv3 OK!<cr><lf>
>>> Mime-Version: 1.0<cr><lf>
>>> Content-type: application/index.cmd.noop<cr><lf>
>>> <cr><lf>
>>> The next line is only a dot:<cr><lf>
>>> ..<cr><lf>
>>> <cr><lf>
>>> .<cr><lf>
<<< % 200 Good MIME message received
>>> Content-type: application/index.cmd.poll; type=index-tagged-1;
    dsi=1.2.3.4<cr><lf>
<<< % 201 Poll request received. Response to follow
<<< Content-type: application/response; code=201
/* Note: the index objects would be in here encoded in MIME format */
<<< .<cr><lf>
    { sender shuts down socket for writing }
<<< % 222 Connection closing in response to CIP shutdown
    { receiver closes its side, resets, and awaits a new CIP }
```

Fig. 6.9 Simple CIP conversation.[4]

----

[4] Note that the line enclosed by "`/*`" and "`*/`" are the author's comments, and not part of the CIP conversation.

The Tagged Index Object

The Tagged Index Object (TIO) format specifies an index format that can be used by a wide variety of directory servers, and is specifically designed to support the LDAP index exchange. The TIO format allows for full updates of the index as well as incremental updates to previously exchanged index information. The ability to support incremental updates of the index information comes at the expense of larger sized indices. TIO is based upon the design of the structures that were defined in Whois++. By exchanging index information, directory servers can route queries that ask questions such as:

☞ What is John Smith's e-mail address? This is much harder than: What e-mail address does John Smith at "o = Prentice-Hall" have since, with only the person's name to go by, LDAP can't narrow the search down to a particular subtree?

☞ What is the X.509 certificate for Fred Smith at aol.com? One certainly doesn't want to search America Online's entire directory tree to find out this one piece of information. I also don't want to have to shadow the entire America Online directory subtree onto my server, as it might contain millions of entries. If this request were being made because Fred is trying to log onto my server using strong authentication in LDAP, I'd certainly want to be able to respond to the bind in real time.

☞ Who are all the people at Novell that have the title of programmer? This is more difficult if you aren't accessing Novell's LDAP server.

By exchanging TIOs via CIP LDAP, servers are able to either immediately answer the client requests or return the appropriate referral. The grammar of the TIO specification in BNF is detailed in Figure 6.10.

```
        index-object = 0*(io-part SEP) io-part
             io-part = header SEP schema-spec SEP index-info
              header = version-spec SEP update-type SEP this-update SEP
                       last-update context-size name-space SEP
        version-spec = "version:" *SPACE "x-tagged-index-1"
         update-type = "updatetype:" *SPACE ( "total" |
                       ("incremental"[*SPACE"tagbased"|"uniqueIDbased"])
         this-update = "thisupdate:" *SPACE TIMESTAMP
         last-update = [ "lastupdate:" *SPACE TIMESTAMP SEP]
        context-size = [ "contextsize:" *SPACE 1*DIGIT SEP]
         schema-spec = "BEGIN IO-Schema" SEP 1*(schema-line SEP)
                       "END IO-Schema"
         schema-line = attribute-name ":" token-type
          token-type = "FULL" | "TOKEN" | "RFC822" | "UUCP" | "DNS"
          index-info = full-index | incremental-index
          full-index = "BEGIN Index-Info" SEP 1*(index-block SEP)
                       "END Index-Info"
 incremental-index = 1*(add-block | delete-block | update-block)
           add-block = "BEGIN Add Block" SEP 1*(index-block SEP)
                       "END Add Block"
        delete-block = "BEGIN Delete Block" SEP 1*(index-block SEP)
                       "END Delete Block"
        update-block = "BEGIN Update Block" SEP
                       0*(old-index-block SEP)
                       1*(new-index-block SEP)
                       "END Update Block"
     old-index-block = "BEGIN Old" SEP 1*(index-block SEP)
                       "END Old"
     new-index-block = "BEGIN New" SEP 1*(index-block SEP)
                       "END New"
         index-block = first-line 0*(SEP cont-line)
          first-line = attr-name ":" *SPACE taglist "/" attr-value
           cont-line = "-" taglist "/" attr-value
             taglist = tag 0*("," tag) | "*"
                 tag = 1*DIGIT ["-" 1*DIGIT]
          attr-value = 1*(UTF8)
           attr-name = 1*(NAMECHAR)
           TIMESTAMP = 1*DIGIT
            NAMECHAR = DIGIT | UPPER | LOWER | "-" | ";" | "."
                 SEP = (CR LF) | LF
```

Fig. 6.10 Tagged Index Object BNF definitions.[5]

---

[5] The definitions of DIGIT, UPPER, LOWER, and UTF8 have been omitted from the BNF above but are included in the actual definition of the Tagged Index Object.

Notice that each index object that conforms to this specification has three parts:

☞ Generic headers
☞ List of attributes that are used in the index object (i.e., the schema)
☞ The actual index object

The format of the index object is a sequence of lines, where each line is terminated by a line feed character. Each line begins with an attribute name, followed by a list of tags, and ends with the values corresponding to the attribute name. Each tag corresponds to a specific entry in the directory from which the index was generated. Tags are applied to the data on a per-entry level. Thus, if two index lines in the same index object contain the same tag, then those two lines always refer to the same "record" in the directory. In LDAP terminology, the two lines would refer to the same directory object. Additionally, if two index lines in the same index object contain different tags, then it is always the case that those two lines refer back to different records in the directory. Each tag is a decimal number represented as a string. It is up to the generating directory to create the tags appropriately.

The *this-update* field in the TIO indicates the time at which the index object was created on the directory server. The *last-update* field in the TIO indicates the time the directory server last created a TIO for this dataset. These times are the number of seconds from 00:00:00 UTC January 1, 1970.[6] The optional *context-size* field gives the number of entries in the dataset from which the TIO was generated.

Consider the index for the "ou=us breeders" subtree that would be generated by the LDAP server DS1. Assume that the three entries in the subtree have values as given in Table 6.4.

Table 6.4 Entries From "OU = US Breeders" Subtree

Distinguished Name	Values
Cn=breeder2, ou=us breeders, ou=SIDK, o=Internet	Cn: breeder2, John Smith ObjectClass: top, person, breeder GivenName: John Surname: Smith Breed: pug, poodle E-mailAddress: *john@SIDK.org, john@us.SIDK.org*

[6] UTC time is Universal Coordinated Time, or the time at the Greenwich Meridian. Local time is not used for these time fields.

Table 6.4 Entries From "OU = US Breeders" Subtree (continued)

Distinguished Name	Values
Cn=emily, ou=us breeders, ou=SIDK, o=Internet	Cn: emily, Emily Jones ObjectClass: top, person, breeder GivenName: Emily Surname: Jones Breed: poodle E-mailAddress: *emily@SIDK.org*
Cn=alice, ou=us breeders, ou=SIDK, o=Internet	Cn: alice, Alice Smith ObjectClass: top, person, breeder GivenName: Alice Surname: Smith Breed: poodle, schnauzer E-mailAddress: *alice@SIDK.org*

In Figure 6.11, the index object will use all of the attribute values from the above entries in Table 6.4, but some index generation schemes may omit certain attributes. The TIO for this subtree generated by DS1 would be:

```
version: tagged-index-1
updatetype: total
thisupdate: 855938804
BEGIN IO-Schema
cn: TOKEN
sn: FULL
givenName: FULL
objectClass: FULL
breed: FULL
e-mailAddress: TOKEN
distinguishedName: FULL
END IO-Schema
BEGIN Index-Info
dn: 1/cn = breeder2, ou = us breeders, ou = SIDK, o = Internet
 -2/cn = emily, ou = us breeders, ou = SIDK, o = Internet
 -3/cn = alice, ou = us breeders, ou = SIDK, o = Internet
cn: 1/breeder2
 -1/John
 -1, 3/Smith
 -2/Emily
 -2/Jones
 -3/Alice
```

```
sn: 1, 3/Smith
 -2/Jones
givenName: 1/John
 -2/Emily
 -3/Alice
objectClass: */top
 -*/person
 -*/breeder
breed: 1/pug
 -*/poodle
 -3/schnauzer
e-mailAddress: */SIDK.org
 -1/john
 -2/emily
 -3/alice
 -1/us.SIDK.org
END Index-Info
```

Fig. 6.11   Tagged Index Object for the "OU = US breeders" subtree.

The tags in the above index object are the numbers of the "*" character that precede the "/" characters. If two different lines both have a tag of "1," then that is an indication that the information on those lines was derived from the same entry. In this case, it would be the entry with the distinguished name: "cn = breeder1, ou = us breeders, ou = SIDK, o = Internet." This entry has two common names. Notice that the names have been broken into tokens (as was indicated in the schema specification portion of the TIO). The tokenization of the attributes breaks them up on any white space character, or any "@" character. Thus, it is known that the entry has the following words or tokens in its cn attribute values:

☞ Breeder2

☞ John

☞ Smith

However, the TIO does not indicate how these tokens might be put back together to form the original attribute values. As far as can be determined from the TIO, these three tokens might all come from one attribute value, or they might have been drawn from three values, or possibly even more. Given these tokens, the following possible cn attribute values for this entry are given in Figure 6.12.

```
 1.  Breeder2
 2.  John
 3.  Smith
 4.  Breeder2 John
 5.  Breeder2 Smith
 6.  John Smith
 7.  John Breeder2
 8.  Smith Breeder2
 9.  Smith John
10.  John Breeder2 Smith
11.  John Smith Breeder2
12.  Breeder2 John Smith
13.  Breeder2 Smith John
14.  Smith John Breeder2
15.  Smith Breeder2 John
```

Fig. 6.12 Possible cn attribute values for the entry.

Of these 15 possible combinations of the tokens from the original entry, there are only two real values that are present. However, when DS1 sends the TIO to DS4, there is no way for DS4 to have any knowledge of the real values. Now consider the TIOs that would be built by DS2 and DS3 from their respective subtrees from the LDAP entries (see Tables 6.5 and 6.6).

Table 6.5 Entries From the "OU = French Breeders" Subtree

Distinguished Name	Values
Cn=breeder1, ou=french breeders, ou=SIDK, o=Internet	Cn: breeder1, Fred Smith ObjectClass: top, person, breeder GivenName: Fred Surname: Smith Breed: pug, poodle, dalmatian E-mailAddress: *fred@SIDK.org*
Cn=louise, ou=french breeders, ou=SIDK, o=Internet	Cn: louise, Hebert ObjectClass: top, person, breeder GivenName: Louise Surname: Hebert Breed: poodle E-mailAddress: *louise@SIDK.org*
Cn=fido's place, ou=french breeders, ou=SIDK, o=Internet	Cn: fido's place, Fred Hebert ObjectClass: top, person, breeder GivenName: Fred Surname: Hebert Breed: poodle E-mailAddress: *fred_hebert@SIDK.org*

Table 6.6   Entries From the "OU = Pug Breeders" Subtree

Distinguished Name	Values
Cn=breeder4, ou=pug breeders, ou=SIDK, o=Internet	Cn: breeder4 ObjectClass: top, person, breeder GivenName: Fred Surname: Smith Breed: pug EmailAddress: *fred_smith@SIDK.org*
Cn=bob, ou=pug breeders, ou=SIDK, o=Internet	Cn: bob, Bob Jones ObjectClass: top, person, breeder GivenName: Bob Surname: Jones Breed: pug EmailAddress: *bob@SIDK.org*

The two subtrees yield the following index objects. First consider the TIO for the "OU = French Breeders" subtree in Figure 6.13.

```
version: tagged-index-1
updatetype: total
thisupdate: 855938804
BEGIN IO-Schema
cn: TOKEN
sn: FULL
givenName: FULL
objectClass: FULL
breed: FULL
e-mailAddress: TOKEN
distinguishedName: FULL
END IO-Schema
BEGIN Index-Info
dn: 1/cn = breeder1, ou = french breeders, ou = SIDK, o = Internet
-2/cn = louise, ou = french breeders, ou = SIDK, o = Internet
-3/cn = fido's place, ou = french breeders, ou = SIDK, o = Internet
cn: 1/breeder1
-1, 3/Fred
-1/Smith
-2/Louise
-2, 3/Hebert
-3/fido's
-3/place
```

```
sn: 1/Smith
-2, 3/Hebert
givenName: 1, 3/Fred
-2/Louise
objectClass: */top
-*/person
-*/breeder
breed: 1/pug
-*/poodle
-1/dalmatian
e-mailAddress: */SIDK.org
-1/fred
-2/louise
-3/fred_hebert
END Index-Info
```

Fig. 6.13 Tagged Index Object for the "OU = French breeders" subtree.

Next consider the TIO for the "OU = Pug Breeders" subtree in Figure 6.14.

```
version: tagged-index-1
updatetype: total
thisupdate: 855938804
BEGIN IO-Schema
cn: TOKEN
sn: FULL
givenName: FULL
objectClass: FULL
breed: FULL
e-mailAddress: TOKEN
distinguishedName: FULL
END IO-Schema
BEGIN Index-Info
dn: 1/cn = breeder4, ou = pug breeders, ou = SIDK, o = Internet
-2/cn = bob, ou = pug breeders, ou = SIDK, o = Internet
cn: 1/breeder4
-2/bob
-1/jones
sn: 1/Smith
-2/Jones
```

```
givenName: 1/Fred
-2/Bob
objectClass: */top
-*/person
-*/breeder
breed: */pug
e-mailAddress: */SIDK.org
-1/fred_smith
-2/bob
END Index-Info
```

Fig. 6.14 Tagged Index Object for the "OU = Pug breeders" subtree.

Query Routing Using CIP

Each of the index objects from the previous section is submitted via CIP to DS4. DS4 can then use the three index objects that it has collected to route queries to the appropriate servers. In LDAP terminology, it will normally create `SearchResultReference` type responses that would point to the appropriate entries on the other servers. Each `SearchResultReference` that is returned by DS4 is an LDAPURL containing the host name of the appropriate LDAP server at the search base that can be used in another search. This is implemented as shown in Figure 6.15.

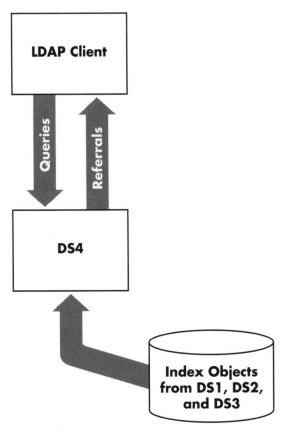

Fig. 6.15 DS4 routing queries based on CIP `index` objects that it has received.

Examples of the LDAP URLs that DS4 returns in response to some sample search filters are given in Table 6.7.

Table 6.7 Example `SearchResultReferences` Returned by DS4 When Using TIOs

Search Filter	Returned `SearchResultReferences`
Sn = Smith	Ldap://ds1/cn=breeder2, ou=us breeders, ou=SIDK, o=Internet
	Ldap://ds1/cn=alice, ou=us breeders, ou=SIDK, o=Internet
	Ldap://ds2/cn=breeder1, ou=french breeders, ou=SIDK, o=Internet
	Ldap://ds3/cn=breeder4, ou=pug breeders, ou=SIDK, o=Internet

Table 6.7 (continued)

Search Filter	**Returned** `SearchResultReferences`
Breed = pug	Ldap://ds1/cn=breeder2, ou=us breeders, ou=SIDK, o=Internet
	Ldap://ds1/cn=breeder1, ou=french breeders, ou=SIDK, o=Internet
	Ldap://ds3/cn=breeder4, ou=pug breeders, ou=SIDK, o=Internet Ldap://ds3/cn=bob, ou=pug breeders, ou=SIDK, o=Internet
(Sn = Smith) & (Breed = pug)	Ldap://ds1/cn=breeder2, ou=us breeders, ou=SIDK, o=Internet
	Ldap://ds2/cn=breeder1, ou=french breeders, ou=SIDK, o=Internet
	Ldap://ds3/cn=breeder4, ou=pug breeders, ou=SIDK, o=Internet
(Sn = Jones) & (Breed = poodle)	Ldap://ds1/cn=emily, ou=us breeders, ou=SIDK, o=Internet
Cn = smith alice	Ldap://ds1/cn=alice, ou=us breeders, ou=SIDK, o=Internet

Thus, even though DS4 does not have complete information on the subtrees that are maintained by the other LDAP servers, it does have enough information to route the clients' requests to the servers that have an excellent chance of answering the request successfully. Notice in the last example, DS4 has returned an LDAPURL in the `SearchResultReference` that will not result in an entry that has the common name that the LDAP client is seeking. This is due to the incomplete information that led to the tokenization that resulted when DS1 created the index object.

The TIO format allows for incremental updates to be issued. Consider the situation in which a single entry is modified in a very large dataset. In this scenario, it would be burdensome to issue a completely new TIO with a total update. The TIO format allows the directory server to issue a new index object that indicates what objects have changed in the dataset. Consider the example in which the entry, "cn=alice, ou=us breeders, ou=SIDK, o=Internet" has been deleted from DS1. DS1 would issue the TIO shown in Figure 6.16 as an incremental update.

```
version: x-tagged-index-1
updatetype: incremental UniqueIDbased
lastupdate: 855938804
thisupdate: 855939525
BEGIN IO-schema
dn: FULL
END IO-Schema
BEGIN Delete Block
dn: 1/ cn=alice, ou=us breeders, ou=SIDK,
o=Internet
END Delete Block
```

Fig. 6.16 Index object resulting from the deletion of "cn=alice, ou=us breeders, ou=SIDK, o=Internet" from DS1.

Similar index objects could be generated when entries are added or modified in the dataset. Notice that the tags in the original full index object, and the subsequent incremental index object, don't match. There is no need to make the index objects match in this case since the entries have a unique identifier, namely, the distinguished name field. This is indicated by the UniqueIDbased keyword in the updatetype header field.

Using Centroids in CIP

Another index object has been defined for use in CIP. The TIO format is based upon the previously defined Centroid format. There are two main differences between the Centroid and the TIO:

☞ The Centroid format does not support incremental updates. Each Centroid is a full update of the index information.

☞ The Centroid does not use tags, so that queries can only be routed to another server (or dataset) as a whole, and not to any particular part or entry of the dataset.

RFC 1913 defines a Centroid as a list of the templates and attributes used by that server, and a word list for each attribute. The word list for a given attribute contains one occurrence of every word that appears at least once in that attribute in some record in that server's data, and nothing else. The Centroid for the "ou=us breeders, ou=SIDK, o=Internet" is seen in Figure 6.17.

```
Template: Breeder
ObjectClass: top
     Breeder
     Person
Cn: breeder2
     John
     Smith
     Emily
     Jones
     Alice
GivenName: John
     Emily
     Alice
Surname: Smith
     Jones
Breed: pug
     Poodle
     Schnauzer
E-mailAddress: John
     SIDK.org
     Us.SIDK.org
     Emily
     Alice
```

Fig. 6.17 Centroid for "ou=us breeders, ou=SIDK, o=Internet."

Notice that the references from the values back to individual entries that are provided by the tags in the TIO format are missing in the Centroid format. The Centroid only provides the reference back to an underlying dataset, which allows queries to be routed back to the server that masters the dataset for some types of queries.

CHAINING LDAP OPERATIONS

LDAP defines a protocol for client-server interaction. In certain circumstances, the contacted LDAP server may not have the information needed to satisfy the client's request. Such a circumstance is given in the previous section on CIP. In the examples in that section, DS4 would not have enough information to return successful search results for most client requests, and would instead return either referrals or SearchResultReferences. Recall in the discussion of DNS that it allows the DNS resolver to request that the name server handle the DNS query recursively instead of returning a referral. LDAP does not include such a request that the server should handle the client's request recursively. This notion of recursion is also known as *request chaining*. The X.500 series of recommendations has designed support for chaining by implementing a separate back end protocol.

An LDAP server could simply repeat the client's operation to a second LDAP server, but this simple repetition presents a problem known as *loop-detection*. Simply put, this problem revolves around the issue of a server detecting when it receives an LDAP request that it has already seen. This is illustrated in Figure 6.18.

In Figure 6.18 the initial client request is submitted to DS1. DS1 is unable to fulfill the request, so it chains the request to DS4, which in turn chains the request to DS2. DS2 then chains the request to DS3, which finally returns the request back to DS4. When the request is returned to DS4, a loop has been created. If DS4 does not detect this loop, it would chain the request again to DS2, and the request would continue among the LDAP servers indefinitely. The LDAP client would not get a response, since nothing would ever be returned to DS1 from the request chaining. DS1 would return a `timeLimitExceeded` return code to the client's request if one was specified in the initial LDAPMessage.

LDAP controls can be defined to assist the servers in loop detection. The simplest mechanism would be to mimic the successful DNS method of using a *hop count* to detect loops. A hop count is an integer kept in the request that is incremented each time the request is passed from one server to another. Whenever a request is chained, the LDAP server initiating the chaining would add a `hopCount` control with an initial value of

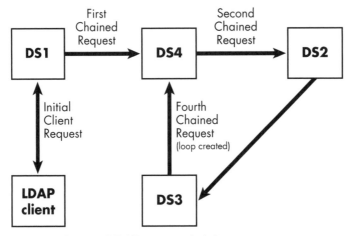

Fig. 6.18 Loop in LDAP request chaining.

zero. Each time a server chains a request that contains a `hopCount` control, the value would be incremented. Whenever the count reaches some specified limit, it can be assumed that a loop has been created and the request will not be fulfilled; an error can then be returned with the value `loopDetect`. This control might be defined as:

```
hopCount ::= SEQUENCE {
    Count INTEGER,
    InitialServer OCTET STRING,
    UniqueOperationIdentifier OCTET STRING }
```

Only the `Count` field in the control is specifically necessary. By including the host name for the first server that chained the request and a unique identifier for the chained request, the directory administrators are aided in identifying the loops that are created and how they might be avoided in the future.

Another technique would be to include a time in the control instead of a hop count. This time would indicate when the request would expire, and when servers should stop attempting to chain it. The success of this mechanism depends on the time clocks of the servers being closely synchronized. Since this expiration time would be specified in terms of seconds, if the servers' clocks were slightly off, one of two problems could happen:

☞ A delay in the detection of the request's expiration could be experienced. This would allow the loop to go undetected for a period of time equal to the difference in the time clocks of the two servers. This delay could occur when the clock of the initial server is later than the clock of a subsequent server. Since the loop would eventually be detected, nothing particularly bad happens in this instance.

☞ The request could expire prematurely. In this circumstance, a server would indicate that the request has expired prior to its actual time of expiration. This would occur when the clock of the initial server is earlier than the clock of a subsequent server. This problem is quite bad in that it results in a denial of service for the client's requests. If the time clocks had been perfectly synchronized, the request would have been chained again and might have returned a successful result.

For reasons such as these, network operating systems and their administrators go to great pains to keep servers' time clocks synchronized. A similar LDAP control to the `hopCount` can be created to implement the following method of loop detection:

```
timeStampControl ::= SEQUENCE {
    TimeStamp TIMESTAMP,
    InitialServer OCTET STRING,
    UniqueOperationIdentifier OCTET STRING }
```

In the X.500 series of recommendations, chaining operations from one directory server to another forms part of a protocol known as Directory Service Protocol (DSP). In addition to allowing for operation chaining, DSP also allows for the chaining of an abandon operation. This `chainedAbandon` operation allows a directory server to attempt to indicate to another server that a previously chained operation need not be performed. It operates in much the same way that an LDAP client might issue an `AbandonRequest` in order to indicate to the LDAP server that the response to a previously issued request is no longer needed. While, X.500 defines other protocols for back end operation in the area of replication, there are no additional Internet protocols that parallel them. For the purposes of replication, LDAP is used for server-to-server communication instead of defining additional complexity and protocols.

CHAPTER SUMMARY

This chapter discussed how directory servers communicate among themselves. We talked about information replication using LDAP and the Common Index Protocol (CIP). Some of the issues involved in replication and synchronization were discussed as well. Techniques involving query routing, chaining, and loop detection were mentioned. With this foundation, the techniques that are used in most LDAP servers can be readily understood.

Directory Management[1]

As a property-based information retrieval service, the directory is a service that may be used to administer, manage, and locate network services, including electronic mail, print services, and portions of the network directory service itself. Used as such, the directory becomes a complex, distributed service that can span multiple hosts in the corporate intranet. Furthermore, by making directory services available via the Internet by providing access to directory information via LDAP, the directory service not only spans the corporate intranet, but also spans the global Internet. Thus, as a complex service that administers a variety of other applications, a directory service requires administration itself. Here, we will discuss two aspects of directory management:

☞ Use of the directory to administer other application services

☞ Management of the directory service itself as a complex network service

In order to use the directory to administer application services, certain management information is made available in the directory. As the Electronic Messaging Association's (EMA) publication, *Messaging Management Implementor's Guide: Use of the Directory and Control Functions,*

---

[1] This chapter is based on an article "Directory Management" that was co-authored with Susan May. It was originally published in the March/April 1997 issue of *Messaging Magazine,* volume 3, number 2. *Messaging Magazine* is the magazine of the Electronic Messaging Association, 1655 N. Fort Myer Drive, Suite 500, Arlington, VA 22209. Telephone: (703) 524-5550. Fax: (703) 524-5558. Web: http://www.ema.org.

states: "when management information is made available in a global directory, this facilitates communication between management domains, and allows for greater coordination between multivendor management applications both within and between domains." For instance, in the case of message tracking, a domain or enterprise might wish to make a management agent available to external users. Message tracking is the function that involves following the path an electronic mail message took on its path from the message's originator to its eventual end point (normally to an intended recipient). As illustrated in Figure 7.1, tracking the message that User1 sends to User2 involves several steps.

Once the message is submitted to the initial host, the user keeps a copy of the message and the unique identifier that has been assigned to the message. In order to find out what has happened to the message (i.e., track the message), the user (or a messaging system administrator operating on

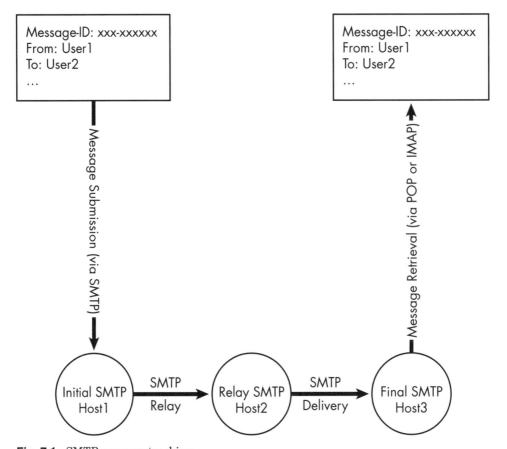

Fig. 7.1 SMTP message tracking.

behalf of the user) will submit a message tracking request containing the unique identifier for the message in question. This request would need to be submitted to a management agent that is associated with SMTP Host1. SMTP Host1 would report back (via SNMP) that it had relayed the message in question to SMTP Host2. SNMP is the Simple Network Management Protocol, and is the standard means for monitoring Internet hosts and applications that run on them. Version 2 of SNMP is defined in RFC 1902 and several accompanying RFCs. The tracking console would use this information to submit a message-tracking request to the management agent associated with SMTP Host2. In response, SMTP Host2 would report back that it had relayed the message in question to SMTP Host3. Finally, in response to another message-tracking request, SMTP Host3 reports that the message in question was successfully delivered and retrieved by User2. This interaction of the management components is illustrated in Figure 7.2.

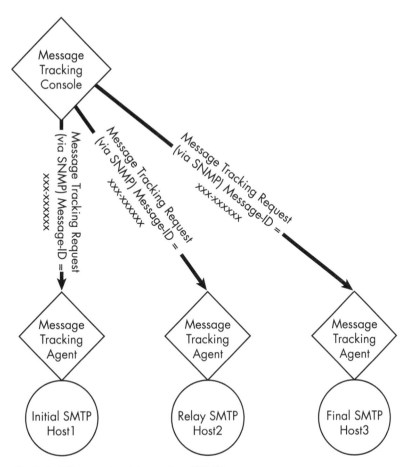

Fig. 7.2 Message-tracking using SNMP.

Notice that each SNMP request from the management console will be a `Get` request that includes the Message-ID of the message as originated. The EMA's publication, *Messaging Management Implementor's Guide: Use of the Directory and Control Functions,* proposes a Management Information Base (MIB) for message-tracking purposes which is indexed by the Message-ID string. In SNMP, the data that each Internet host or application server makes available is defined in the format of an MIB. When an Internet host makes information available via SNMP, the host has been *instrumented* for SNMP. In this situation, the directory comes into play in order that the message-tracking console can look up (via LDAP) configuration information for each of the SNMP agents that it needs to contact. The principal piece of information needed is the host name for the agent, since it is possible that the SNMP agent and the SMTP host that it monitors are located on different TCP/IP hosts. There is currently no standardized LDAP schema for retrieving this configuration information, though several vendors are supplying proprietary schemas with their message-tracking products.

This message-tracking example illustrates that there are several cases when the directory might be used for management purposes:

☞ A user or application needs information about the management components. In this example, the message-tracking console needs configuration information for the management agents that are associated with each of the SMTP hosts.

☞ A user or application needs information about a management component responsible for managing a messaging component. In this example, the message-tracking console needs to find out what management agent is associated with each of SMTP hosts.

☞ A management component needs information about itself or other components. In this situation, the agent for SMTP Host1 wants to contact the agent for SMTP Host1 in order to assist in the message-tracking request.

Using SNMP to Monitor LDAP Servers

A primary way in which the needs mentioned in the previous section can be met is by creating an appropriate set of LDAP object classes and attributes and a subsequent population of the directory with these objects. However, once the management console becomes dependent upon the LDAP server for certain configuration information, it is critical that the LDAP server itself be instrumented for monitoring via SNMP as well. This interaction between management components, messaging components, and the directory is illustrated in Figure 7.3.

In this figure, both the Network Management Console and the Messaging Server are acting as LDAP clients. The Network Management Agents normally collect status information from the Messaging Servers via some local proprietary interfaces, making it available for collection via the SNMP. SNMP is a general-purpose protocol that has as its principal goal the centralized monitoring of network resources. The main aspects of SNMP's version 2 are defined in RFCs 1902 and 1905, though several other RFCs contribute to the overall definition. SNMP has three main protocol operations:

☞ Get—gets the first matching entry in the specified table.

☞ GetNext—gets the next matching entry in the specified table; must be preceded by an earlier Get operation.

☞ Set—adds or changes a value in the specified table. Typically not used in monitoring applications, since all data is normally updated via the local interface between the SNMP agent and the managed service.

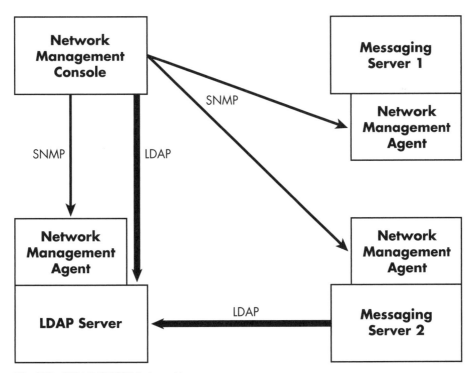

Fig. 7.3 LDAP SNMP interaction.

The Network Management Console will periodically poll various Network Management Agents to determine the various parameters available for the network services and devices in which the network administrator is interested in monitoring. Issuing a `Get` operation for a specific table followed by a sequence of (zero or more) `GetNext` operations implements SNMP polling. The SNMP agent will issue a special response "endOfMibView" when the last entry in the table has been retrieved. Since SNMP agents normally listen on the well-known UDP port number assigned to SNMP (port 161), there is only one SNMP agent per Internet host listening on this port. Other SNMP agents would need to be configured to listen on other port numbers. These agents provide a programmatic interface that allows network services to instrument themselves for monitoring via SNMP. There are numerous services that can be monitored simultaneously, on a typical network server. Some include:

☞ File Services (e.g., NFS)

☞ Print Services

☞ TCP Routing Services

☞ DNS

☞ Messaging Services (e.g., SMTP, POP, and IMAP)

☞ Directory Services

The SNMP console will periodically poll the agent for information about each of the instrumented services that have registered with the agent. The agent is responsible for collecting the information that is needed to fulfill the console's requests. Each service is responsible for defining the information that is of interest to the administrators of its services. An MIB is a tabular arrangement of data. For example, RFC 2248, which defines a SNMP MIB for network application servers (such as LDAP servers and messaging servers), has this ASN.1 definition for the information that should be kept available for monitoring these servers:

```
ApplEntry ::= SEQUENCE {
    applIndex    INTEGER,
    applName     DisplayString,
    applDirectoryName     DistinguishedName,
    applVersion    DisplayString,
    applUptime    TimeStamp,
    applOperStatus    INTEGER,
    applLastChange    TimeStamp,
    applInboundAssociations    Gauge32,
    applOutboundAssociations    Gauge32,
```

```
        applAccumulatedInboundAssociations     Counter32,
        applAccumulatedOutboundAssociations     Counter32,
        applLastInboundActivity     TimeStamp,
        applLastOutboundActivity     TimeStamp,
        applRejectedInboundAssociations     Counter32,
        applFailedOutboundAssociations     Counter32,
        applDescription     DisplayString,
        applURL     URLString
}
```

If there were a messaging server and an LDAP server both running on the same Internet host, then there would be an `applEntry` available for each server, and there would be two entries in the `applTable` that is defined. The `applTable` is defined in Figure 7.4.

The notation above is specific to SNMP MIB definitions. The *not-accessible* value is an indication that the SNMP console may only retrieve, not modify, the `applTable`. The information that is available in the `applEntry` for each monitored network server is intended to be generic and of interest for any network server. The `applEntry` includes a Distinguished Name (DN), which can be used to access the directory entry for the monitored server. Note that the `applDirectoryName` field does not contain a host name for this DN, so the SNMP console should contact its local LDAP server first. If that server does not contain the entry referred to by the DN, then it will return a referral to another LDAP server that will hopefully have the entry in its DIT. There is also an indication of when the application server was started, what its current status is (e.g., up, down), and the current activity at the server. This activity is denoted in terms of the number of *associations* that are active with the server. RFC 2248 uses the generic term *association* rather than a more specific term like *TCP socket* because not every service that will

```
applTable OBJECT-TYPE
  SYNTAX SEQUENCE OF ApplEntry
  MAX-ACCESS not-accessible
  STATUS current
  DESCRIPTION
    "The table holding objects which apply to all different
    kinds of applications providing network services.
    Each network service application capable of being
    monitored should have a single entry in this table."
  ::= {application 1}
```

Fig. 7.4 The `applTable` definitions.

be monitored using the definitions of this MIB needs to make use of TCP sockets. However, since network application servers are the intended users of the MIB, they will all need to communicate with their peers using some mechanism. This communication mechanism is called an association in the RFC. Not only can the number of currently active associations be determined, the MIB also allows the retrieval of the number of associations that have taken place since the server was started.

In order to retrieve information about all the entries in the applTable, the SNMP console would issue a Get request, and the agent would return the first entry in the MIB. Then, using the applIndex from this entry, the console would issue a GetNext request, and the agent would return the second entry in the MIB. Now, using the applIndex from the second entry in the MIB, the agent issues another GetNext request. This time there are no more entries in the MIB, and the agent responds with an endOfMibView response. This interaction is illustrated in Figure 7.5.

In Figure 7.5 the sequence of requests and responses is from the top of the figure to the bottom. If there were more than two entries in the applTable that were maintained on this Internet host, then the GetNext requests would continue on until the SNMP agent returned an endOfMibView request. A companion to the generic applTable that contains information that is specific to directory servers is found in RFC 1567 (which has not been

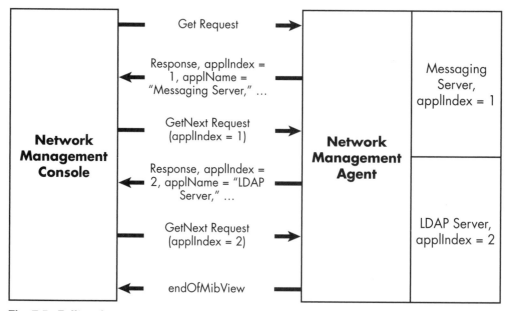

Fig. 7.5 Polling the applTable.

updated by the IETF). RFC 1567 defines three separate MIBs that are designed to hold statistics of interest about the operational state of the directory server. RFC 1567 uses the term Directory Service Agent (DSA) to refer to a directory server. For our purposes here, it will be assumed that a DSA refers to an LDAP server. These three MIBs are:

☞ `DsaOpsTable`—provides summary statistics on the accesses, operations, and errors.

☞ `DsaEntriesTable`—provides summary statistics on the entries held by the DSA.

☞ `DsaIntTable`—provides some useful information on the interaction of the monitored DSA with peer DSAs.

Only the first two MIBs will be discussed here, since the `DsaInt-Table` provides information that is useful in more complex installations. For those installations with a single LDAP server, only the `DsaOpsTable` and the `DsaEntriesTable` provide useful information. The `DsaOpsTable` has the following MIB definition (see Figure 7.6).

```
dsaOpsTable OBJECT-TYPE
  SYNTAX SEQUENCE OF DsaOpsEntry
  MAX-ACCESS not-accessible
  STATUS current
  DESCRIPTION
    " The table holding information related to the
      DSA operations."
  ::= {dsaMIB 1}

dsaOpsEntry OBJECT-TYPE
  SYNTAX DsaOpsEntry
  MAX-ACCESS not-accessible
  STATUS current
  DESCRIPTION
    " Entry containing operations related statistics
      for a DSA."
  INDEX { applIndex }
  ::= {dsaOpsTable 1}

DsaOpsEntry ::= SEQUENCE {
```

```
1) Bindings
   dsaAnonymousBinds
      Counter32,
   dsaUnauthBinds
      Counter32,
   dsaSimpleAuthBinds
      Counter32,
   dsaStrongAuthBinds
      Counter32,
   dsaBindSecurityErrors
      Counter32,

2) Incoming Operations
   dsaInOps
      Counter32,
   dsaReadOps
      Counter32,
   dsaCompareOps
      Counter32,
   dsaAddEntryOps
      Counter32,
   dsaRemoveEntryOps
      Counter32,
   dsaModifyEntryOps
      Counter32,
   dsaModifyRDNOps
      Counter32,
   dsaListOps
      Counter32,
   dsaSearchOps
      Counter32,
   dsaOneLevelSearchOps
      Counter32,
   dsaWholeTreeSearchOps
      Counter32,

 3) Outgoing Operations
  dsaReferrals
     Counter32,
  dsaChainings
     Counter32,

 4) Errors
  dsaSecurityErrors
     Counter32,
  dsaErrors
        Counter32
     }
```

Fig. 7.6 MIB definitions for the `DsaOpsTable`.

This MIB divides the LDAP operations into binds and all the other types. For the incoming bind attempts, the counters indicate how many binds were attempted using each form of authentication. The failed attempts are recorded in the dsaBindSecurityErrors counter. By monitoring the number of connections, the directory adminstrator can monitor the traffic at the LDAP server. For example, if no binds are successfully made to the LDAP server over a period of time, the administrator could conclude that there is a problem with the network or with the LDAP server that is preventing the user from connecting.

There is a counter that is defined to hold the number of attempted operations for each of the other types of LDAP operations. Note that the dsaListOps and the dsaReadOps will always be zero for an LDAP server. This is because the List and Read operations are not defined in LDAP, and are X.500-only operations. The other counters are all applicable to LDAP servers. They will show the amount of activity that has taken place since the LDAP server came up. The entries in the dsaOpsTable are aligned with the entries in the previously discussed applTable. Thus, the counter dsaInOps holds the number of operations that the LDAP server has received since it came up. The time that the LDAP server came up can be determined by looking at the applUptime timestamp in the applTable. The other table of interest for most LDAP server implementations is the dsaEntriesTable defined in Figure 7.7.

```
dsaEntriesTable OBJECT-TYPE
  SYNTAX SEQUENCE OF DsaEntriesEntry
  MAX-ACCESS not-accessible
  STATUS current
  DESCRIPTION
    " The table holding information related to the
      entry statistics and cache performance of the DSAs."
  ::= {dsaMIB 2}

dsaEntriesEntry OBJECT-TYPE
  SYNTAX DsaEntriesEntry
  MAX-ACCESS not-accessible
  STATUS current
  DESCRIPTION
    " Entry containing statistics pertaining to entries
      held by a DSA."
  INDEX { applIndex }
  ::= {dsaEntriesTable 1}
```

```
DsaEntriesEntry ::= SEQUENCE {
  dsaMasterEntries
    Gauge32,
  dsaCopyEntries
    Gauge32,
  dsaCacheEntries
    Gauge32,
  dsaCacheHits
    Counter32,
  dsaSlaveHits
    Counter32
  }
```

Fig. 7.7 `DsaEntriesTable` definitions.

For LDAP servers that aren't replicated, the only nonzero value in
the table will be the `dsaMasterEntries`. If two (or more) LDAP servers
hold the data for the same DN entry, then the one entry that is guaranteed
to hold the authentic information is presumed to be the "master" entry,
and all the other LDAP servers are only holding "copies" of that entry.[2]

The IETF has currently created a specification that allows for the
directory server to make use of the SNMP trap mechanism to alert the
administrator of certain unusual situations. In SNMP, the trap mechanism is sent from the SNMP agent to the consoles. The trap is used
when unusual events happen at an instrumented host. This specification
is not yet available as an RFC. Most of the definitions in this specification are peculiar to messaging servers and not directory servers. However, the specification does define the mechanism whereby the directory
administrator can be alerted in several situations, such as:

☞ When the directory server is unavailable when it should be.
☞ When connectivity fails (the directory server is unable to contain
  another peer directory server).
☞ When security failure (the directory server is unable to successfully
  authenticate to a peer directory server) has occurred.

Once the LDAP server has been appropriately instrumented, it can
participate effectively in the management of the network components. In

---

[2] Some LDAP implementations allow more than one LDAP server to be the master for an entry.
Such multimaster implementations have more complex definitions for master entries and copy entries.

order to find the management agent responsible for monitoring a given directory server, the management console can make use of information stored in an LDAP accessible directory. The EMA's *Messaging Management Implementor's Guide: Use of the Directory and Control Functions* proposes a schema for just such information. A DIT conforming to this schema would have a structure similar to the one shown in Figure 7.8.

In this schema, the principal object classes of interest are those for the management agents (in this DIT, the management agents are cn=ma1 and cn=ma2), and those for the messaging components (in this DIT, the messaging component is cn=mta1). The schema is defined in the EMA document using X.500 terminology. It has been slightly simplified for presentation here:

```
( NAME 'managedMTA' SUP mhs-message-transfer-agent — from X.402, Sect. A.1.3
  MAY ( managementAgentName)

( NAME 'managementAgentName' EQUALITY distinguishedNameMatch SYNTAX
1.3.6.1.4.1.1466.115.121.1.12 )

( NAME 'managementAgent' SUP 'top' MUST ( commonName )
  MAY ( managedMTAName $ mgmtFunctionDescription $ mgmtFunctionAddresses $
mgmtConsoleAddress $ alarmDestAddresses $ mgmtConformance)

(NAME 'managedMTAName' EQUALITY distinguishedNameMatch SYNTAX
1.3.6.1.4.1.1466.115.121.1.12 )
```

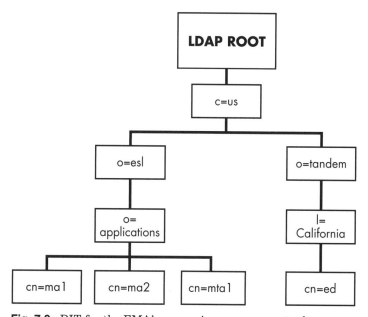

Fig. 7.8 DIT for the EMA's messaging management schema.

The two managed objects that are defined and given object class definitions are the messaging server (i.e., `managedMTA`) and the management agent. The `managedMTA` object class is defined as a subclass of the X.400-based messaging server definition "mhs-message-transfer-agent," while the `managementAgent` object class is defined from scratch. The `managementAgent` object class lists the names of the messaging servers that it manages by giving their DNs. It also lists the management functions that it supports. The attribute syntaxes for these functions are not shown above, but they have the following meanings:

`MgmtFunctionDescription`—type of function, e.g., dynamic monitoring.

`MgmtFunctionAddresses`—address-protocol pairs for each in this function.

`MgmtConsoleAddress`—address of management console; IP, e-mail, or other.

`AlarmDestAddresses`—place to send traps; may be same as management console.

`MgmtConformance`—MADMAN or MADMAN plus EMA extensions.

The actual schema has these management functions grouped together so that each management agent can have several management functions. This schema definition is made using new X.500 constructs that are not supported by LDAP. Here is one way this schema can be used.

A user is interested in the performance of the local messaging servers. So the MTA object is looked up in the directory using an LDAP search. This LDAP search operation retrieves the distinguished names (among other items) of one or more management agents that are monitoring this MTA. The user then performs an LDAP search to retrieve the information from each of the management agents. For at least one of the retrieved management agents, the user will send an SNMP request to the IP address given in the `mgmtFunctionAddresses` attribute in order to retrieve the dynamic monitoring information for the MTA. This schema allows the management agent operations to be logically and physically separated from the messaging servers that are being managed.

Directory Support and Management of Other Applications and Services

The industry has recognized the value in using a "data repository," such as a directory, to hold information that is needed by applications. Often, the applications are completely independent of the directory service. In this case, the directory is used as a device that aids in the interaction and management of the application's components. Instead of actually locating the application on the network, the directory helps the application locate information it needs to complete the transaction between components of the application. The users of the directory in this case are typically not people, but computer programs. Several examples of directory-supported applications available today are:

☞ MHS routing, as described in RFC 1801

☞ Trading partner information for facilitating EDI transactions

☞ Security certificates used for encryption and digital signatures

☞ Translation of e-mail formats between dissimilar e-mail systems (e.g., from Lotus Notes mail to MS-Exchange, or between an e-mail system and X.400 or SMTP/MIME) and addressing

☞ Voicemail Address Resolution (from the VPIM work of the EMA)

In the case of routing electronic mail by the Message Handling System (MHS), the directory assists in message routing. The directory is used to enter all routing information that MHS needs to route messages throughout its domain. In some organizations it is impractical, perhaps impossible, to update all routing tables in the MHS at the same time, (or in a timely manner) when the MHS has a configuration change. Historically, the e-mail routing tables had to be updated when an addition or deletion of a messaging server occured in the network. However, this information may be entered once in a directory and then made available using LDAP to all of the messaging servers. In this model, the messaging server makes an LDAP call to retrieve its routing table from the directory when it first starts up.

Alternatively, a messaging server may access a directory for its routing information prior to making a routing decision. Both types of implementation are on the market today. Each has its merits and disadvantages. But both schemes allow easier management of the MHS by using a directory as a data repository. Novell employed a very simple MHS routing scheme in the messaging system that was delivered with its NetWare 4.1 network operating system. This scheme put all of the routing information in the directory, and the messaging servers would access the directory for each routing decision. While LDAP was not used in this system (as Novell had deployed its Novell Directory Service (NDS) prior to the widespread deployment of LDAP) it used a schema and protocol that were compatible with the LDAP technology.

The schema for the messaging users included a special attribute that contained the messaging server name and a file system location where the mail could be spooled. The schema also included an object class for a messaging server, and an object class for a grouping of messaging servers into a message routing group. A modified version of this schema is given in Figure 7.9.

The other messaging attributes are all strings. The postmaster attribute contains the e-mail address of a user to notify when problems arise and where undeliverable mail can be forwarded. The `messaging-DatabaseLocation` contains the location on the Novell file server where connecting file servers should deposit inbound messages. In an Internet environment, this would be analogous to the port number on the host. The `supportedGateway` attribute lists the types of non-Novell messaging connections that are supported from this `messagingServer` (e.g., SMTP). The `messageRoutingGroup` is defined as a subclass of the group, yet adds

```
(NAME 'messagingUser' SUP top AUXILIARY MUST (messagingServerName $
mailboxLocation ))

(NAME 'messagingServer' SUP server STRUCTURAL MUST (messageRouting-
GroupName $ messagingDatabaseLocation $ postmaster) MAY (supportedGate-
way))

(NAME 'messagingRoutingGroup' SUP group STRUCTURAL)

(NAME 'messagingServerName' EQUALITY distinguishedNameMatch
   SYNTAX 1.3.6.1.4.1.1466.115.121.1.12 SINGLE-VALUE )

(NAME 'messagingServerName' EQUALITY distinguishedNameMatch
   SYNTAX 1.3.6.1.4.1.1466.115.121.1.12 SINGLE-VALUE )

(NAME 'mailboxLocation' EQUALITY caseIgnoreMatch
   SUBSTR caseIgnoreSubstringsMatch
   SYNTAX 1.3.6.1.4.1.1466.115.121.1.15{64} )

(NAME 'messageRoutingGroupName' EQUALITY distinguishedNameMatch SYNTAX
1.3.6.1.4.1.1466.115.121.1.12 SINGLE-VALUE )
```

Fig. 7.9 Schema for messaging servers and users in NDS.

no new attributes. The expectation is that messaging servers are members of the `messageRoutingGroup`.

In this example, the messaging servers are acting as LDAP clients. They will use the directory to look up configuration information and to determine routing information for the messages they receive. When a messaging server first comes up, it will know its own distinguished name. Using this, it can query the directory via LDAP to retrieve the information from its own directory object, such as:

☞ what routing group it is in

☞ where its incoming messages are stored

☞ the name of its postmaster

☞ any messaging gateways that it is configured to support

The next step in the messaging server's configuration is the retrieval of the `messageRoutingGroup` object from the directory. The retrieval of this object allows the messaging server to know all of the other messaging servers to which it can connect directly, i.e., the ones to which it can attempt to open a socket connection. Once the messaging server has configured itself with the information that it has retrieved from the directory via LDAP, it can begin processing messages that are queued up for delivery (in the place indicated by its `messagingDatabase-Location` attribute). In this environment, the messages are addressed by using a special form of the distinguished name. This form allows the messaging server to use the e-mail address of the recipient as a key for an LDAP lookup. The messaging server looks up the `messagingServerName` attribute for each recipient. This allows the messaging server to route the message to the appropriate servers for each of the recipients. For those recipients that are not users of the Novell messaging system, the messaging server must find an appropriate messaging gateway. The gateway is found by querying the `messagingGateway` attribute of each of the servers in the `messageRoutingGroup` object in which this messaging server is a member.

This simple mechanism for configuring the messaging servers and their routing table by using LDAP has the following benefits:

☞ The messaging server doesn't need any special configuration application.

☞ The messaging server doesn't even need to be running in order to be configured.

☞ The messaging server can be administered from anywhere that an LDAP server is available. This is due to the distribution and replication available in modern directory services.

☞ The messaging server can be added to the network at will, and its peer messaging server will find it as soon as it needs to route e-mail to users on the new messaging server.

Using the Directory to Support a Public Key Infrastructure

The definitions of the strongAuthenticationUser and certification-Authority object classes are one means by which the Public Key Infrastructure (PKI) can be supported by LDAP. The example of secure electronic mail using the S/MIME specifications (defined in RFCs 2311 and 2312) will be used to illustrate how this works. S/MIME makes use of public key cryptography to digitally sign and encrypt MIME messages. Public keys that belong to a user may be stored in the form of an X.509 certificate in the user's directory entry in the userCertificate attribute. Certificate issuers store their public keys in the form of an X.509 certificate as well, but instead they store them in the cACertificate attribute.

If user1 needs to send an encrypted message to user2, then it needs user2's public key. This public key is retrieved from the directory by issuing an LDAP search request that includes the userCertificate in the list of requested attributes. The information in the X.509 certificates (included in the public key) is digitally signed with the private key of the certificate issuer. If user1 does not have knowledge of (or, in fact, trust) the issuer of user2's certificate, then the directory can be consulted again. This time the LDAP search request will target the issuer name field in user2's certificate and indicate that the cACertificate attribute is included in the list of requested attributes. User1 can examine the issuer name that is included in this certificate as well to determine if it is known and trusted. If this certificate is not trusted either, user1 can then retrieve the cACertificate of this certificate's issuer.

This certificate retrieval continues until a known and trusted certificate is found. In addition to retrieving the cACertificate from each of the certificate issuers' LDAP entries, user1 will also want to retrieve the CRL attribute as well. The CRL contains a list of unique identifiers for all the certificates that have been issued, but subsequently "revoked" by the certificate issuer (i.e., the certificate revocation list (CRL)). Each CRL is examined to make sure the issuer has not revoked the certificate that user1 is attempting to verify. Since CRLs contain an identifier for every certificate that has ever been revoked, their size continues to grow over time.

Schema Management Considerations

The design, implementation, and subsequent support of a directory that will support specific application requirements has far more items to consider than the simple White Pages Service directory. The first and foremost item is to ensure that the application can find information in the directory quickly and efficiently. Therefore, the directory information tree (DIT) structure used should be one that makes the most sense in the context of the search that the application will perform when looking for information. In many cases, this type of support requires a separate and very specific subtree in the DIT.

Most people are very familiar with the traditional White Pages Service (WPS) DIT structure that supports information being read by human users. The DIT is usually constructed around organizations or geographies, because this is what human users associate with people in WPS directories. However, applications often need numbers to make associations between components of an application. Therefore, an application-oriented DIT may have a structure that is incomprehensible to humans, but extremely well optimized for, and understood by, an application's use.

As shown in the example from the NetWare 4.1 messaging schema (see Figure 7.9), much of the information stored in the `messagingServer` and `messageRoutingGroup` objects is intended for the use of messaging servers, and is not necessarily intended to be viewed by humans. Another example of a directory application assisting in routing is the voice mail address resolution. The Voice Profile for Internet Mail (VPIM) specifies a method of using Internet ESMTP and MIME protocols for use in digital voice messaging relay between dissimilar voice messaging systems. The key data element that must be provided in this application is a fully qualified RFC822 address format, such as a map to the voice mail mailbox. Using a directory, a lookup process can be developed which, when supplied with the voice mail box number for a recipient, is mapped to an RFC822 address that allows the message to be forwarded to the correct voice messaging system. This DIT, as illustrated by the EMA VPIM working group, in shown in Figure 7.10.

In this DIT structure, the knowledge of the appropriate telephone prefix (attribute TP above) is required for navigation through the entries in the tree. The second consideration in schema management would be the selection and maintenance of object classes and attributes that reflect the data elements needed by an application. This analysis involves a thorough review of the specific data items needed by an application in order to perform its tasks. Prior to the definition of data elements, one should have a

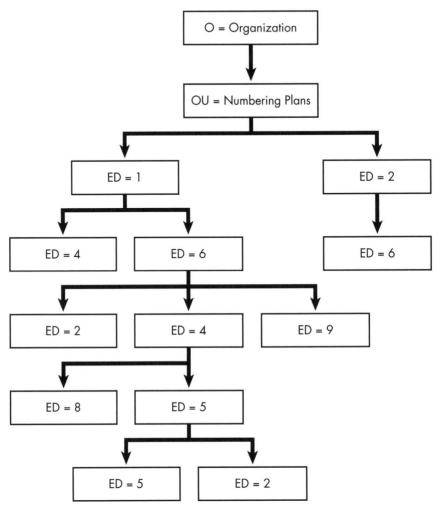

Fig. 7.10 Voice Mail DIT.

very clear understanding of what the application will do, even to the point of flow-charting (e.g., inputs/outputs) common data interactions.

The VPIM directory is structured in a hierarchy whereby each node in the tree represents a single digit of an E.164 telephone number.[3] The higher in the tree a digit is, the higher its significance in the telephone number. The e164Digit attribute type is used for naming nodes in the tree. Since a single digit names the nodes in the tree, the e164Digit attribute shall have a length of one digit. The e164Digit attribute type name is abbreviated to "ed."

---

[3] E.164 is the ITU recommendation that defines what telephone numbers look like.

A telephone number of +1 613 765 1234 would have the following corresponding Distinguished Name in the above VPIM directory:

```
ed=4, ed=3, ed=2, ed=1, ed=5, ed=6, ed=7, ed=3, ed=1, ed=6,
ed=1, ou=numbering plans, o=organization
```

Once the data elements have been defined, then a specific profile for the application using directory language should be developed. In the case of X.500 directories, the profile would consist of the standard schema definition items such as syntax, single or multivalued, attribute type, matching rules, structure rules, name forms, etc, and result in a documented schema that includes object identifiers. Once the schema is documented, it may be given to directory vendors who will include these definitions into their directory products that will support the application. For example, a profile has been put forward that supports EDI transactions using an X.500 directory. ISO/IEC DISP 12073 "International Standardized Profile FD16-Directory Data Definitions - EDI Use of the Directory" specifies the support of EDI transactions in an X.500 manner. EDI stands for Electronic Data Interchange, and is one way in which electronic commerce transactions are exchanged among trading partners. EDI transaction formats are typically electronic versions of documents that are used in a paper format in normal business transactions. Various data formats have been specified by several industry organizations. These formats include electronic versions of:

☞ Purchase Orders
☞ Purchase Order Changes
☞ Order Receipts/Acknowledgments
☞ Requests for Catalog Listings
☞ Shipping Manifests
☞ Request for Quotation (RFQ)
☞ Billing Invoices

An object class from that document is shown in Figure 7.11.

Notice the slight difference in the syntax of the ITU object class and attribute specification from the IETF representation that was used in Chapter 3. The eDITradingProfile object class is used to represent information in the directory about entities that actively engage in electronic commerce using EDI. Each of the different types of EDI transactions that are used are listed in the eDIMessageTypes attribute. The eDIInterchangeRoles attribute indicates whether the entity is willing to send EDI transactions, receive EDI transactions, or both. The other attributes of the eDITrading-

```
eDITradingProfile OBJECT CLASS
SUBCLASS OF top
MUST CONTAIN {commonName}
MAY CONTAIN {eDIProfileReference, eDIMessageTypes, eDIInterchangeRoles,
eDIApplicationPriority, eDIBusinessFunctionQualifier}
::= {fdi-6-oc7}


eDIInterchangeRoles ATTRIBUTE
WITH ATTRIBUTE-SYNTAX BIT STRING {
sender (0)
receiver (1)}
MATCHES FOR EQUALITY
::= {fdi-6-at4}
```

Fig. 7.11 An EDI object class.

`Profile` object class are not of interest here. The information contained in an object of class `eDITradingProfile` can be retrieved using a simple LDAP query. Thus, if there were a directory that had this type of information, a potential trading partner could examine the `eDITradingProfile` object for a potential trading partner. The `eDIMessageTypes` attribute would be examined to determine if a compatible set of EDI transactions existed between the two potential trading partners. If an appropriate level of compatibility was determined to exist, then the electronic commerce transactions could begin to be exchanged.

The final consideration is the overall management of the application/directory interaction. There should be, at least, one person who is extremely familiar with the data aspects of the application and their implementation into the directory system. The mapping of the application data elements to the directory schema should be well documented (usually in some offline manner, e.g., a spreadsheet or table). In addition, the system management team must recognize that the directory and application have now become a single system. If the application is considered to be business-critical, then the directory that supports the application must also be considered business-critical and supported accordingly.

AUTHENTICATION TECHNIQUES TO IDENTIFY CLIENT TO SERVER (AND VICE VERSA)

One of the most important aspects of administrating the directory service is the control of how information that is stored in the directory is made available to various requesters, and how the directory identifies the requester of the data. This identification is often termed *user authentication*, or just *authentication*. Directory servers typically authenticate the user by means of a bind operation in whatever protocol the directory server supports (e.g., DAP, LDAP, etc.) While this section does not pretend to present a complete list of all of the possible means of authenticating users to directory services, the most commonly discussed means are presented. Various authentication means that have been defined for directory services are as follows:

☞ Anonymous authentication

☞ User ID and password in the clear, also known as *simple authentication*

☞ User ID and password across an encrypted TLS link, often called *protected authentication*

☞ Challenge response mechanisms

☞ Exchange of X.509 credentials, known as *strong authentication* via:
  • TLS
  • Simple Authentication and Session Layer (SASL)
  • as defined in X.509

In anonymous authentication, the bind operation does not contain any information that can be used to identify the requesting user. Typically, all anonymous users are given identical access to directory information. In simple authentication, the bind operation contains the name of the user and a sequence of bytes that is known only by the named user. This sequence of bytes is known as the password. If this password matches the password stored by the directory service, then the bind operation is presumed to be successful, and the connecting user is given access to the directory information according to the access granted to that user.

In protected authentication, the directory server is "listening" on a TLS port in accordance to the definitions of TLS as defined in RFC 2246. Once the TLS client and TLS server finish their negotiation, a session key has been exchanged that is used by both the LDAP client and the LDAP server to secure the communications across the TLS connection. The session is secured due to the fact that all data that is passed over the connection is encrypted using the negotiated key. Thus, the entire bind operation that contains the user name and password is encrypted for protection, as that information travels across the Internet.

An interesting alternative to the submission of the user's password across the LDAP connection is the use of a challenge response mechanism.

One example of such a mechanism is defined in RFC 2195. This mechanism, known as CRAM-MD5, stands for Challenge Response Authentication Mechanism-MD5. MD5 is the secure message digest algorithm defined in RFC 1321. MD5 has the special property of producing 16 bytes of output data from arbitrary input data. By using CRAM-MD5 as an authentication method, the LDAP client is allowed to bind to the LDAP server without sending the password across the network. A challenge response mechanism works in the client server paradigm as follows:

1. The client contacts the server in order to authenticate.
2. The server responds with some string of bytes, possibly including a randomly generated byte sequence. This string of bytes is known as the "challenge."
3. The client combines its password with the server's challenge in a special way that is defined by the challenge response mechanism, and sends this combination back to the server. This combination is known as the response.
4. The server examines the response to determine if it confirms that the responding client has knowledge of the user's password that is attempting the authentication.

In addition to allowing the client to authenticate itself to the server, some challenge response mechanisms allow the server to authenticate itself to the client. The server authentication normally takes place before the client authentication that is described above. The above challenge response mechanism allows for only a single challenge before the password derived response is generated. Some challenge response mechanisms allow for multiple challenges to be exchanged before the password-derived response is created. In the single challenge response mechanisms, if for some reason the client contacts a "rogue" server, it may be possible for the client's password to be discovered. This is due to the fact that the rogue server may use the client's response as part of a "dictionary" attack. In this scenario, the rogue server will use a list of possible passwords and generate responses for each possibility in the list until it finds one that matches the response provided by the client. For this reason, single challenge response mechanisms may be inappropriate when authenticating across the Internet, although it is a very reasonable choice when authenticating within the corporate intranet. Note that the challenge response mechanisms never distribute the client's password, so they have attractive characteristics when compared to the simple and protected authentication mechanisms.

CRAM-MD5 is a single challenge response mechanism. The data encoded in the server's challenge contains a presumptively arbitrary string of random digits, a timestamp, and the fully-qualified primary host name of the server. The syntax of the unencoded form must correspond to that of an RFC 822 'msg-id' as described in RFC 1939 (which defines POP3). The client makes note of the data and then responds with a string consisting of the user name, a space, and a 'digest.' The latter is computed by applying the keyed MD5 algorithm from (RFC 2104) where the key is a shared secret and the digested text is the timestamp (including angle-brackets). This shared secret (i.e., the password) is a string known only to the client and server. The "digest" parameter itself is a 16-octet value that is sent in hexadecimal format, using lower-case ASCII characters. When the server receives this client response, it verifies the digest provided. If the digest is correct, the server should consider the client authenticated and respond appropriately. An example from RFC 2195 using the IMAP protocol is shown below. The base64 encoding of the challenges and responses is part of the IMAP4 AUTHENTICATE command, not part of the CRAM specification itself.

```
S: * OK IMAP4 Server
C: A0001 AUTHENTICATE CRAM-MD5
S: + PDE4OTYuNjk3MTcwOTUyQHBvc3RvZmZpY2UucmVzdG9uLm1ja
   S5uZXQ+
C: dGltIGI5MTNhNjAyYzdlZGE3YTQ5NWI0ZTZlNzMzNGQzODkw
S: A0001 OK CRAM authentication successful
```

In this example, the shared secret is the string `tanstaaftanstaaf`. Hence, the keyed MD5 digest is produced by calculating the following:

```
MD5((tanstaaftanstaaf XOR opad),
MD5((tanstaaftanstaaf XOR ipad),
<1896.697170952@postoffice.reston.mci.net>))
```

where ipad and opad are as defined in the keyed-MD5 RFC.

When using TLS for protected authentication, an important side effect that results from its use is the ability of the LDAP client to gain access to the LDAP server's certificate. The LDAP client can then use this certificate in order to validate that it is "talking" to the appropriate LDAP server. This verification is performed by validating the authenticity of the server certificate against its set of known certificate authority (CA) certificates. The LDAP server's certificate will have been digitally signed by one of these CA certificates. If the LDAP client is able to verify the signature on the LDAP server's certificate by using the public key from the appropriate CA, then the client can be assured that the LDAP server is authentic. The LDAP client should periodically check the directory entries of its cached CAs in order to retrieve the CRLs. This allows the LDAP client to determine if the LDAP server's certificate is still in effect, or whether it has been revoked.

The current accepted format of certificates that is used in directory authentication is that defined as X.509 version 3 certificates. Note that whether simple authentication or protected authentication is used, the name that is transmitted to the directory is normally the complete distinguished name that the user is known to the directory (e.g., cn=bruceg, o=prentice hall, c=us).

Strong authentication provides the most powerful means of authentication between directory clients and directory servers. One of the most important aspects of strong authentication that distinguishes it from the other authentication means is that the user's name and password never cross the network, even in encrypted form. As in the protected form defined above, the directory client has the ability to authenticate the directory server. But, in the strong authentication technique, the certificate of the directory client is transmitted to the directory server, along with proof that the directory client knows about the private key that corresponds to the public key contained in the user certificate information. Typically, the private key is locked in the directory client by means of a password that must be entered by the end user in order to unlock it for use in the strong authentication. Note that the private key never leaves the client workstation. Once the Directory Server receives the client Certificate, information in the certificate is used to authenticate the client to the directory. One common area to place the user identity is in the certificate subject-name field, but the user identity can be placed in other fields as well (e.g., the other-names extension field). The forms of strong authentication that are available in LDAP are placed inside of the SASL authentication choice on the bind operation. Some available strong authentication choices using SASL are as follows:

☞ the mechanism defined in the TLS specification mentioned above.
☞ the strong authentication technique defined in the X.509 recommendation (can be placed inside of SASL).
☞ Kerberos authentication (can be placed inside of SASL as well, although it doesn't use X.509 certificates).

Whichever of these techniques is used, the high level view of the exchange of X.509 certificates between directory client and directory server is the same. Directory servers may or may not support all of these defined authentication techniques. Furthermore, directory servers normally give administrators the capability to turn off weaker authentication means in order to protect the integrity of the directory information.

CHAPTER SUMMARY

This chapter discussed how the directory (in particular LDAP) can be used as a management tool. Additionally, some of the issues surrounding the management of the directory server itself were given attention. We saw how SNMP can be used to monitor the activity of directory servers. We also showed how schema management concerns play an important role in how well the LDAP server can manage applications.

## CHAPTER 8

Building an LDAP Browser in Java[1]

T he typical general-purpose application desired for LDAP environments is one that allows the end user to view the contents of the DIT. The user would be able to visualize the DIT by examining each entry in the hierarchy, and expanding an entry by viewing its children and siblings. This application is referred to as an *LDAP Browser*. The idea behind an LDAP browser is much the same as the idea behind a web browser, except that an LDAP browser brings the information in an LDAP server to the view of a user rather than bringing it in a web server.

An LDAP browser could be written in many ways. This chapter will discuss in detail how an LDAP browser can be written to run inside a web browser in the browser's Java environment. It will be assumed that the reader has some familiarity with the Java programming language, but all of the features of the LDAP browser implementation will be completely discussed. Thus, it is not necessary to have written numerous Java applications to continue with this chapter. In order to gain access to the LDAP server, the browser makes use of the LDAP Java client API as defined in an Internet draft, which has not progressed to the RFC stage as of the writing of this book. The browser also uses the version of Java and its Abstract Windowing Toolkit (AWT) as defined in the Java language specification version 1.1.

---

[1] The Java programming language is defined in *The Java Language Specification*, by James Gosling, Bill Joy, and Guy Steele. Publisher: Addison-Wesley, 1996.

This discussion will include screen shots of the browser in action, as well as the full source code for the browser. Unlike the web browser that allows connections to most web sites without collecting any authentication information from the users, this LDAP browser must first collect all of the information that is needed for the LDAP bind operation. The information that is needed for a typical bind operation is:

☞ LDAP server's host name

☞ LDAP user's distinguished name

☞ LDAP user's password

☞ The initial search base

After this information has been collected, it will be stored so that it can be used later if necessary. The main reason that the information might need to be used later is if the connection to the LDAP server is somehow invalidated. Some LDAP servers will invalidate a connection if there is no activity for a certain period of time. When the connection is invalidated, it is necessary for the LDAP client to submit another bind operation to the server. When the rebind is required, the browser will retrieve the stored bind configuration and use the data to bind again, without any additional user interaction.

Since the LDAP browser will not be its own application, but will instead be running inside of a web browser, it will be built as applets. In this situation, it is appropriate to store the values in a global area so that they can be shared among the different components that need them, since there isn't an easy way of passing data from one applet to another. Thus, this class is used to store the browser's global data (see Figure 8.1).

```
1 import netscape.ldap.*;
2
3 class browserGlobals {

4    public static LDAPConnection ld = null;
5    public static String USER_DN = "";
6    public static String USER_PW = "";
7    public static String MY_HOST = "localhost";
8    public static String SEARCHBASE = "";
9    public static int MY_PORT = 389;
10   static final int CLICKTHRESHOLD = 250;
11 }
```

Fig. 8.1 Global data for the LDAP browser.

Notice that the four variables USER_DN, USER_PW, MY_HOST, and SEARCHBASE match the previously mentioned pieces of information that are needed for the typical `bind` operation. A variable is also defined for the port on which the LDAP server is listening. The browser won't actually allow the user to change this value, but it would be simple enough to provide a field to do that. The other critical variable that is defined in `the browserGlobals` class is `ld`. It is of type `ldapConnection`. The `ldapConnection` is the central LDAP class that is defined in the LDAP Java API. The import statement at the top of the code segment brings in support for this LDAP Java API. It provides methods to establish an authenticated or anonymous connection to an LDAP server, as well as methods to search for, modify, compare, and delete entries in the directory. The LDAPConnection class also provides fields for storing settings that are specific to the LDAP session (such as limits on the number of results returned or timeouts). Notice that all of these variables are defined as `static;`. This is an indication that they can only be instantiated once. No matter how many different times a program creates an instance of `browserGlobals`, all references to USER_DN will point back to the same underlying data item. The CLICKTHRESHOLD constant that is defined represents the maximum number of milliseconds that can elapse between consecutive mouse clicks before they are considered to be a double-click event. Each Java application needs to define such a mechanism since Java, unlike other windowing systems,[2] does not define a double-click event.

THE DATA COLLECTION APPLET

The browser will be built using two screens. The first screen will collect the `bind` configuration data, and the second screen will handle all of the displaying and navigation of the DIT. Each of the screens will be implemented as a separate Java applet using the Java Development Kit (JDK) version 1.1 implementation of the Abstract Windowing Toolkit (AWT). AWT defines all of the components used in this version of the JDK for implementing graphical user interfaces (GUI). Subsequent versions of the JDK have defined other mechanisms for building GUIs. The definitions needed to hold the `bind` configuration data are shown in Figure 8.2.

TextField objects allow the user to enter characters. Label objects simply display data on the screen and cannot be changed by the user. The

---

[2] Windowing systems such as Microsoft Windows and OS/2 have built-in support for the double-click event.

variable myGlobals holds the bind configuration data after the user enters it so that it can be passed along to the navigation screen. When a web page that contains a Java applet is viewed in the browser, the browser calls the applet's init() routine (see Figure 8.3). This routine for the collection

```
java.awt.TextField LDAPServerTextField;
java.awt.Label LDAPServerLabel;
java.awt.TextField searchBaseTextField;
java.awt.Label searchBaseLabel;
java.awt.TextField nameTextField;
java.awt.Label nameLabel;
java.awt.TextField passwordTextField;
java.awt.Label passwordLabel;
java.awt.Button okButton;
browserGlobals myGlobals;
```

Fig. 8.2 Variables for holding bind configuration data.

```
 1  public void init()
 2  {
 3    setLayout(null);
 4    setSize(430,270);
 5    LDAPServerTextField = new java.awt.TextField();
 6    LDAPServerTextField.setBounds(168,24,156,24);
 7    add(LDAPServerTextField);
 8    LDAPServerLabel =
 9        new java.awt.Label("LDAP Server");
10    LDAPServerLabel.setBounds(36,24,100,24);
11    add(LDAPServerLabel);
12    searchBaseTextField = new java.awt.TextField();
13    searchBaseTextField.setBounds(168,72,156,24);
14    add(searchBaseTextField);
15    searchBaseLabel =
16        new java.awt.Label("LDAP Search Base");
17    searchBaseLabel.setBounds(36,72,108,24);
18    add(searchBaseLabel);
19    nameTextField = new java.awt.TextField();
20    nameTextField.setBounds(168,120,156,24);
21    add(nameTextField);
22    nameLabel = new java.awt.Label("Name");
23    nameLabel.setBounds(36,120,100,24);
```

```
24      add(nameLabel);
25      passwordTextField = new java.awt.TextField();
26      passwordTextField.setBounds(168,168,156,24);
27      add(passwordTextField);
28      passwordLabel = new java.awt.Label("Password");
29      passwordLabel.setBounds(36,168,100,24);
30      add(passwordLabel);
31      okButton = new java.awt.Button();
32      okButton.setLabel("OK");
33      okButton.setBounds(132,216,60,40);
34      okButton.setBackground(new Color(12632256));
35      okButton.addActionListener
36          (new okButtonListener());
37      add(okButton);
38  }
```

Fig. 8.3 Init routine for the data collection applet.

applet needs to place the GUI objects in the appropriate locations on the screen and then wait for the user to enter some configuration data.

The init() starts out on line 3 by indicating that it won't need any of AWT's built-in screen layout routines. Instead, init() will place each of the GUI objects in a specified location on the screen. Next, the size of the applet window in pixels is specified on line 4. The rest of the routine creates each of the GUI objects, defines their sizes, and then places them in specific locations on the screen. Of particular interest are the lines that impact the okButton object. Lines 35 and 36 make use of the addActionListener() method of AWT. This is an indication that whenever something affects the state of the okButton object, the method okButtonListener() should be called. It is up to the browser application to define this routine, as it is not provided by the AWT. The init() routine defines nine GUI objects to be placed on the screen. There are four text fields that allow the user to enter data, four labels that indicate what should be typed into the text field, and one button that is to be pressed when the user is finished entering data. After the init() routine completes, the initial screen of the browser applet appears, as seen in Figure 8.4.

Notice in Figure 8.4 the user has entered data in the server name and search base fields only, and that no distinguished name and password have been entered. This is an indication that the browser should perform an anonymous bind to the LDAP server. Once the OK button has been pressed by the user, the browser's Java runtime support will call the okButtonListener() routine that the browser provides. This routine

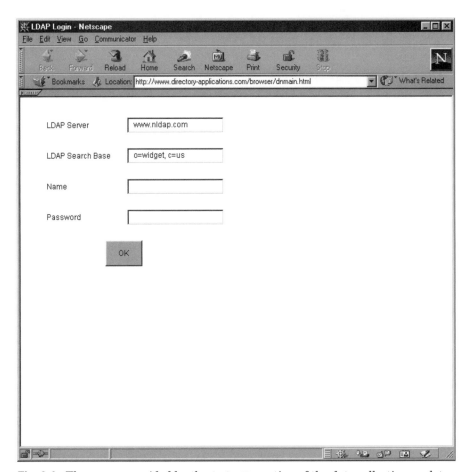

Fig. 8.4 The screen provided by the `init()` routine of the data collection applet.

needs to store the data that the user entered into the global variables
that are defined and then call the DIT navigation routine. This is implemented in the code in Figure 8.5.

This routine uses the `getText()` method of the various AWT GUI
components in order to retrieve the text that has been entered by the
user. After `okButtonListener()` stores the data in the `myGlobals` object,
it then tries to load the web page that contains the DIT navigation applet.
In this case, the web page is named "dnDialog.html" and is located in the
same directory on the same web server as the web page that contains the
data collection applet. The `getCodeBase()` method returns a URL that
holds the web server and directory in which the web page that contains
the data collection applet is located. In this case the URL is
http://www.directory-applications.com/browser. The `thisURL` variable adds

```
 1  class okButtonListener implements ActionListener {
 2    public void actionPerformed(ActionEvent event) {
 3      String password = passwordTextField.getText();
 4      String name = nameTextField.getText();
 5      String searchBase =
 6        searchBaseTextField.getText();
 7      String serverName =
 8        LDAPServerTextField.getText();
 9      myGlobals.MGR_DN = name;
10      myGlobals.MGR_PW = password;
11      myGlobals.MY_HOST = serverName;
12      myGlobals.SEARCHBASE = searchBase;
13      try {
14        URL thisURL =
15          new URL(getCodeBase() + "dnDialog.html");
16        getAppletContext().showDocument(thisURL);
17      } catch ( MalformedURLException e) {
18        add(new Label("Error creating URL"));
19      }
20    }
21  }
```

Fig. 8.5 `okButtonListener` routine for the data collection applet.

the page named "dnDialog.html" to this URL. Java's `showDocument()` method transfers control to the page given in the `thisURL` variable.

THE DIT NAVIGATION APPLET

The DIT navigation applet will have the following four components:

☞ A list control to hold the LDAP entries in the container at the current level of the DIT

☞ A text field to show which LDAP entry is currently selected

☞ A larger text area to show the attributes and values of the selected LDAP entry

☞ A button that can be pressed to move up one level in the DIT hierarchy

No specific control is defined to move down in the DIT. Instead, the user must double-click on an entry in the list control. Additionally, the applet needs a local variable to hold the currently selected DN, and a variable to hold the `browserGlobals` that were stored by the data collection applet. Finally, a variable is needed to hold the time at which the mouse button was last pressed. If the time between two mouse-clicks is ever less than the CLICKTHRESHOLD defined in the global object, then the user has double-clicked the mouse. These objects are defined in Figure 8.6.

The `init()` routine of the DIT navigation applet starts out the same as the `init()` routine of the data collection applet (see Figure 8.7). It creates new GUI components, defines their sizes, and places the components in specific locations on the screen.

```
java.awt.Button selectDNButton;
java.awt.TextField selectDNTextField;
java.awt.TextArea entryDisplay;
java.awt.List DNlist;
browserGlobals myGlobals;
long lastClick = 0;
String currentSelection = "";
```

Fig. 8.6 Variables for the DIT navigation applet.

```
 1  public void init()
 2  {
 3      setLayout(null);
 4      setSize(426,450);
 5      selectDNButton = new java.awt.Button();
 6      selectDNButton.setLabel("up");
 7      selectDNButton.setBounds(264,60,60,24);
 8      selectDNButton.setBackground(new Color(12632256));
 9      selectDNButton.addActionListener
10          (new dnButtonListener());
11      add(selectDNButton);
12      selectDNTextField = new java.awt.TextField();
13      selectDNTextField.setBounds(36,60,208,24);
14      add(selectDNTextField);
15      DNlist = new java.awt.List(0);
16      add(DNlist);
17      DNlist.setBounds(36,100,312,144);
18      DNlist.addMouseListener(new myMouseCatcher());
19      entryDisplay = new java.awt.TextArea();
20      entryDisplay.setBounds(36,275,312,125);
21      add(entryDisplay);
```

Fig. 8.7 Start of the init routine of the DIT navigation applet.

Next, the `init()` routine must submit a `bind` operation to the LDAP server, and then retrieve the contents of the container specified in the SEARCHBASE variable of the browser object. Once the contents of the LDAP container have been retrieved, each entry's DN is placed in the DNlist component. Prior to accessing the LDAP server, the applet must ask permission to make a network connection. This requirement to ask permission is a property of the Java security model for applets. In normal circumstances, applets are only allowed to connect back to the web server from where they were initially loaded. Version 1.2 of the JDK defines certain extensions to the security model that allow more flexible access to the Internet. Netscape has defined extensions to version 1.1 of the JDK that allow the applet to request these same capabilities. These extensions are contained in the Netscape Capabilities classes. One such capability that can be requested is the UniversalConnect privilege that allows the applet to connect to any other network server, instead of just the server from which the applet was loaded. This call is implemented by the following line of code:

```
netscape.security.PrivilegeManager.enablePrivilege
   ("UniversalConnect");
```

When the web browser executes this line of code, a dialog box is displayed which allows the user to grant or deny this request (see Figure 8.8).

If the user presses the Grant button, then the program can continue execution. If the user presses the Deny button, then the applet is not allowed to connect, and a Java runtime exception is raised. Notice that this panel has a button with the title, Certificate. This button is present

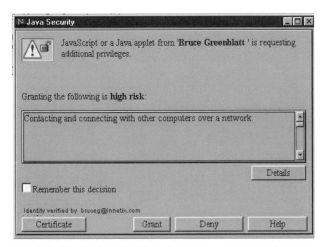

Fig. 8.8 Dialog box to allow the user to grant or deny UniversalConnect privilege.

because the compiled Java code is stored on the web server in the form of a digitally signed Java archive (JAR) file. Pressing the `Certificate` button will display certain information from the certificate of the signer of the JAR file, such as the name of the signer, the issuing authority for the certificate, and an e-mail address.

The code to bind to the LDAP server, retrieve the entries from the container specified in the `SEARCHBASE` variable, and display them in the `Dnlist` GUI component is shown in Figure 8.9.

This code segment makes use of the Java LDAP API to access the LDAP server specified in the `MY_HOST` variable of the globals class. The first task is to check and see if the connection to the LDAP server is valid. This is done on line 2 by checking if the variable `ld` is equal to the value `NULL`. If this is the case, then a connection must be created, which is done on line 3. Next, the connection across the network is checked on line 4. If there is no valid TCP connection to the host machine on which the LDAP server is running, one is created on lines 5 and 6. Next, the connection to the server is tested to see if a `bind` operation has been issued. If one has not been successfully issued, then a `bind` operation is sent to the LDAP server on lines 8 and 9 by using the `authenticate()`

```
 1  try {
 2    if (myGlobals.ld == null)
 3      myGlobals.ld = new LDAPConnection();
 4    if (!(myGlobals.ld.isConnected()))
 5      myGlobals.ld.connect( myGlobals.MY_HOST,
 6        myGlobals.MY_PORT );
 7    if (!(myGlobals.ld.isAuthenticated()))
 8      myGlobals.ld.authenticate( myGlobals.MGR_DN,
 9        myGlobals.MGR_PW );
10    Vector listVector = new Vector();
11    String MY_FILTER = "objectclass=*";
12    String MY_SEARCHBASE = myGlobals.SEARCHBASE;
13    LDAPSearchConstraints cons =
14      myGlobals.ld.getSearchConstraints();
15    cons.setBatchSize( 1 );
16    LDAPSearchResults res = myGlobals.ld.search(
17    MY_SEARCHBASE, LDAPConnection.SCOPE_ONE,
18    MY_FILTER, null, false, cons );
```

Fig. 8.9 Second code segment of the init routine for the DIT navigation applet.

method. Once the authenticated connection has been established to the LDAP server, the search operation can be issued. The three important parameters of the search operation are:

☞ Search Base
☞ Search Scope
☞ Search Filter

The search base was entered by the user in the data collection applet, and has been retrieved into the MY_SEARCHBASE variable. The browser will only show information that is in a single container at a time. This is simply a design choice so that the user is only viewing information in a single container at a time. This scope is indicated in the second parameter of the search method on line 17: `LDAPConnection.SCOPE_ONE`. Since all objects in the container need to be retrieved, a search filter must be chosen that will match any object. Since the `objectClass` attribute is a mandatory attribute of the Top object class, every LDAP object must have such an attribute. Thus, a wild card match against this attribute is used, and is shown on line 11: `"objectclass=*"`. Alternatively, an LDAP *present* filter could have been used with the `objectClass` attribute, and would achieve the same result of matching each entry in the specified container.

The final three parameters to the search method indicate:

☞ Which attributes are to be returned?
☞ Should only attribute types be returned, or should attribute values be returned as well?
☞ What constraints (if any) need to be applied to the search?

Search constraints allow the LDAP application to indicate size and time limits for the search (among other settings). Line 15 has set a single constraint that returns the search results as they come in, rather than wait for all of the results to be returned. In theory, this allows the LDAP browser to get the results onto the screen a little more efficiently by processing them as they come in. By setting the `attrs` (the fourth) parameter to `null`, the browser has indicated that all attributes in the matched entry are to be returned. By setting the `attrsOnly` (the fifth) parameter to `false`, the browser has indicated that both attribute types and values are to be returned. Notice that the parameters to the `search` method match well against the fields of the LDAP search operation. Once the search operation has been submitted, the browser must fetch the results and place the matched DNs into the `Dnlist` GUI component as shown in Figure 8.10.

```
1        int numberOfItems = 0;
2        while ( res.hasMoreElements() ) {
3          LDAPEntry findEntry =
4             (LDAPEntry)res.nextElement();
5          listVector.addElement
6             (findEntry.getDN());
7          numberOfItems += 1;
8        }
9        for (int i = 0; i < numberOfItems; i++)
10         DNlist.add((String)(listVector.
11            elementAt(i)));
12     } catch( LDAPException e ) {
13       DNlist.add("Error: " + e.toString());
14     } catch ( Exception e) {
15       DNlist.add("Some other error: " + e.toString());
16     }
17  }
```

Fig. 8.10 Third code segment of the init routine of the DIT navigation applet.

The variable res will hold the results that have been returned from the LDAP server. The LDAPSearchResult type is defined by the Java LDAP API and is a container for holding LDAP entries that have been retrieved by an LDAP search operation. The code segment above pulls the matched entries, one at a time, from res, and stores them into a vector. Once all of the results have been placed in the vector, they are then inserted, one at a time, into the DNlist GUI component using the add method (on lines 10 and 11) that has been defined by the AWT. Notice that any errors are handled by entering the string representation of the error code into the DNlist. Once the results have been placed into the DNlist, the result is a screen that appears similar to the one in Figure 8.11.

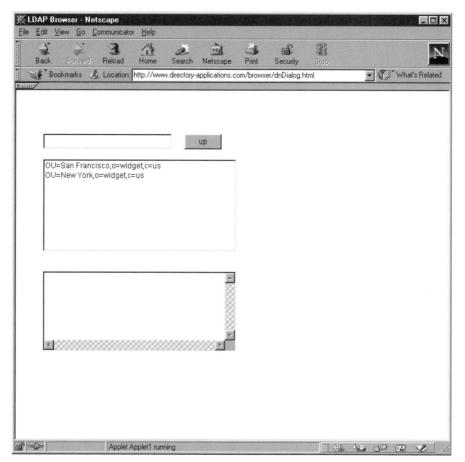

Fig. 8.11 Screen displayed after completion of the init routine of the DIT navigation applet.

Upon completion of the `init()` method, the applet waits for the user to perform one of three actions:

☞ Select one of the entries in the list of distinguished names
☞ Double-click on one of the entries in the list of distinguished names
☞ Click on the "up" button

When an entry in the list of distinguished names is selected, all of the attributes and values from that entry are displayed in the text area at the bottom of the panel. When an entry in the list of distinguished names is double-clicked, the list box is cleared, and the entry which was double-clicked is used as the new base for an LDAP search, the results of which are displayed in the list of distinguished names. Similarly, if the "up" button is selected, the list box is cleared, and the parent entry of the current container is used as the new base for an LDAP search, the results of which are displayed in the list of distinguished names.

In the AWT, *action listeners* are classes that are defined to handle GUI events. In order to handle these events, the action listeners must define certain methods that are called by the AWT when various events occur. The first two types of user actions are handled by the action listener, myMouseCatcher, which is registered on line 18 of Figure 8.7. Java will call the actionPerformed() method of the myMouseCatcher class any time a GUI mouse event happens over the DNlist object. A mouse event happens when the user clicks (or double-clicks) the mouse. The third type is handled by the action listener, dnButtonListener, which is registered on lines 9 and 10 of Figure 8.7. Java will call the actionPerformed() method of the dnButtonListener class whenever the "up" button is pressed. Since dnButtonListener is less complex, it will be shown first (see Figure 8.12).

```
 1  class dnButtonListener implements ActionListener {
 2  public void actionPerformed(ActionEvent event) {
 3    DN myDN = new DN(currentSelection);
 4    DN parentDN = myDN.getParent();
 5    String selectedDN = parentDN.toString();
 6    selectDNTextField.setText(selectedDN);
 7    DNlist.removeAll();
 8    netscape.security.PrivilegeManager.
 9      enablePrivilege("UniversalConnect");
10    try {
11      if (myGlobals.ld == null)
12        myGlobals.ld = new LDAPConnection();
13      if (!(myGlobals.ld.isConnected()))
14        myGlobals.ld.connect( myGlobals.MY_HOST,
15          myGlobals.MY_PORT );
16      if (!(myGlobals.ld.isAuthenticated()))
17        myGlobals.ld.authenticate( myGlobals.MGR_DN,
18          myGlobals.MGR_PW );
19      Vector listVector = new Vector();
20      String MY_FILTER = "objectclass=*";
21      String MY_SEARCHBASE = selectedDN;
22      LDAPSearchConstraints cons =
23        myGlobals.ld.getSearchConstraints();
24      cons.setBatchSize( 1 );
```

```
25        LDAPSearchResults res =
26          myGlobals.ld.search( MY_SEARCHBASE,
27        LDAPConnection.SCOPE_ONE, MY_FILTER, null,
28          false, cons );
29        int numberOfItems = 0;
30        while ( res.hasMoreElements() ) {
31          LDAPEntry findEntry =
32            (LDAPEntry)res.nextElement();
33          listVector.addElement
34            (findEntry.getDN());
34          numberOfItems += 1;
35        }
36          for (int i = 0; i < numberOfItems; i++)
37            DNlist.add( (String)
38              (listVector.elementAt(i)));
39          currentSelection = selectedDN;
40        } catch( LDAPException lde ) {
41          DNlist.add("Error: " + lde.toString());
42        }
43      }
44  }
```

Fig. 8.12 DNButtonListener action listener for the DIT navigation applet.

This routine allows the user to move up one level in the DIT. When actionPerformed() is called, the contents of the currentSelection variable are retrieved. Recall that this variable is initialized to the empty string in Figure 8.6. It will be set again any time that an entry is selected in the list in the myMouseCatcher action listener. Notice that it is also set on line 39 above before leaving. Once the currentSelection is retrieved, a method from the Java LDAP API is used to get the parent container from the supplied DN. For example, if currentSelection holds the DN: "o = Prentice Hall, c = US," then its parent would hold the DN: "c = US." Notice that currentSelection is a string variable, and the getParent() method operates on DN objects. The DN class is defined in the Java LDAP API. Once the parent DN is retrieved, it is placed in the selectDNTextField, and the list of DNs is cleared from the DNlist GUI component. Next, on lines 8–18, a connection to the LDAP server is reestablished, if necessary. Then, a new search is submitted, and the results are placed into the DNlist GUI component, just as in the case of the init() routine.

The MyMouseCatcher action listener handles both the single-click and double-click events. The first portion of the code that handles the double-click event is laid out in Figure 8.13.

```
 1  class myMouseCatcher extends MouseAdapter {
 2    public myMouseCatcher () { }
 3    public void mouseClicked (MouseEvent e) {
 4      long x = e.getWhen() - lastClick;
 5      int selectedIndex = DNlist.getSelectedIndex();
 6      String selectedDN =
 7        DNlist.getItem(selectedIndex);
 8      selectDNTextField.setText(selectedDN);
 9      if (x <= myGlobals.CLICKTHRESHOLD) {
10        DNlist.removeAll();
11        netscape.security.PrivilegeManager.
12          enablePrivilege("UniversalConnect");
13        try {
14          if (myGlobals.ld == null)
15            myGlobals.ld = new LDAPConnection();
16          if (!(myGlobals.ld.isConnected()))
17            myGlobals.ld.connect( myGlobals.MY_HOST,
18              myGlobals.MY_PORT );
19          if (!(myGlobals.ld.isAuthenticated()))
19            myGlobals.ld.authenticate
20              (myGlobals.MGR_DN, myGlobals.MGR_PW );
21          Vector listVector = new Vector();
22          String MY_FILTER = "objectclass=*";
23          String MY_SEARCHBASE = selectedDN;
24          LDAPSearchConstraints cons =
25            myGlobals.ld.getSearchConstraints();
26          cons.setBatchSize( 1 );
27          LDAPSearchResults res =
28            myGlobals.ld.search( MY_SEARCHBASE,
29            LDAPConnection.SCOPE_ONE, MY_FILTER, null,
30            false, cons );
31          int numberOfItems = 0;
32        while ( res.hasMoreElements() ) {
33          LDAPEntry findEntry =
34            (LDAPEntry)res.nextElement();
35          listVector.addElement
36            (findEntry.getDN() );
37          numberOfItems += 1;
38        }
39        for (int i = 0; i < numberOfItems; i++)
40          DNlist.add((String)
41            (listVector.elementAt(i)));
42        currentSelection = selectedDN;
43      } catch( LDAPException lde ) {
44        DNlist.add("Error: " + lde.toString());
45        }
```

Fig. 8.13 Handler for the double-click mouse event in the DIT navigation applet.

Notice on line 2 in Figure 8.13 that this class includes a constructor. This is because the AWT requires mouse adapters to include a constructor. In this case, the constructor is empty. The first action that the `mouseClicked()` method performs is to determine the time at which the mouse was clicked. By comparing this to the previous time that the mouse was clicked, it can be determined if the event is a single-click or double-click event. This comparison is performed on line 13. This is where the `CLICKTHRESHOLD` global variable comes into play. It can be adjusted to allow for a greater time between clicks in order to give slow mouse users a chance to double-click. If this is a double-click event, the method retrieves the selected entry from the `DNlist,` and uses that entry's DN as the search base for a new search to be submitted to the LDAP server. Notice that the code to set up the search and to fill the `Dnlist` (lines14–45) remains the same as in previous listings (such as lines 10–42 of Figure 8.12). The only difference is how the search base has been configured.

If, after processing the event, the "OU = San Francisco" entry is double-clicked, the screen appears as shown in Figure 8.14.

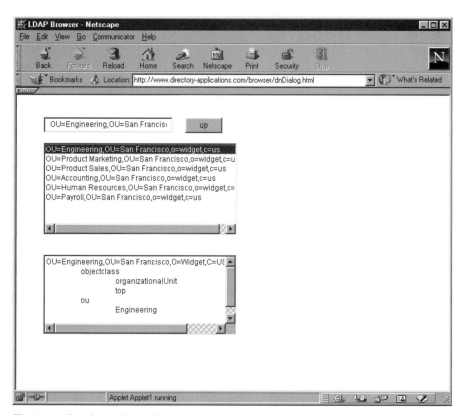

Fig. 8.14 Display of the "OU=San Francisco" container in the DIT navigation applet.

If the "OU = Engineering" entry is double-clicked, the screen appears as in Figure 8.15.

Notice in Figures 8.14 and 8.15 the text area at the bottom of the screen has been filled with the attributes and values from an entry. This action is the result of processing the single-click event in the code segment seen in Figure 8.16.

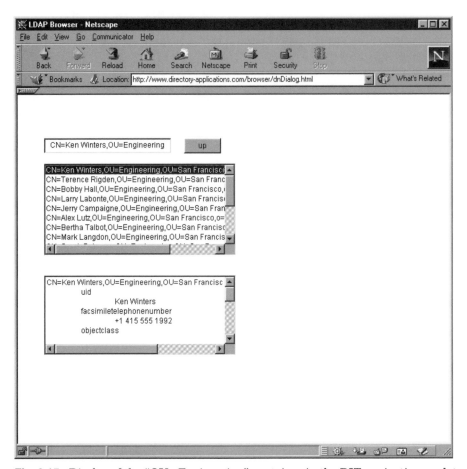

Fig. 8.15 Display of the "OU=Engineering" container in the DIT navigation applet.

```
 1  } else {
 2    netscape.security.PrivilegeManager.enablePrivilege
 3      ("UniversalConnect");
 4    try {
 5      if (myGlobals.ld == null)
 6        myGlobals.ld = new LDAPConnection();
 7      if (!(myGlobals.ld.isConnected()))
 8        myGlobals.ld.connect( myGlobals.MY_HOST,
 9          myGlobals.MY_PORT );
10      if (!(myGlobals.ld.isAuthenticated()))
11        myGlobals.ld.authenticate( myGlobals.MGR_DN,
12          myGlobals.MGR_PW );
13      Vector programListVector = new Vector();
14      String MY_FILTER = "objectclass=*";
15      String MY_SEARCHBASE = selectedDN;
16      LDAPSearchConstraints cons =
17        myGlobals.ld.getSearchConstraints();
18      cons.setBatchSize( 1 );
19      LDAPSearchResults res =
20        myGlobals.ld.search( MY_SEARCHBASE,
21        LDAPConnection.SCOPE_BASE, MY_FILTER, null,
22        false, cons );
23      LDAPEntry findEntry =
24        (LDAPEntry)res.nextElement();
25      entryDisplay.setText("");
26      entryDisplay.append( findEntry.getDN() );
27      LDAPAttributeSet findAttrs =
28        findEntry.getAttributeSet();
29      Enumeration enumAttrs =
30        findAttrs.getAttributes();
31      entryDisplay.append( "Attributes: \n" );
32      while ( enumAttrs.hasMoreElements() ) {
33        LDAPAttribute anAttr =
34          (LDAPAttribute)enumAttrs.nextElement();
35          String attrName = anAttr.getName();
35          entryDisplay.append( "\t" + attrName +
36          "\n" );
37          Enumeration enumVals =
38            anAttr.getStringValues();
39          while ( enumVals.hasMoreElements() ) {
39            String aVal =
40              (String)enumVals.nextElement();
41            entryDisplay.append( "\t\t" + aVal + "\n");
42          }
43      }
44      entryDisplay.setCaretPosition(0);
45    } catch( LDAPException lde ) {
46      DNlist.add("Error: " + lde.toString());
47    }
48  }
```

Fig. 8.16 Handling the single-click event in the DIT navigation applet.

Recall that the `selectedDN` variable was already set up on lines 6 and 7 of Figure 8.13. This is used as the search base for a new search to be submitted. Notice that in this search, the search scope is changed to `SCOPE_BASE` on line 21. This is because all of the attributes and values of the selected entry are to be displayed in the `entryDisplay` text area. The statement on line 25 clears the text area. The first line of the display is the distinguished name of the selected item. The `getDN()` method of the `LDAPEntry` class of the Java LDAP API returns the distinguished name so that it can be placed in the text area. Next, the attributes and values from the selected entry are displayed in the text area. The `getAttributes()` method of the `LDAPEntry` class of the Java LDAP API returns the attributes from the entry into a Java enumeration object. Each element of the enumeration is a separate attribute and its associated values. The code in the `while` loop starting at line 32 steps through each element of the enumeration.

Each element in the enumeration is retrieved by using the standard Java method `nextElement()`, and casting the returned value as an `LDAPAttribute` object. The `LDAPAttribute` class is defined in the Java LDAP API. The name of the attribute is returned by using the `getName()` method of the `LDAPAttribute` class. The values of each attribute are also stored in a Java enumeration object. Each of the values in the enumeration is retrieved with the `nextElement()` method, casting it as a string object. Each value is individually added to the text area on line 41. After selecting the "OU = San Francisco" entry from Figure 8.11, the display in Figure 8.17 appears.

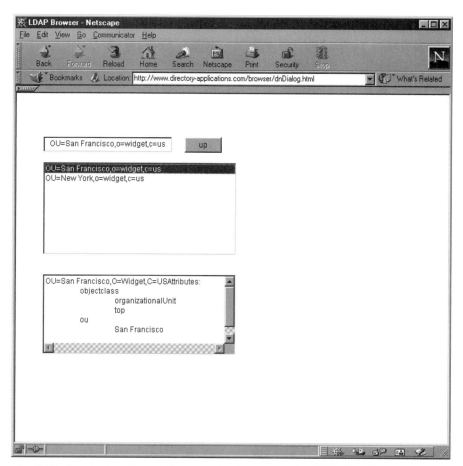

Fig. 8.17 Displaying the attributes and values from the "OU=San Francisco" entry in the DIT navigation applet.

This is all there is to the LDAP browser. In only a few hundred lines of code, a complete application has been written that allows for viewing all types of objects in the DIT. The only remaining item is the creation of an HTML page to display the applet (see Figure 8.18). This is the easiest part.

A similar page is created for the DIT navigation applet. The only change is to the CODE parameter of the APPLET tag. The ARCHIVE parameter of the APPLET specifies the name of the Java archive file that contains the compiled Java applets. This file needs to be digitally signed in order for the Netscape Capabilities Classes to work properly.

```
<HTML>
<HEAD>
<TITLE>LDAP Browser</TITLE>
</HEAD>
<BODY>
<APPLET ARCHIVE="dndialog.jar"
 CODE="collectData.class"
 WIDTH=426 HEIGHT=500></APPLET>
</BODY>
</HTML>
```

Fig. 8.18 HTML page for the data collection applet.

ENHANCING THE BROWSER

The most obvious enhancements that could be made to the browser are to allow for modifications to the entries in the DIT, addition of new entries into the DIT, and deletion of existing entries from the DIT. In this way, the browser has been turned into an editor as well. Much of the code in these enhancements lies in the implementation of data collection screens, such as the code in Figure 8.4, which is the `init()` routine for the data collection applet. In this case, the data collected is for the `bind` operation. In the case of a delete operation, a screen would be displayed that allowed for the distinguished name entry to be deleted. Fortunately, the DIT navigation applet serves this purpose perfectly. All that is needed is the addition of a delete button to the screen, and the creation of an action handler for the button when it is pressed.

The delete button can be added to the screen by placing the code displayed in Figure 8.19 after line 11 in Figure 8.7.

```
1  deleteDNButton = new java.awt.Button();
2  deleteDNButton.setLabel("delete");
3  deleteDNButton.setBounds(264,160,60,24);
4  deleteDNButton.setBackground(new Color(12632256));
5  deleteDNButton.addActionListener
6    (new deleteButtonListener());
7    add(deleteDNButton);
```

Fig. 8.19 Code to add a delete button on the DIT navigation screen.

The code for the `deleteButtonListener` class, displayed in Figure 8.20, is more straightforward.

The actual method from the Java LDAP API that deletes the entry from the DIT is shown on line 16 above. The `delete()` method is simply passed from the string from the list of currently selected distinguished names. If no exception is raised, then the next line is executed, removing that line from the list control. Other enhancements to the browser are more complex because more data must be collected. For example, in adding a new entry to the DIT, the entire set of proposed attribute types and values must be collected from the user. They need to be collected and saved in an `LDAPEntry` object. This is the reverse of the search operation. `LDAPAttribute` objects are collected into `LDAPAttributeSet` objects, which are then combined into an `LDAPEntry`. Once all of the data for the new entry is collected, the `add()` method of the `LDAPConnection` class is called. A similar design works for the implementation of a `modify` operation.

```
 1  class deleteButtonListener implements ActionListener {
 2    public void actionPerformed(ActionEvent event) {
 3      int selectedIndex = DNlist.getSelectedIndex();
 4      String selectedDN = DNlist.getItem(selectedIndex);
 5      netscape.security.PrivilegeManager.
 6        enablePrivilege("UniversalConnect");
 7      try {
 8        if (myGlobals.ld == null)
 9          myGlobals.ld = new LDAPConnection();
10        if (!(myGlobals.ld.isConnected()))
11          myGlobals.ld.connect( myGlobals.MY_HOST,
12            myGlobals.MY_PORT );
13        if (!(myGlobals.ld.isAuthenticated()))
14          myGlobals.ld.authenticate( myGlobals.MGR_DN,
15            myGlobals.MGR_PW );
16          ld.delete(myDN.toString());
17          Dnlist.remove(selectedIndex);
18      } catch( LDAPException lde ) {
19        DNlist.add("Error: " + lde.toString());
20      }
21  }
21    }
```

Fig. 8.20 Code for the `deleteButtonHandler` enhancement of the DIT navigation applet.

CHAPTER SUMMARY

This chapter used the Java programming language to show how an LDAP client application that reads and modifies LDAP information can be built. This application is built using the industry standard Java LDAP API. This API has unfortunately not yet progressed to the RFC stage, and is still an Internet draft. While the code in this application is written using the AWT specification, it could easily be modified to use later Java windowing specifications, such as Swing. We showed how the application that simply reads the information from the LDAP server can be enhanced in such a way that information is written into the directory as well.

Building Applications That Use the Directory

Throughout this book, various Internet directory technologies have been discussed, and the use of LDAP directories to manage other applications has also been covered in some detail. In any particular application, there will always be several different ways that it can be integrated with the Internet directory service. These different ways of integration relate to the degree in which the application makes use of the directory. This level of dependence may be categorized as follows:

☞ directory ignorant
☞ directory aware
☞ directory enabled
☞ directory dependent

This chapter will cover how directory technology can be used in applications in ways other than management roles. Directory ignorant applications are not integrated with the directory at all, and make no use of any type of directory information. Any infrastructure that a directory ignorant application needs is provided by the application itself. An example of such a self-provided infrastructure may be found in most electronic mail applications. These applications normally provide some sort of address book service to the end users. This address book service typically displays an alphabetized list of user names and their corresponding addresses. While this information could be retrieved from an LDAP or Whois++ source, most electronic mail applications have historically provided this service for themselves, and provided the appropriate administrative interfaces that allowed for the creation of the user records in the address book service.

The first level of directory integration in which the information in the directory is actually used by the application is the directory aware application. This application acknowledges the existence of the directory, but works in approximately the same manner whether the directory is present or absent. Consider an application that forces the user to authenticate prior to being used. In the absence of the directory, this application maintains its own credentials database. When the directory is present, the application instead presents the user's credentials to the directory for processing. In the case of an LDAP directory, the credentials are presented to the directory in the form of a bind operation. Once the user has authenticated, the application proceeds normally. The process of a directory aware application is illustrated in the flowchart in Figure 9.1.

Notice that the LDAP aware application works in a nearly identical manner whether the LDAP directory is present or not. The only difference is in the source of the credentials database. The LDAP aware application typically makes some minimal use of the directory, but the user experience is not altered in any way. This implementation, in which the end user leverages the same credentials to access LDAP as are used to access the application, is known as *Single Sign On* (SSO). SSO is a feature that allows the end user to know only a single set of credentials. SSO also simplifies administration since there is only one credentials database that needs to be administered. The main drawback to SSO is the same as the main benefit. SSO creates a single point of attack on the network. If the credentials database is compromised, unauthorized people or applications can use any part of the retrieved credentials to gain access to any of the network. Great care must therefore be taken in safeguarding access to the LDAP credentials database.

The next step in the evolution of integrating the application with the directory is the directory-enabled application. In this application, features are available that work only when an LDAP directory is available. However, many other features that are provided are completely independent of the LDAP directory. As an example of an LDAP enabled application, consider an enhanced electronic mail application. The simplest use of LDAP by such an application would be to make use of LDAP for a White Pages Service. This would allow the end user or administrator to configure any number of sources to be used to provide a list of users and

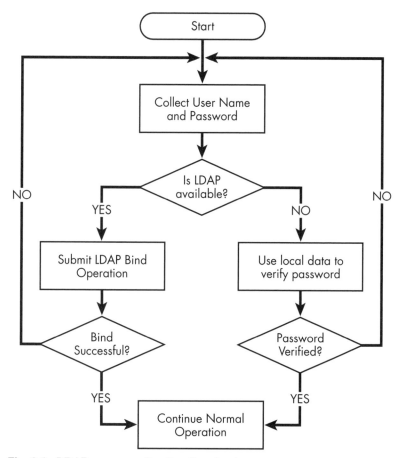

Fig. 9.1 LDAP aware application flowchart.

their e-mail address information (i.e., an address book). In order to configure the application, the following information must be collected:

1. LDAP server host name
2. LDAP server port
3. Using TLS/SSL (yes or no)
4. LDAP distinguished name for base object (DN)
5. LDAP bind credentials (normally a password)
6. LDAP search context (another LDAP DN)

Once this information is collected and saved by the e-mail application, it can be used to retrieve an address book for the user. The host name and port number are used to open a TCP socket. If the use of TLS is indicated, then a TLS session is negotiated on top of the previously opened TCP socket. The LDAP DN from the fourth item and the credentials from the fifth item are used in the LDAP bind. Finally, the sixth item is used as the search base of an LDAP search operation. The parameters of the LDAP search operation should be set according to those in Table 9.1.

Table 9.1 LDAP Search Fields for Address Book

LDAP Search Parameter	Value
Base Object	LDAP DN from Configuration
Scope	Whole Subtree
DerefAliases	DerefAlways
SizeLimit	0
TimeLimit	0
TypesOnly	False
Filter	"e-mailAddress present"
Attributes	NULL (get all attributes)

This search retrieves all objects in the DIT that contain an `emailAddress` attribute. An alternative approach would be to display the addresses in an organizational hierarchy as indicated by the containment used in the DIT. If this approach was taken, then the searches would all use the "singleLevel" scope, and the client-server interaction would work the same way as in the Java LDAP browser application of the previous chapter. Additional features that take advantage of the directory can be added to the e-mail application. One such feature is a *group mailbox,* which is an e-mail account with a single address that is accessed by multiple users. Customer support accounts are famous for using this functionality. In order to control access to the group mailbox, each `groupMailbox` that is created on the server is associated with a `groupOfNames` object. Recall that `groupOfNames` is an object class defined in RFC 2256 as:

```
( 2.5.6.9 NAME 'groupOfNames' SUP top STRUCTURAL MUST ( mem-
ber $ cn ) MAY ( businessCategory $ seeAlso $ owner $ ou $ o
$ description ) )
```

When someone attempts to retrieve mail from a group mailbox, the mail server checks to see if that user is a member on that authorized list. Assume that the e-mail application is already using LDAP for its authentication mechanism, as shown in the left branch of the flowchart in Figure 9.1. Whatever LDAP DN was used in the bind operation is checked against the member attribute of the groupOfNames object that is associated with the group mailbox. The association of the DN of the groupOfNames object with the group mailbox can be stored locally with the mail server. The administrator initially makes the association at the time that the group mailbox is created. The determination for whether the user attempting to gain access to the group mailbox has been granted access can be done with a simple search operation using the parameters shown in Table 9.2. Assume the following values:

☞ `groupMailbox` DN is "cn=support, o=acme.com"
☞ user's DN from bind is "cn=fred, o=acme.com"

Table 9.2 LDAP Search to Determine Access Rights for Group Mailbox

LDAP Search Parameter	Value
Base Object	"cn=support, o=acme.com"
Scope	Single Object
DerefAliases	DerefAlways
SizeLimit	0
TimeLimit	0
TypesOnly	True
Filter	member = "cn=fred, o=acme.com"
Attributes	ObjectClass

By storing this group authorization information in the directory, the authorization list can be administered from anywhere in the network using standard LDAP access mechanisms, making access directly into the mail server unnecessary. The notion of central administration is a typical feature of directory-enabled applications. The principal distinction between the directory aware application and the directory enabled application is illustrated here. In the directory aware case, the application takes advantage of the directory when it is available in such a way that no features are lost when the application is installed on a network without a directory. In the directory enabled case, the application has features that only work in situations where it is installed on a network with a directory. In the case of the e-mail application, the group mailbox feature is not available unless there is an LDAP directory available. However, the application as a whole still works even though there is no directory present, albeit with missing features.

The final class of directory integrated applications is the directory dependent application. In contrast with the previous classes of directory integration, the directory dependent application does not work unless there is a directory present. The obvious example of the directory dependent application is the LDAP browser application of the previous chapter. Other examples of directory dependent applications were found in Chapter 7 in the discussion of Directory Management. The use of the directory by Novell in its messaging server for routing of electronic mail was dependent on the existence of a directory. This is a good example, since most electronic mail servers do not rely on the directory for storage and exchange of routing information. That chapter also discusses how the directory is leveraged for use in the implementation of a public key infrastructure. The remainder of this chapter consists of several examples of how existing applications might be implemented in such a way that they are directory dependent.

USE OF THE DIRECTORY IN STORAGE MANAGEMENT APPLICATIONS

A storage management application (SMA) is a special-purpose network service that interconnects different kinds of data storage devices with associated data servers on behalf of a larger network of users. Typically, an SMA is part of the overall network of computing resources for an enterprise. The SMA allows network administrators to configure the storage infrastructure in a variety of complex ways that typically make use of a storage technology called Redundant Array of Independent Disks (RAID).[1] RAID is a way of storing the same data in different places (i.e., redundantly) on multiple hard disks. By placing data on multiple disks, input/output (I/O) operations can overlap in a balanced and controlled way, often dramatically improving performance. Since multiple disks increase the mean time between failure (MTBF), storing data also redundantly increases fault-tolerance.

A RAID appears to the operating system to be a single logical hard disk. RAID employs the technique of *striping*, which involves partitioning each drive's storage space into units ranging from a sector (512 bytes) up to several megabytes. The stripes of all the disks are interleaved and addressed in order. In a single-user system, where large records such as medical or other scientific images are stored, the stripes are typically set up to be small (perhaps 512 bytes) so that a single record

---

[1] The definition of RAID technology presented here is taken from the definitions at the web site, http://www.whatis.com.

spans all disks and can be accessed quickly by reading all disks at the same time. In a multiuser system, better performance requires establishing a stripe wide enough to hold the typical or maximum size record. This allows overlapped disk I/O across drives. There are several different levels of RAID technology, plus a non-redundant array (RAID-0). Some of the more common RAID levels are:

- ☞ RAID-0: This technique has striping but no redundancy of data. It offers the best performance but no fault-tolerance.
- ☞ RAID-1: This type is also known as disk mirroring and consists of at least two drives that duplicate the storage of data. There is no striping. Read performance is improved since either disk can be read at the same time. Write performance is the same as for single disk storage. RAID-1 provides the best performance and the best fault-tolerance in a multiuser system.
- ☞ RAID-2: This type uses striping across disks with some disks storing error checking and correcting (ECC) information. It has no advantage over RAID-3.
- ☞ RAID-3: This type uses striping and dedicates one drive to storing parity information. The ECC information is used to detect errors. Data recovery is accomplished by calculating the exclusive OR (XOR) of the information recorded on the other drives. Since I/O operations address all drives at the same time, RAID-3 cannot overlap I/O. For this reason, RAID-3 is best for single-user systems with long record applications.
- ☞ RAID-4: This type uses large stripes, which means you can read records from any single drive. This allows you to take advantage of overlapped I/O for read operations. Since all write operations have to update the parity drive, no I/O overlapping is possible. RAID-4 offers no advantage over RAID-5.
- ☞ RAID-5: This type includes a rotating parity array, thereby addressing the write limitation in RAID-4. Thus, all read and write operations can be overlapped. RAID-5 stores parity information but no redundant data (although parity information can be used to reconstruct data). RAID-5 requires at least three (and usually five) disks for the array. It is best for multiuser systems in which performance is not critical and few write operations are done.

SMAs allow the administrator to change different parameters of the storage system, and to also display the non-modifiable parameters to the users. The level of RAID support of an individual disk array would be a non-modifiable parameter, while the striping unit size would be a modifiable parameter. DNS can be used to enable discovery of managed storage servers by making use of the service type (SRV) records. LDAP can be used for authentication and access control to the disk subsystem. For the purposes of this example, SMA clients and SMA servers interact with DNS and LDAP, as shown in Figure 9.2.

Notice that both the SMA client and SMA server access LDAP via means of a local LDAP client. The SMA client will make use of a DNS resolver in order to discover Internet hosts that have SMA servers. The SMA client and SMA server continue to communicate via their proprietary SMA protocol for services that are not appropriate to be delivered via LDAP or DNS. By making the information about the SMA servers

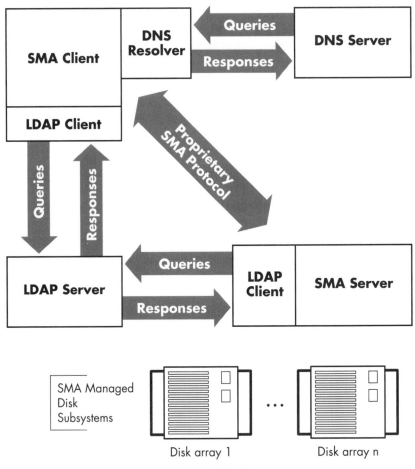

Fig. 9.2 SMA interaction with DNS and LDAP.

and the managed disk arrays available via LDAP, it is made available to all LDAP capable clients in the network, not just those machines that have installed the SMA client software.

Information Stored about SMA Servers in DNS

Whenever an SMA server is installed on an Internet host, an SRV record should be added to DNS. This allows SMA clients to use DNS to locate SMA servers. The typical SRV records for a server in the domain acme.com is:

sma.tcp.acme.com	SRV 0 0 8000 diskserver1.acme.com
sma.tcp.acme.com	SRV 0 0 8001 diskserver1.acme.com
sma.tcp.acme.com	SRV 0 0 8001 diskserver2.acme.com

Notice that there are two SMA servers running on the host diskserver1.acme.com. They need to listen on different ports in order to avoid conflicts. A third SMA server is located on diskserver2.acme.com. The SMA client must do a lookup for QNAME=sma.tcp.acme.com, QCLASS=IN, QTYPE=SRV. RFC 2052 specifies that if only the root domain is returned in the response, then no SRV records are available. Using SRV records allows the client to discover all of the SMA servers available in the network. The installation may also add TXT records to DNS to add extra information. For example,

> Diskserver1.acme.com   IN   TXT "There are two SMA servers running on me, and my LDAP server is ldap.acme.com."

Once the SRV records for the SMA servers have been retrieved from DNS, SRV records for the LDAP servers in that domain may have to be retrieved from DNS as well. In order to access DNS information, the code of a DNS resolver would be embedded as part of the SMA client. The GNU public distribution (see *http://www.gnu.org*) has the source code available for a resolver that is available for use in such a manner.

Store Other Information in LDAP

Once the SMA servers have been discovered in DNS by the SMA client, various information about the servers can be discovered and configured via LDAP and the proprietary SMA protocol. The SMA schema must be defined in order for anything to be done with the SMA server via LDAP.

The schema will allow for the definition of SMA server objects as well as the disk arrays that they manage. The object class used for SMA servers is:

```
( NAME 'sMAServer' SUP top STRUCTURAL MUST ( cn $ hostName $
portNumber ) MAY ( description $ authorizedCreators ) )
```

Each SMA server manages disk arrays, which are represented in LDAP by this object class:

```
( NAME 'diskArray' SUP top STRUCTURAL MUST ( cn $ raidLevel $
numberOfDisks $ megaBytesAvailable ) MAY ( description $
authorizedModifiers $ stripePartitionSize ) )
```

All of the attributes in the above object class definitions use the directory string syntax, with the exception of the `authorizedModifiers` and `authorizedCreators` attributes. They use the DN syntax and refer to another object in the directory that is of the `groupOfNames` object class.

Thus, the `raidLevel` and `authorizedModifiers` attribute types have these definitions:

```
(NAME 'raidLevel' EQUALITY caseIgnoreMatch
  SUBSTR caseIgnoreSubstringsMatch
  SYNTAX 1.3.6.1.4.1.1466.115.121.1.15{64} SINGLE-VALUE)
```

```
(NAME 'authorizedModifiers' EQUALITY distinguishedNameMatch
  SYNTAX 1.3.6.1.4.1.1466.115.121.1.12 )
```

The other attribute type definitions are similar to that of the `raidLevel`. Even though the raid level is actually an integer, the choice has been made to use a string syntax during transfer. This makes it easier to view the protocol in the data stream, and to display the received values to the end user. Recall that the `groupOfNames` object class has this definition:

```
( 2.5.6.9 NAME 'groupOfNames' SUP top STRUCTURAL MUST ( member
$ cn ) MAY ( businessCategory $ seeAlso $ owner $ ou $ o $
description ) )
```

The member attribute of the `groupOfName` object contains a list of DNs that have been authorized to perform the indicated SMA operation. The intention is that SMA server objects in the directory will act as containers, and beneath them in the LDAP hierarchy will be the disk arrays that they manage. Figure 9.3 shows this hierarchical organization.

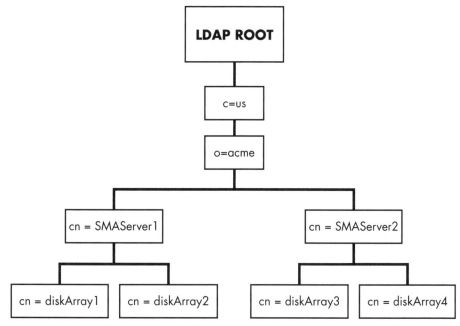

Fig. 9.3 LDAP hierarchy for SMA objects.

In the above DIT, there are two SMA servers represented:

☞ CN=SMAServer1, O=acme, C=US
☞ CN=SMAServer2, O=acme, C=US

And four managed disk array objects:

☞ CN=diskArray1, CN=SMAServer1, O=acme, C=US
☞ CN=diskArray2, CN=SMAServer1, O=acme, C=US
☞ CN=diskArray3, CN=SMAServer2, O=acme, C=US
☞ CN=diskArray4, CN=SMAServer2, O=acme, C=US

Notice that the SMA server that manages a disk array can be found by removing the RDN of the object and looking for its parent object in the tree. For example, the SMA server, CN=SMAServer1, O=acme, C=US, manages the disk array, CN=diskArray1, CN=SMAServer1, O=acme, C=US. In order to find the SMA servers in the directory, an LDAP search operation must be submitted. Once the SRV record has been retrieved from DNS, the following three attributes are discovered about the SMA server's object in the directory:

☞ objectClass

☞ hostName

☞ portNumber

These known attributes are used in the construction of the search filter. The typical search operation to read the current values from the directory entry for an SMA server is shown in Table 9.3.

Table 9.3 Search Operation to Find an SMA Server in LDAP

LDAP Search Parameter	Value
Base Object	" "
Scope	Whole Subtree
DerefAliases	DerefAlways
SizeLimit	1
TimeLimit	0
TypesOnly	False
Filter	"objectClass = sMAServer" and "hostName = diskserver1.acme.com" and "portNumber = 8001"
Attributes	NULL (get all attributes)

Notice that the base object field remains empty. Since the SRV record format doesn't allow for the specification of a search base (or any other extra information), the entire subtree must be searched. Once the SMA server is found in the directory, the managed disk arrays can be easily found. Assume that the DN returned by the search operation in Table 9.3 is CN=SMAServer1, O=acme, C=US. The appropriate search operation to find the entire set of managed disk arrays for this SMA server is shown in Table 9.4.

Table 9.4 Search Operation to Find Disk Arrays in LDAP

LDAP Search Parameter	Value
Base Object	"CN=SMAServer1, O=acme, C=US"
Scope	SingleLevel
DerefAliases	DerefAlways
SizeLimit	0
TimeLimit	0
TypesOnly	False
Filter	"objectClass = diskArray"
Attributes	NULL (get all attributes)

The combination of these search operations allows for the retrieval of the SMA servers and disk arrays in the DIT. The sequence of the two searches can be repeated for each of the SMA servers that have SRV records in DNS. In this scenario, the SMA client reconfigures the disk arrays by directly communicating with the SMA server via their non-LDAP protocol. Once the disk array has been reconfigured, the SMA server updates the directory information via LDAP. Two example operations that are issued as part of this SMA protocol are:

☞ Add disk array
☞ Change partition size on disk array

When the SMA server receives either of these operations it must verify the authorization information that is associated with the appropriate object. For the disk array addition operation, the `authorizedCreators` attribute of the `sMAServer` object is checked. The partition size change operation uses the `authorizedModifiers` attribute of the `diskArray` object. In order to verify the identity of the user initiating the SMA operations, the SMA protocol must include some sort of authentication mechanism. This authentication mechanism is just the LDAP Bind operation. At the beginning of the SMA protocol, elements of the bind operation are included. The SMA server then transmits these protocol elements to an LDAP server for verification. If the LDAP server confirms that the bind information is correct, then the SMA accepts the identity of the SMA client as given in the name field of the bind request. The SMA server maintains a separate connection to the LDAP server for each incoming connection from an SMA client. This interaction between the SMA application and LDAP implements the notion of Single Sign On (SSO). It allows the user of SMA to use the same identity and credentials when using an LDAP client or an SMA client. This interaction is illustrated in Figure 9.4.

Notice that the SMA server is simply repeating the responses from the LDAP server back to the SMA client. Once the bind is successful, other SMA operations can proceed. When the SMA server receives a request to "Add a Disk Array," it must do three things:

1. Make the new disk array available as part of the network infrastructure.
2. Check that the user making the request is a member of the `authorizedCreators` group.
3. Perform LDAP operations in order to indicate to the network at large that the disk array is available.

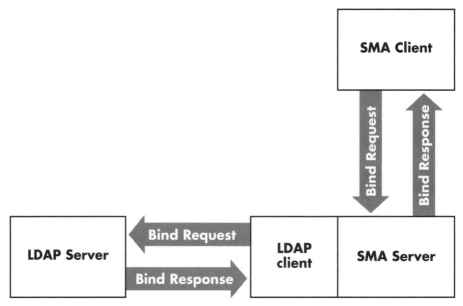

Fig. 9.4 Single Sign On between LDAP and SMA.

The `authorizedCreators` group is known as an access control list (ACL). ACLs are a very common use of LDAP. There are two ways of implementing the ACL check:

☞ use the LDAP compare operation
☞ use the LDAP search operation

The benefit of using the compare operation is that the SMA server doesn't have to retrieve the membership list of the ACL in order to perform the check. The LDAP server is doing all the work. The SMA server needs to create an LDAP AttributeValueAssertion as part of the compare operation. The compare operation has the following format:

```
CompareRequest ::=  [APPLICATION 14] SEQUENCE {
            entry  LDAPDN,
              ava  AttributeValueAssertion }
```

The `AttributeValueAssertion` allows the SMA server to supply the attribute name and value. If the DN in the entry has an attribute with the value supplied in the `AssertionValue` field of the `AttributeValueAssertion`, then the LDAP server will return a result code of `compareTrue`; otherwise, it will return `compareFalse`. The `AttributeValueAssertion` has the following format:

```
AttributeValueAssertion ::=  SEQUENCE {
            attributeDesc   AttributeDescription,
            assertionValue  AssertionValue }
```

In order to add a new disk array to the DIT, the SMA server uses the connection to the LDAP server that was created during the previous bind, and issues a compare operation with the fields listed in Table 9.5.

Table 9.5 LDAP Compare Operation to Check the ACL for the Disk Array Creation

LDAP Compare Parameter	Value
Entry	"CN=diskArrayCreators, O=acme, C=US"
Ava: attributeDesc	"member"
Ave: assertionValue	"CN=Admin, O=acme, C=US"

The above operation presumes that the `authorizedCreators` attribute of the `sMAServer` object has an attribute value equal to "CN=diskArrayCreators, O=acme, C=US." It also assumes that the bound user has the DN, "CN=Admin, O=acme, C=US." If the LDAP server returns the result code `compareTrue`, then the SMA Server next submits an `add` operation to create a new `diskArray` object in the DIT. Recall that the `add` operation has the following format:

```
AddRequest ::= [APPLICATION 8] SEQUENCE {
          entry LDAPDN,
          attributes AttributeList }

AttributeList ::= SEQUENCE OF SEQUENCE {
          type AttributeDescription,
          vals SET OF AttributeValue }
```

The `add` operation to create the entry would contain the fields listed in Table 9.6.

Table 9.6 Add Operation to Create a `diskArray` Object in the DIT

LDAP Add Parameter	Value
ObjectClass	"diskArray"
Entry	"CN=newDiskArray, CN=SMAServer1, O=acme, C=US"
Type: raidLevel	"3"
Type: numberOfDisks	"4"
Type: megaBytesAvailable	"100000"
Type: description	"A new fancy disk array"
Type: authorizedModifiers	"CN=arrayModifiers, O=acme, C=US"
Type: stripePartitionSize	"1000"

Notice that all fields, including the optional attributes, have been included in the add operation. Once the `diskArray` object has been added to the DIT, `modify` operations can be applied to it. When the SMA server receives a request from the SMA client to change the partition size, it performs actions similar to those when it receives a request to add the disk array:

☞ check the `authorizedModifiers` ACL

☞ modify the `diskArray` entry in the DIT

The ACL check for modification can be performed using the compare operation in a manner similar to the ACL check performed when the `diskArray` object is added to the DIT. In order to indicate that the partition size has been changed, the entry in the DIT must be modified. Recall that the `modify` operation has the following format:

```
ModifyRequest ::= [APPLICATION 6] SEQUENCE {
    object   LDAPDN,
    modification SEQUENCE OF SEQUENCE {
    operation  ENUMERATED {
            add   (0),
            delete (1),
            replace (2) },
    modification AttributeTypeAndValues } }

AttributeTypeAndValues ::= SEQUENCE {
    type AttributeDescription,
    vals SET OF AttributeValue }
```

The `modify` operation to update the partition size would contain the fields seen in Table 9.7.

Table 9.7 `Modify` Operation to Change the Partition Size of an Entry in the DIT

LDAP Modify Parameter	Value
Object	"CN=newDiskArray, CN=SMAServer1, O=acme, C=US"
Modification: operation	2
Modification: type	"stripePartitionSize"
Modification: vals	"500"

In this scenario, LDAP has been used to control access to the SMA servers and the disk arrays that they manage. LDAP is also used to publish the information about the storage management components to the network at large. Furthermore, the authentication framework of LDAP is used to identify the users of the SMA clients that are accessing the SMA servers. Other applications that are managed by network administrators are candidates for LDAP-enabling using similar techniques. For example, LDAP-enabling printer management applications can also allow for these features:

☞ Discovery of printers and print servers on the network using DNS and LDAP

☞ Support for Single Sign On (SSO)

☞ Controlled access to the printers by end users

As each application becomes integrated with the Internet directories, that infrastructure becomes incrementally more powerful in terms of its ability to administer those applications. For example, each application that integrates its authentication components with LDAP represents one less password per user that must be maintained by the administrators and remembered by the users of that application.

USE OF THE DIRECTORY FOR LDAP-ENABLED CHAT ROOMS

A modern Internet application is the chat room. A chat room provides a setting on the Internet in which several users can instantaneously exchange messages in order to provide for an ongoing conversation. A user connects to the chat room server, and that user either joins an existing conversation or creates a new conversation. Once a user participates in a conversation, that user is able to view all of the messages that are submitted to the chat room server by any of the conversation's participants. The conversation ends when there are no longer any participants. In addition to providing a forum for the users to converse, the chat room server must also maintain a long-term record of all conversations that have taken place as it must broadcast each message that it receives from a user to all of the participants in the conversation.

Much of the work that needs to be done by the chat room Server can be implemented by directory enabling of the server. The chat room servers are found by placing SRV records in the DNS. In this case, the protocol that can be used is the "chat," which results in the following records:

chat.tcp.acme.com	SRV 0 0 8000 chatserver1.acme.com
chat.tcp.acme.com	SRV 0 0 8001 chatserver1.acme.com
chat.tcp.acme.com	SRV 0 0 8001 chatserver2.acme.com

Notice that there are two chat root servers running on the host chatserver1.acme.com. They need to listen on different ports in order to avoid conflicts. A third chat room server is located on *chatserver2.acme.com*. Just as in the case of the storage management application, the chat room server and the chat room client make use of a proprietary protocol in addition to making use of LDAP and DNS. The view of the chat room application's interaction with the directories is similar to that of the SMA interaction, and is shown in Figure 9.5.

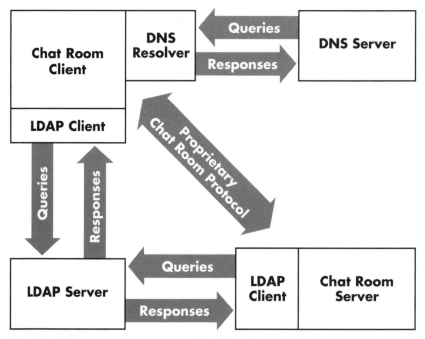

Fig. 9.5 Chat room interaction with DNS and LDAP.

The chat room protocol consists of the following requests, all of which are initiated by the client and received by the server:

1. Logon to chat room server
2. Create new conversation
3. Join an existing conversation
4. Leave an existing conversation
5. Submit message to conversation

A by-product of item 5 is that the submitted message is distributed to all conversation participants, via the chat room protocol. The chat room application uses the following LDAP object definitions:

```
( NAME 'chatRoomServer' SUP top STRUCTURAL MUST ( cn $ host-
Name $ portNumber ) MAY ( description $ authorizedCreators ) )
```

Each SMA server manages disk arrays, which are represented in LDAP by this object class:

```
( NAME 'chatRoomConversation' SUP top STRUCTURAL MUST ( cn $
startTime ) MAY ( description $ endTime ) )
```

```
( NAME 'chatRoomMessage' SUP top STRUCTURAL MUST ( cn $
createdBy $ createdTime $ messageText ))
```

```
( NAME ' participantInfo' SUP top STRUCTURAL MUST ( cn $
joinTime $ participantDN ) MAY leaveTime )
```

With the exception of the `authorizedCreators` and the `participantDN` attributes, all of the attributes in the above object class definitions use the directory string syntax. These attributes use the DN syntax. They refer to another object in the directory that is of the `groupOfNames` object class. (See the attribute type definitions in the SMA example above, since they are similar to the attribute type definitions that are to be used here.)

In LDAP, the `chatRoomConversation` objects are created immediately beneath the `chatRoomServer` object on which they are created. Similarly, the `chatRoomMessage` and `participantInfo` objects are created immediately beneath the `chatRoomConversation` object to which they belong. Thus, each time a new conversation is created on a chat room server, a new `chatRoomConversation` object is created in LDAP. Each time a new user joins a conversation, a new `participantInfo` object is created in LDAP. That object is subsequently modified when that user leaves the conversation. If the user rejoins the conversation, a new `participantInfo` object is created with a new `joinTime` attribute. Additionally, each message that is exchanged by the users creates a new `chatRoomMessage` object in LDAP. Obviously, the chat room application will be creating many more LDAP objects than did the SMA. A typical chat room DIT hierarchy is illustrated in Figure 9.6.

The chat room Login procedure is implemented on top of the LDAP bind operation in precisely the same manner as the SMA login operation shown in Figure 9.4. The other operations cause changes to the DIT as described below. Assume that the user has connected and is successfully bound to CN=Chat Server1, O=acme, C=US. The chat room protocol (CRP) operations are implemented as follows:

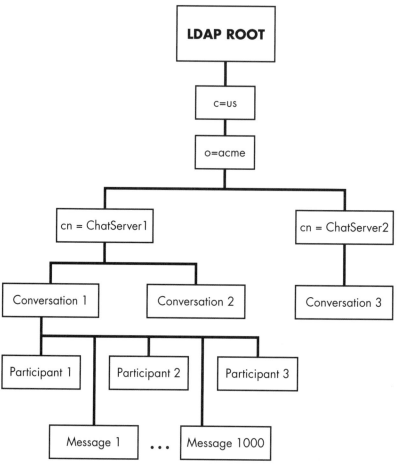

Fig. 9.6 LDAP hierarchy for chat room objects.

1. Create New Conversation—Check the `authorizedCreators` attribute of the chat room server's LDAP object to make sure that the bound user has sufficient access to start a new conversation. Take conversation title from the CRP operation and use it as the cn attribute of the new conversation object that is added in LDAP. This new `chatRoom-Conversation` object is added directly beneath the chat room server object in the DIT.

2. Join an Existing Conversation—Add a new `participantInfo` object in LDAP. The `cn` attribute is taken from the DN of the bound user. The `joinTime` attribute is the current time on the server, specified in GMT time. For example, 10:55 PM on March 28, 1999 is represented as `19990328105500Z`. In this object, the combination of the cn and the `joinTime` are needed to form the RDN of the object, since neither attribute alone is guaranteed to be unique. The new object is added directly beneath the `chatRoomConversation` object that the user joined.

3. Leave an Existing Conversation—This operation modifies the `participantInfo` object that was created above by the addition of the `leaveTime` attribute.

4. Submit Message to Conversation—Add a new `chatRoomMessage` object in LDAP. The new object is added directly beneath the `chatRoomConversation` object in which the user is participating. The chat room server generates the cn attribute of this object. The other attributes of the object are taken from the CRP.

The implementation of the LDAP interaction is in addition to whatever behavior needs to happen in the CRP. Users can find conversations to join by browsing the DIT. The chat room servers don't need to create support for any extensive search and retrieval facility. They only need to concentrate on the capability of supporting simultaneous conversations. Note that in a distributed environment, the LDAP information is replicated among several LDAP servers. Thus, a user browsing the DIT for a conversation to join may find an ongoing conversation in which he (or she) is interested in joining, only to find that the conversation has ended. This is due to the fact that the user has connected to an LDAP server that is different from the LDAP server to which the chat room server connects.

CHAPTER SUMMARY

This chapter discussed different ways in which common applications can make use of the directory. We introduced a classification that can describe to what degree an application has integrated itself with the directory using the following four categories:

- ☞ directory ignorant
- ☞ directory aware
- ☞ directory enabled
- ☞ directory dependent

Then we showed how several real-world applications could make use of the directory, including storage management, the chat room, and electronic mail. In integrating these applications, we combined the use of DNS and LDAP.

Microsoft's Active Directory Service (ADS) and Novell's Directory Service (NDS)

Starting with the release of the Active Directory Service (ADS) component of Windows 2000, Microsoft makes available an LDAP server that is an integrated feature of the network operating system. Using its Novell Directory Service (NDS), Novell has available since 1992 an LDAP-style directory in its NetWare operating system with its NetWare 4 version. LDAP support was added to NDS in 1997 with the availability of the LDAP services for NDS components that was offered as an add-on to versions of NDS that were already in the marketplace. Subsequent versions of NDS have the LDAP component offered as an integrated feature.

Thus, users of the two most popular network operating systems (NetWare and Windows NT) now have available an LDAP server that comes with the operating system as an integrated feature. As of this writing, no version of Unix is available that comes with an integrated LDAP server although Netscape and Novell make their LDAP servers available for various Unix platforms. Thus, Unix users will have to pay an additional fee and undertake an additional installation to place an LDAP server in their network.[1] This chapter is intended to serve as a brief

---

[1] Currently, the OpenLDAP consortium makes available the source code for an LDAP server that can be compiled and built and will run on Unix; contact their web site at: http://www.openldap.org.

overview of these two LDAP servers, and introduce the reader to some of the major features that they provide. Several fine books provide detailed information on both NDS and ADS.[2]

Both NDS and ADS do more than just provide a generic LDAP server. They are the focal point for the administration of their respective networks. NDS and ADS make a list of and provide access to every resource in the network. They allow the administrator to manage relationships between users and the network devices, network applications, and other information in the network. Both Microsoft and Novell will tell you that their respective offering is substantially superior to its competition. While both offerings have many advanced features, there are far more similarities than differences for the typical user.

The most important aspects that distinguish these two directories from generic LDAP servers are those that revolve around the ongoing administration of the network. Thus, for both NDS and ADS, this chapter will discuss what types of objects are normally created in the DIT, how basic access to those objects is controlled, and how the directories replicate the information in the DIT across the network from one directory server to another.

A TYPICAL NDS INSTALLATION

Let us consider what happens when a NetWare administrator installs NDS. First, an administrator creates the NetWare version 4 or later server in the network.[3] When the first NetWare server is installed, NDS is installed as well. Additionally, several objects are created in the directory at that time. These objects are representative of real objects that need to be administered. The principal objects that are created upon NDS initialization are:

☞ A user entry that represents the administrator of the network
☞ A server entry that represents the NetWare server that was installed

---

[2] Chris Andrew et. al., *Novell's NDS Developer Guide,* IDG Books, 1999; Alistair Lowe-Norris, *Windows 2000 Active Directory,* O'Reilly, 2000; Jeffrey Hughes and Blair Thomas, *NDS for NT,* IDG Books, 1998.

[3] NDS is also installable as a feature on other operating systems, not just as an integral feature of the NetWare operating system.

☞ A volume object for each volume that is created on the NetWare server. In NetWare, each server must have at least one volume on which files are stored. The server may have additional volumes. Each volume is represented by its own entry in NDS.

☞ An organization container into which the above objects are placed

The object classes for these entries are not standard LDAP object classes. Instead, Novell has defined new object classes that are subclasses of the standard object classes. For example, consider the `user` object class that is defined by NDS. The `user` object class is defined as a subclass of the LDAP `organizationalPerson` object class, which is in turn defined as a subclass of the `person` object. Recall that the `person` object class is defined as:

```
( 2.5.6.6 NAME 'person' SUP top STRUCTURAL MUST ( sn $ cn )
  MAY ( userPassword $ telephoneNumber $ seeAlso $ description ) )
```

The `organizationalPerson` object class is defined in RFC 2256 as:

```
( 2.5.6.7 NAME 'organizationalPerson' SUP person STRUCTURAL
  MAY ( title $ x121Address $ registeredAddress $ destinationIndicator $
  preferredDeliveryMethod $ telexNumber $ teletexTerminalIdentifier $
  telephoneNumber $ internationaliSDNNumber $
  facsimileTelephoneNumber $ street $ postOfficeBox $ postalCode $
  postalAddress $ physicalDeliveryOfficeName $ ou $ st $ l ) )
```

Finally, NDS defines the `user` object class as:[4]

```
( NAME 'user' SUP organizationalPerson STRUCTURAL MAY (accountBalance $
allowUnlimitedCredit $ groupMembership $ higherPriveleges $ homeDirec-
tory $ language $ lastLoginTime $ lockedByIntruder $ loginAllowed-
TimeMap $ loginDisabled $ loginExpirationTime $ loginGraceLimit $
loginGraceRemaining $ loginIntruderAddress $ loginIntruderAttempts $
loginIntruderResetTime $ loginMaximumSimultaneous $ loginScript $
loginTime $ messageServer $ minimumAccountBalance $ networkAddress $
networkAddressRestriction $ passwordAllowChange $ passwordExpira-
tionInterval $ passwordExpirationTime $ passwordMinimumLength $ pass-
wordRequired $ passwordUniqueRequired $ passwordUsed $
printJobConfiguration $ printerControl $ provateKey $ profile $ profile-
Membership $ publicKey $ securityEquals $ securityFlags $ serverHolds $
typeCreatorMap $ uID )
```

---

[4] In NDS' definition, both attribute names and object class names can have spaces. The spaces have been removed in this presentation for compatibility with LDAP requirements.

Notice how many additional attributes NDS includes in the defini-tion of the `user` object class. NDS uses these additional attributes to administer users. As an example, consider the `loginScript` attribute. Whenever a NetWare user connects to the network, a series of commands is executed for the user in order to set up the user's environment appro-priately. For example, various NetWare volumes can be mapped as local drives for the user's convenience. This attribute contains the login script for users. NDS also allows a loginScript attribute for organization and organizationalUnit containers. At the container level, this script is exe-cuted in addition to the user's login script. When a user logs in, NetWare's LOGIN program searches one level above (to either the organization or organizational Unit) and runs the container login script before the user's login script (if any). Because NDS replicates information across each server in which the `user` entry is stored, the same login script will be exe-cuted by NDS no matter where in the network a user logs in.

Immediately after creation of an NDS tree and the installation of a NetWare server (both of which normally occur at the same time), a typi-cal DIT appears (see Figure 10.1).

As more users, printers, and other objects are added to the NDS, the top-level organization gets more crowded, so it is subdivided into organi-zational units. After a few entries are added to NDS, the DIT might appear more like the tree in Figure 10.2.

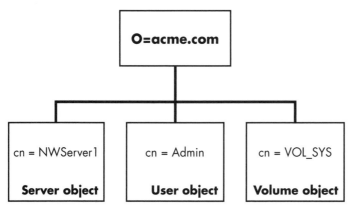

Fig. 10.1 NDS DIT upon system initialization.

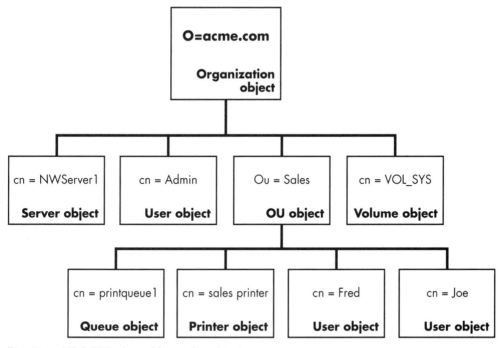

Fig. 10.2 NDS DIT after adding a few objects.

Notice that the NDS administrator has added a new organizational unit to the tree for the sales organization within acme.com. Two new users, a printer and an associated print queue, have also been added to this new organizational unit container. Thus, there are now nine objects in the NDS DIT, as shown in Table 10.1.

Table 10.1   Objects and Object Classes in a Typical NDS DIT

NDS Name	NDS Object Class
O=acme.com	Organization
Cn=NWServer, o=acme.com	NCP Server
Cn=admin, o=acme.com	User
Ou=sales, o=acme.com	OrganizationalUnit
Cn=VOL_SYS, o=acme.com	Volume
Cn=PrintQueue1, ou=sales, o=acme.com	Queue
Cn=SalesPrinter, ou=sales, o=acme.com	Printer
Cn=Fred, ou=sales, o=acme.com	User
Cn=Joe, ou=sales, o=acme.com	User

In NDS it is typical to group users and the resources that they use in the same containers. This allows for easy creation of access control rights for the users and those resources. In addition to the user's login script attribute mentioned above, there are other attributes in the user object class that allow for the control of how and from which locations in the network the user may log in, and what resources that user may use. Every entry in NDS contains an Access Control List (ACL) attribute that has been added to the top object class. In NDS, the ACL is the key component in determining directory access control. The ACL determines which operations a trustee entry can do on another entry and its attributes. In the schema, the ACL is a multivalued attribute type assigned as an optional attribute to the object class, Top.[5] Because all object classes inherit the characteristics of Top, all entries could have an ACL attribute. Since it is an optional attribute in Top, not all entries in NDS will have an ACL. In NDS, the ACL has the following three fields:

☞ Protected attribute name
☞ Subject name
☞ Privileges

An ACL value can protect either an object or an attribute. The protected object is always the one that contains the ACL attribute. If an ACL entry is to apply to the object as a whole, the protected attribute name is empty. If a specific attribute is to be protected, it is named in the ACL entry. Note that even though the ACL can only contain one attribute name, since it can be multivalued, a separate ACL can be included for each attribute that is to be protected. The privileges field is a bit-mask representing the kind of access being granted (value 1) or denied (value 0). The interpretation depends on how the bits are used, as shown in Table 10.2.

Table 10.2 NDS ACL Privileges Interpretation

Bit Mask	Individual Attributes	Entry Rights
0x00000001	Compare Attributes	Browse Entry
0x00000002	Read Attribute	Add Entry
0x00000004	Write, Add, Delete Attr	Delete Entry
0x00000008	Add/Delete Self	Rename Entry
0x00000010	(none)	Supervisory
0x00000020	Supervisory	(none)

---

[5] The original implementation did not support auxiliary object classes. Instead, it added attributes to the standard object class, such as adding the ACL attribute to the Top object class.

Since the `privileges` value of the ACL is a bit-mask, two bit-mask values are combined if the rights are to be granted. For example, to grant browse, creation, and deletion rights to an entry, the three bit-mask values are added together to create a `privileges` value of `0x00000007`. The ACL is interpreted in a slightly different manner, depending on whether an individual attribute is being protected, or whether the entry as a whole is being protected. The add entry right (i.e, bit-mask value `0x00000002`) gives the user identified in the subject name field of the ACL the right to create entries in the DIT beneath the object to which the ACL is attached. If this same bit-mask value mentions an attribute type name in the protected attribute name field, then the user identified in the subject name field is given the right to read the attribute in question.

Normally, the subject name field in an ACL contains a distinguished name. However, NDS has defined several values that have special significance. The two most useful values that can be used here are:

☞ `[Root]`—Denotes the Directory tree root object.
☞ `[Public]`—Includes all objects in the tree.

Thus, if an ACL contains the value `[Public]` in the subject name field, then that is an indication that all users in the tree have been granted the privilege mentioned in the ACL. Not only does NDS allow for individual entries to be used in the subject name field, it also allows for containers to be used. Remember that the ACL is an attribute on the object that is being accessed. The ACL attribute lists the trustees and the rights they have to the object. For example, if object Joe in Figure 10.2 had browse [entry rights] over OU=Engineering, the ACL on the object OU=Engineering would look like that in Table 10.3.

Table 10.3 Sample NDS ACL

ACL Field	Value
Subject Name (Trustee Name)	CN=Joe, OU=sales, O=acme.com
Protected Attribute ID	`[Entry Rights]` (rights apply to the whole entry, not just an attribute)
Privilege Set	Browse

Now, consider an ACL on the CN=sales printer object in Figure 10.2 that allows everyone to print. This ACL, which is attached as an attribute to the printer object, would look like that in Table 10.4.

Table 10.4   Sample NDS ACL to Allow Access to the Sales Printer

ACL Field	Value
Subject Name (Trustee Name)	OU=sales, O=acme.com
Protected Attribute ID	[Entry Rights] (rights apply to the whole entry, not just an attribute)
Privilege Set	Browse, Add

This ACL works because access rights in the NDS are inherited. All users in a container inherit the rights that have been assigned to the container. So, in the ACL of Table 10.4 Joe and Fred now have rights to use the sales printer. Not only do Joe and Fred have these rights, but whenever a new user is added to the OU=Sales container, that new user will automatically inherit these rights as well. NDS allows administrators to control how rights are inherited. A special kind of ACL, called an Inherited Rights Filter (IRF), specifies which rights can be inherited from an object to entries below it in the directory. The IRF (sometimes called an inheritance mask) takes the place of the trustee name in the ACL ([Inherited Rights Filter] appears in the Trustee ID field). It can be applied to [Entry Rights], [All Attributes Rights], or specific attribute rights. Consider the following ACLs (see Table 10.5) that are applied to the NDS tree in Figure 10.2 after a new user, Bob, has been added in a new organizational unit called Engineering.

Table 10.5   Sample NDS ACLs

ACL #	Object Holding ACL	Trustee	Protected Attribute	Privilege Set
1	O=acme.com	Sales	[Entry Rights]	Browse + Delete
2	OU=Engineering	Fred	[Entry Rights]	Create
3	Bob	Joe	[Entry Rights]	Delete

If no object in the directory has an Inherited Rights Filter, Joe would have the following effective rights:

☞ The delete right to Fred because Fred's ACL grants this right to Joe in ACL #3.

☞ The delete right to acme.com and ou=engineering, o=acme.com, because sales is part of Joe's distinguished name (this makes Joe *security-equivalent* to sales). Two NDS objects are said to be security-equivalent when granting a right to one of the objects automatically grants that right to the other object. In this case, granting the rights to ou=sales automatically grants those rights to all of the objects in the sales container because of the way NDS objects inherit rights.

☞ The browse right to Bob, Engineering, and acme.com because Joe is security-equivalent to sales.

Notice that even though Joe has been named as the trustee in only one of the ACLs above, he has been granted additional rights through NDS' notions of ACL inheritance and security equivalence. Remember from the definition of the user object class that there is an attribute called securityEquals. This multivalued attribute lists all of the other entries in NDS that are security-equivalent to this user. If Joe's securityEquals attribute lists Fred, then Joe will also have the following right granted in the ACLs listed in Table 10.5:

☞ The create right to Engineering and Bob because Joe is security-equivalent to Fred.

Now, suppose that OU=engineering has an Inherited Rights Filter that masks the delete right. This ACL resembles that in Table 10.6.

Table 10.6 Sample Inherited Rights Filter

Object Holding ACL	Trustee	Protected Attribute	Privilege Set
OU=Engineering	[Inherited Rights Filter]	[Entry Rights]	Delete

This means that if Joe had been granted delete rights to the O=acme.com container, then that right would be filtered out for all objects in the OU=Engineering container. In order to calculate the access rights that any NDS object A has to any other NDS object B, the following rights are taken into account:

☞ Rights specifically granted to A.

☞ Rights granted to all containers (all the way back to the root container) that A is in. These are *inherited* rights.

☞ Rights granted to any object to which A is security-equivalent, including any rights that these security-equivalent objects inherit.

☞ Rights that have been filtered out to A and any objects to which it is security-equivalent.

☞ Rights that have been granted to the special NDS object [Public].

Fortunately, NDS always calculates these rights; they never need to be calculated by the NDS user. NDS has a command, NWDSGetEffectiveRights, that allows the NDS user, to retrieve the rights that any NDS object has to any other NDS object. Furthermore, whenever a user A attempts to access an object B, NDS calculates A's rights to B before allowing the access. NDS uses this mechanism to control access to printers, files that are stored in the NetWare file system, and many other network resources. Network administrators can therefore control access to any network resource that is represented in NDS.

NDS PARTITIONS

An interesting feature of NDS is the way it controls how data is repli-cated across the network. On each NDS server some part of the DIT is stored. NDS allows the administrator to divide the DIT up into pieces known as *partitions*. Each partition contains a subtree of the entire DIT. Each partition is stored on one or more NDS servers. The example NDS DIT from Figure 10.2 has been expanded in Figure 10.3 with a few more objects and dotted boxes to show some example partitions.

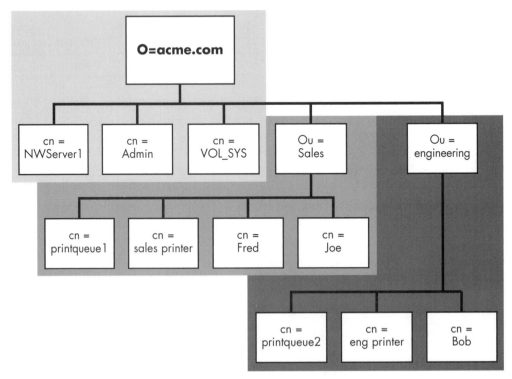

Fig. 10.3 Example of NDS partitions.

The one object in each of the three NDS partitions that is closest to the root names the partition. In this case, the three partitions are:

☞ [root]

☞ OU=sales

☞ OU=engineering

A single instance of a partition is called a *replica*. Partitions can have multiple replicas. NDS servers can hold more than one replica, as long as each replica is of a different partition. One of the replicas (usually the first created) of a given partition must be designated the *master replica*. Each partition can have only one master replica; the other replicas are designated as either read/write or read-only replicas. You can only use the read-only replica to read the information in the partition replica. Thus, only LDAP search operations will be directed to read-only partitions. You cannot write to a read-only partition. For example, an LDAP modify operation cannot be implemented against a read-only replica. NDS automatically redirects the modify operation to a writable replica. Replication adds fault tolerance to the database because the database has more than one copy of its information. Thus, even if one NDS server is down or unavailable, the NDS client can still access and possibly change data in a partition if another replica of the server's partitions is available someplace else in the network.

Synchronization is the process of ensuring that all changes to a particular partition are made to every replica of that partition. Most NDS replication is implemented using a peer-to-peer mechanism.[6] In a peer-to-peer synchronization system, updates can be made to any read/write or master replica. At a predetermined interval, all servers holding copies of the same partition communicate with each other to determine who holds the latest information for each object. The servers update their replicas with the latest information for each replica. Consider the following example. Assume that there are four NDS servers in the network on which are stored the partitions outlined in Table 10.7.

---

[6] Some objects in NDS are replicated using a master/slave mechanism. This replication mechanism is also used in Microsoft's ADS, where it is the primary replication mechanism. It will be discussed in the following section in which ADS is covered.

Table 10.7 Example of Distributing Partitions across NDS Servers

NDS Server	NDS Partition	Partition Type
NDS1	[root]	Master
NDS1	OU=sales	Master
NDS1	OU=engineering	Read/write
NDS2	[root]	Read/write
NDS2	OU=sales	Read/write
NDS3	OU=engineering	Master
NDS4	[root]	Read-only
NDS4	OU=sales	Read-only
NDS4	OU=engineering	Read-only

Notice that in this layout, there are two writable replicas of each partition. Each master partition is writable, as are the read/write partitions. There are three replicas of each partition, since the server NDS4 holds read-only replicas of all of the partitions. As changes are made to objects in the writable replicas, NDS synchronizes these changes to all replicas of the modified partition. NDS allows the administrator to control the interval at which information is replicated across the network. The time period between the synchronization attempts by an NDS server ranges from nearly immediately to many hours. Because the NDS must synchronize many replicas, not all replicas hold the latest changes at any given time. In other words, as soon as a change is made to NDS, all of the other replicas will hold out-of-date information until the next synchronization attempt.

Assume that a change is made to the object: Cn=Joe, ou=sales, o=acme.com on server NDS2. At the next synchronization attempt, this change must be passed on to the replicas of the OU=sales partition that is held on servers NDS1 and NDS4. If a synchronization attempt fails because an NDS server is down or due to some network connectivity failure, NDS will transmit the changes to the replicas on the affected servers and those replicas will receive updates when the problem is resolved. Because NDS allows changes to be made to two replicas simultaneously, NDS must resolve scenarios in which the same object is modified on two writable replicas. If this happens, NDS will resolve the changes at the next time that the two NDS servers attempt to synchronize.

The first thing that happens during the synchronization of two replicas is *time synchronization*. Time synchronization ensures that multiple changes to NDS are done in the order they occur. Time synchronization ensures that all servers in a directory tree report a consistent time. NDS keeps this time using Universal Time Coordinated (UTC), which is the time at Greenwich, United Kingdom.[7] NDS needs this consistent time to establish the order of different operations done on different replicas in the directory tree. Time synchronization may not provide the correct time of day exactly, but it ensures that the servers in the tree remain synchronized. With time synchronization, NDS can stamp directory events with a unique time stamp, which identifies an event and associates it with a time. Time synchronization makes sure that all time stamps are based on the same time across the network.

Assume that four changes are made to Cn=Joe, ou=sales, o=acme.com as outlined in Figure 10.4.

If the next synchronization attempt occurs at 10:40 between NDS1 and NDS2, the state of each partition would appear as that in Table 10.8, assuming that the description attribute previously held the value "Apprentice salesperson."

Table 10.8 Example NDS Synchronization

Time	NDS1 Description	NDS2 Description
10:30	[empty]	"Apprentice salesperson"
10:32	[empty]	"Joe sells lots of stuff"
10:34	"Joe doesn't sell much stuff"	"Joe sells lots of stuff"
10:35	"Joe doesn't sell much stuff"	"Joe sells lots of stuff," "Joe is the number one salesperson"
10:40	"Joe doesn't sell much stuff," "Joe is the number one salesperson"	"Joe doesn't sell much stuff," "Joe is the number one salesperson"

- At 10:30 on NDS1 the description attribute is deleted.

- At 10:32 on NDS2 the description attribute is modified (using the replace sub-operation) to hold the character string "Joe sells lots of stuff."

- At 10:34 on NDS1 the description attribute is modified (using the replace sub-operation) to hold the character string "Joe doesn't sell much stuff."

- At 10:35 on NDS2 the description attribute is modified (using the add sub-operation) to hold the character string "Joe is the number one salesperson."

Fig. 10.4 NDS collision in distributed entries.

---

[7] UTC is also known as Greenwich Mean Time (GMT).

Notice that after the first change is made to the object, each replica holds different values for the description attribute. Also, the final result of the four changes that have been made is probably different than each administrator had expected. So, even though NDS has applied all of the changes in the exact order in which they were entered, the end result is that the description attribute holds information that looks unusual to humans, but looks absolutely correct to NDS. Thus, even though NDS has sophisticated time synchronization and data synchronization mechanisms, external administrative controls must be in place when a complex distributed NDS infrastructure is deployed. In the example above, the NDS1 and NDS2 administrators must contact each other and resolve the value of Joe's description attribute manually, and then modify the attribute value again, as appropriate.

A Typical ADS Installation

Just as in the discussion of NDS, our investigation of ADS will cover what happens during installation, some aspects of the directory schema that are peculiar to ADS, and how data is replicated across the network. Let us consider what happens when a Windows administrator installs ADS. First, an administrator creates Windows 2000 server in the network.[8] When the first Windows 2000 server is installed, ADS is installed as well. The server on which ADS is installed is called a *domain controller*. Just as in NDS, several objects are created in the directory. These objects are representative of real objects that need to be administered. The principal objects that are created upon ADS initialization are:

- ☞ A user entry that represents the administrator of the network.
- ☞ A computer entry that represents the domain controller for the Windows 2000 server that was just installed.
- ☞ Various default groups for managing security relationships in Windows 2000.
- ☞ A domain context container into which the above objects are placed.

The object classes for these entries are not standard LDAP object classes. Instead, just as Novell did, Microsoft has defined new object classes that are subclasses of the standard object classes. For example,

---

[8] Microsoft has also made available a special version of ADS that runs on the Windows NT operating system. Since I don't expect it to be widely deployed at all in comparison to the Windows 2000 version of ADS, I will ignore it (as will most people).

consider the `user` object class that is defined by ADS. Even though this
has the same name as the NDS object class, it is very different, and can
be distinguished as such by the unique object identifier that Microsoft
has assigned for it. Recall that each LDAP object class has two names,
the string representation and the OID representation, as shown here:

```
( 1.2.840.113556.1.5.9 NAME 'user' SUP top STRUCTURAL MUST (governsID
$ defaultObjectCategory $ defaultSecurityDescriptor $ rDNAttID $
lDAPDisplayName $ schemaIDGUID $ subClassOf $ systemAuxiliaryClass $
systemMayContain $ objectClassCategory $ systemPossSuperiors $ syste-
mOnly) MAY (accountExpires $ lastLogon $ lastLogoff $ networkAddress
$ scriptPath $ userCertificate $ … )⁹
```

Notice that Microsoft's definition of the `user` object class is a subclass of `Top`, whereas Novell's definition of the `user` object class is a subclass of the X.500/LDAP `OrganizationalPerson`. It is also interesting to
note that Microsoft has taken the liberty of augmenting the `Top` object
class with numerous additional attributes not defined as part of the
LDAP schema.

While Novell uses the X.500-style `Organization` and `Organization-
alUnit` as the primary containers in the DIT, Microsoft has decided to use
the `domainContext` as the primary container for structuring the DIT. This
approach (known as *dc-naming*) allows a natural progression from the
Windows NT 4.0 directory model in which most objects are stored in a single domain. In NT 4.0, users, printers, etc., are organized into *domains*.
When a user logs into a domain, access is given to the printers and shared
file systems in that domain depending upon the privileges the user has
been granted. Each domain has one or more servers that are assigned as
domain controllers. There is no hierarchy in the domain. All objects are
stored at the top level. If an enterprise has more than one domain in their
network, then the administrator may configure the domain controllers to
share user authentication information. This allows a user to log into one
domain, and access printers in another domain.

Each ADS `domainContext` is analogous to a single Windows NT
domain. This mapping allows for easy migration of data from the domain
system to ADS. Because Microsoft also stores DNS information in the
DIT, each `domainContext` maps to a single Internet domain name. It is
not clear if either of the NDS or ADS naming approaches is any better
than the other (especially since NDS stores DNS information without

---

⁹ The ADS schema actually defines numerous other attributes for the user object class, but they
have been omitted here. This description is the author's understanding of the ADS schema based on
an installation of Beta 3 of Windows 2000 server.

using dc-naming), they are just different ways of approaching the same problem. So, upon installation, a typical ADS DIT appears as seen in Figure 10.5.

Notice how similar this DIT is to the one shown in Figure 10.1, even though it has several more objects. This is because NDS and ADS are fulfilling similar roles. ADS is the central repository for all Windows 2000 administrative information, while NDS is the central repository for all NetWare administrative information. There is much more to NetWare and Windows 2000 than just the network directory, but ADS and NDS are the mechanisms that allow the administrator to control the other features of these modern operating systems. The initial DIT of ADS actually contains several more objects than are shown above. Notice that the computers container is initially empty. This is due to the fact that when ADS is first installed, the only computer in the network will be the domain controller on which ADS is located. This computer is placed in the domain controllers container instead. Notice also that there is no object in the DIT comparable to the volume object in the NDS's initial DIT. This is because in ADS the administrator must decide which shared volumes get published into the ADS DIT.

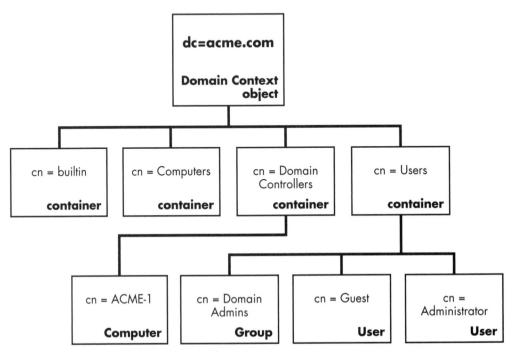

Fig. 10.5 ADS DIT upon system initialization.

Just as in NDS, as more users, printers, and other objects are added to the ADS DIT, the top-level organization gets more crowded, prompting organizational units to be subdivided. After a few entries are added to NDS, the DIT might resemble the tree in Figure 10.6.

Notice that the ADS administrator has added a new organizational unit to the tree for the sales organization within acme.com. Two new users, a printer and an associated print queue, have also been added to this new organizational unit container.

Just as in NDS, in ADS it is appropriate to group users and their resources in the same containers. This allows for easy creation of access control rights for the users and those resources. Just as every entry in NDS contains an ACL attribute, every object in ADS contains a *security descriptor* that has been added to the top object class. This security

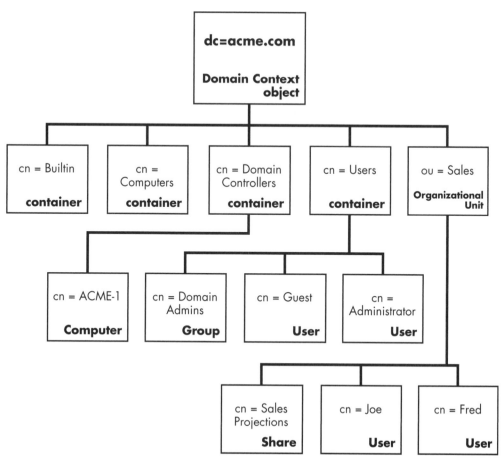

Fig. 10.6 ADS DIT after adding a few objects.

descriptor contains the entry's *Discretionary Access Control List (DACL)*. In ADS, the DACL is the key component in determining directory access control. The DACL contains a list of *Access Control Entries* (ACEs). The DACL determines which operations a user entry can do on another entry and its attributes. In the schema, the ACL is a single-valued attribute type assigned as an attribute to the object class, `Top`. Because all object classes inherit the characteristics of `Top`, all entries will have an ACL attribute. In ADS, the ACE has five fields, as shown in Table 10.9.

Table 10.9 ADS ACE Fields

ADS ACE Field	NDS ACL Analog
AccessMask	Privileges
AceType	Protected Attribute Name
Trustee	Subject Name
AceFlags	N/A
Flags, ObjectType, InheritedObjectType	Protected Attribute Name

Just as in NDS, an ACE value can protect either an object or an attribute. The protected object is always the one that contains the ACE attribute. Whether an ACE entry applies to the object as a whole is determined by the flags subfield. The flags subfield has four possible values:

☞ `Neither`

☞ `Both`

☞ `ObjectType` only

☞ `InheritedObjectType` only

The `neither` and `both` values refer to whether the `ObjectType` or `InheritedObjectType` subfields apply. If the ACE applies to the object as a whole, then flags is neither, while `ObjectType` or `InheritedObjectType` are both empty. If a specific attribute is to be protected, then flags is `ObjectType` only, and the `ObjectType` subfield contains the attribute to be protected. The `ObjectType` subfield does not actually contain the name of the attribute that is protected by the ACE. Instead, it contains a special identifier called a Globally Unique Identifier (GUID). In ADS, a GUID is a 16-byte value that is assigned to every object in the DIT upon creation. This GUID is kept in the object's `objectGUID` attribute. ADS has added the `objectGUID` attribute to the `Top` object class. In this case, the GUID refers to a `schemaIDGUID` that is held in the schema object, which ADS holds in the DIT. This `schemaIDGUID` defines the attribute in the ADS schema. Note that even though the ACE can only contain one attribute name, a separate ACE can be included for each attribute that is to be protected, since the DACL can have many ACEs. The `ObjectType` and `InheritedObjectType` subfields store GUIDs that indicate what the ACE actually applies to.

ADS allows the ACE to apply to child objects as well by using the `AceFlags` field. This field indicates whether the ACE will apply to child objects or not. Additionally, ADS will set the `AceFlags` to indicate whether the ACE has been inherited. If the `AceFlags` indicates that the ACE should apply to child objects, then assigning the `Both` value or the `InheritedObjectType` value to the flags subfield will finish the job. It appears that the NDS approach, with its multivalued ACL attributes, is cleaner and easier to administer, but the ADS approach seems viable as well.

ADS REPLICATION

ADS allows directory data to be replicated across the network between the directory servers. ADS divides the servers in a network into *sites*. ADS performs replication more frequently among servers within a site than to servers in other sites. Thus, if servers A and B are in the same site, and server C is in another site, then server A replicates data more frequently to server B than it does to server C. ADS replications are made to domain controllers in each site. However, a site does not actually determine what data is replicated and how the data is partitioned. The ADS domain is the unit of replication. So, in order to create an analog to the NDS *partition*, multiple domain contexts are created. Consider the example shown in Figure 10.7.

In this example, there are eight separate domains that are defined in the ADS DIT. Each one has its own domain controller, and may have many containers, users, and other objects inside of the domain. As entries are modified within each domain, they are replicated across the various sites. Since a server may hold information for multiple domains, this organization of the data has similar flexibility to the NDS partition replication scheme. Note that since the data is replicated across multiple servers, collisions may occur in ADS just as they were described for NDS in Figure 10.4. Each ADS domain controller (there may be more than one for each domain) has a read/write copy of the DIT for that domain. Only domain controllers in a domain have writable replicas of the DIT for that domain. Domain controllers may have replicas of the DIT for other domains, but those replicas are read-only. In this scenario, domain controllers within a domain are the "masters" of the domain data. Domain controllers outside of that domain

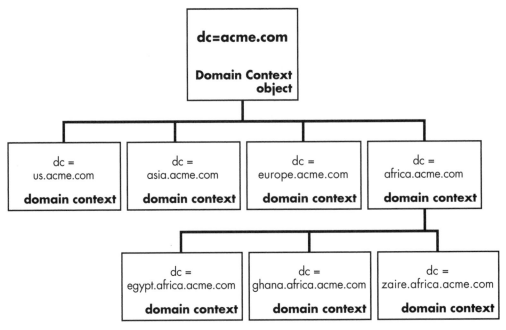

Fig. 10.7 ADS DIT using multiple domains.

are considered "slaves." Updates flow from the masters to the slaves. Since ADS allows for more than one domain controller for a domain, the replication technique that it uses is called *multimaster replication.*

CHAPTER SUMMARY

Both Novell and Microsoft have published white papers that go to great lengths to point out the superiority of their own offering. This chapter has pointed out that, for the commonly used features of the directories, there are more similarities than differences. Furthermore, both are conformant implementations of the LDAPv3 protocol. While this may be seen as cheating somewhat, from a pure directory perspective both NDS and ADS are effective implementations of LDAP. They both provide an effective way of replicating their information across the network, and they both set a good foundation for tools that are used to manage their respective networks. While there may very well be certain differences in performance, security implementation, and other features, I don't believe that these difference come into play when trying to decide between the directories themselves, but instead are more of a factor in the underlying network which they manage.

Glossary

A

A   DNS record type that gives the IP address for a host. A is the abbreviation for address.

Abandon   LDAP operation that allows the client to request cancellation of a previously submitted operation. It is normally used to cancel a search operation that seems to be taking long to complete.

Abstract Object Class   The keyword ABSTRACT in the definition of an LDAP object class indicates that no additional objects of that type may be created. For example, the Top object class may only be used in the definition of other object classes.

Active Directory   Component of Microsoft's Windows 2000 that implements an LDAP server as an integrated feature of the network operating system.

Agent   Name for the server component used in the Simple Network Management Protocol (SNMP).

Alias   A special LDAP object class whose sole purpose is to "point" to some other LDAP object.

Anonymous authentication   A form of authentication that can be used when the client either does not have an account with the server, or is not willing to identify itself.

Applet   Special type of program used in the Java programming language that allows the program to run inside of a web page that is being viewed by a web browser.

Abstract Syntax Notation One (ASN.1)   ITU's mechanism of defining the language that its peer entities use to communicate across a data communications network. ASN.1 defines not only the type of data that is used in communications, but also the mapping of the data layouts into the binary network order.

Authentication   The process of determining whether someone or something is, in fact, who or what it is declared to be. In its simplest form, a client authenticates itself to a server by providing a user name and a password.

Auxiliary Object Class   An object class whose attributes can be added to an existing object in the directory.

B

Backus-Naur Form (BNF)   Grammar used in many IETF documents to define the elements of the protocol that passes between clients and servers.

Bind   LDAP operation that allows the LDAP client and server to mutually authenticate. Also (but unrelated), BIND (Berkeley Internet Name Domain) is the name of the most common DNS name server and resolver implementations.

C

Certificate   Contains the public keys of a user, together with some other information (such as the user's name and e-mail address), rendered unforgeable by encryption with the private key of the issuer of the certificate.

Certification Authority (CA)   A server that issues certificates.

Common Indexing Protocol (CIP)   A back-end protocol that is used by directory servers to exchange index objects. Each index object contains a summary of the information known by a directory server.

Connection LDAP (CLDAP)   Implementation of the LDAP protocol over UDP.

CNAME   DNS record type that indicates a record which is an alias for some other record. It gives the canonical name for the record.

Compare   LDAP operation that allows the LDAP client to specify a single attribute type and value and have it compared to the same attribute of an existing entry in the DIT.

CRAM-MD5   (Challenge Response Authentication Mechanism-MD5) A single challenge response mechanism. The data encoded in the server's challenge contains an arbitrary string of random digits, a time stamp, and the fully-qualified primary host name of the server. The client then responds with a string consisting of the user name, a space, and a 'digest' of the data supplied by the server. The digest is computed using the MD5 message digest algorithm.

D

Delete   The LDAP operation that allows for the removal of an entry from the DIT.

Digest   A message digest algorithm takes any size document as input (i.e., the message) and produces a fixed-size data block as output. This fixed-sized data block is called the message digest. A good message digest algorithm has the property that it is computationally infeasible to produce two messages having the same message digest.

Directory   A property-based information retrieval system. A directory provides a set of names and properties in such a way that directory users can easily search them. Each name in the directory and its associated properties are collected together as a directory entry.

Distinguished Name (DN)   Unique identifier for an entry in an LDAP-accessible DIT. The distinguished name of an entry is the concatenation of all of the name components of each parent entry in the hierarchy.

Directory Information Tree (DIT)   The collection of all entries held in the database of an LDAP server.

Domain Naming Service (DNS)   A directory service whose primary goal is to provide for the mapping of Internet host names to IP addresses. It also provides other information about Internet hosts.

F

Filter   The field in the LDAP search operation that specifies which objects in the DIT are to be returned in the search results.

G

Grammar   Rules for defining protocol elements are created using grammar. IETF protocols are normally defined using an augmented BNF grammar. LDAP is defined using the ASN.1 grammar notation.

H

Handshaking   During the handshaking process, the client and server each exchange some information before a connection can be created. If either side is not satisfied with the information that is provided by the other side (known as its peer), then the attempt to create the socket is broken off, and no connection is created.

Hierarchy   In a hierarchy, data is arranged in such a fashion that each member of the hierarchy has a parent, and may have one or more children. The hierarchy has one special member, called the root, which has no parent. Entries in DNS and LDAP accessible directories are arranged in hierarchies.

Host   A computer that is accessible via Internet protocols.

I

IANA   (The Internet Assigned Numbers Authority) An organization associated with the IETF that has responsibility for the registry of any "unique parameters and protocol values" for Internet operations. These include port numbers and SASL authentication types.

IETF   (The Internet Engineering Task Force) The body that defines standard Internet communication protocols. Examples of the protocols are DNS, LDAP, and Finger. The protocols are defined in documents known as Request for Comments (RFCs).

Index Object   Information that is exchanged between directory servers that use the Common Indexing Protocol. Directory servers can exchange index information that allows them to know the kinds of information that are held by other servers. For example, a server could create an index object that contains the last names of all of the users in its local repository, and exchange this information with another directory server. This exchange allows each of the servers to know about the users' names that are in each other's repositories.

J

Java   A programming language expressly designed for use in the distributed environment of the Internet. It was designed to have the "look and feel" of the C++ language. It can be used to build small application modules or applets for use as part of a web page. Applets make it possible for a web page user to interact with the page.

K

Key   In DNS, the record that gives the public key for the host. Key is not an abbreviation for anything.

L

LDAP   (The Lightweight Directory Access Protocol) A sophisticated client-server protocol used to access a directory. Version 3 of LDAP is defined in RFC 2251. LDAP is based on the ITU X.500 series of recommendations.

M

Mesh   The collection of directory servers which mutually exchange index information.

Modify   LDAP operation which lets a client make changes to a single entry in the DIT.

ModifyDN   LDAP operation that lets a client change the name of an entry in the DIT. Essentially, the ModifyDN operation moves an entry from one place in the DIT to another.

MX (Mail eXchange)   In DNS, the record that holds information about where to deliver mail destined for users with e-mail addresses on this host.

N

Name Server   The server component of DNS.

Novell Directory Service   Component of Novell's NetWare that implements an LDAP server as an integrated feature of the network operating system.

NS (Name Server)   In DNS, the resource record that gives information about the name servers that are available in a particular domain.

O

Object Class   In LDAP, the attributes that can be used in an entry are defined by that entry's object class. Object class definitions list out the attributes that must be in entries of that type and other attributes that may appear in entries, but are not required to be there.

Object Identifier (OIDs)   Numeric identifiers that are defined in ASN.1 and can be used in LDAP to uniquely identify elements in the protocol such as attribute types and object classes.

P

Public Key Infrastructure (PKI)   A tool used to provide aid in the support of public-key encryption. The basic feature allows for retrieval of users' public keys in order to allow for the exchange of encrypted and digitally signed information.

Port   In TCP and other Internet protocols, this allows many application servers to operate on the same host simultaneously. Each port is identified by an integer. Some port numbers are specifically allocated to certain protocols. LDAP normally operates over TCP using port number 389.

Protocol   Definition of the set of rules used for communication between application programs running on hosts when they send data back and forth. Examples of protocols defined in Internet RFCs are LDAP and DNS.

PTR   In DNS, this resource record includes a pointer from one point in the DNS name space to another. PTR is the abbreviation for pointer.

R

Record   An entry in the DNS directory. Each record is of a specific type. All DNS records share a common format.

Recursion   In DNS, this allows a query to be forwarded from one name server to a second name server. This relieves the DNS resolver of submitting the same query to numerous name servers until it finds the right one.

Referral   In LDAP, when a server does not have the ability to respond to a client operation (normally a search operation), it can return a referral to the client. The referral contains the name of another LDAP server and perhaps a starting search base to use for this operation, should the client resubmit it.

Resolver   The client component in DNS.

RFC (Request For Comments)   Where IETF defines its protocols in documents.

RP (Responsible Person)   In DNS, a record that gives the e-mail address for a responsible person for this host.

RUIP (Remote User Information Program)   In Finger, the server component.

S

SASL (The Simple Authentication and Security Layer)   Defined in RFC 2222, a method for adding authentication support to connection-based protocols such as LDAP.

Schema   Defines the types of objects and properties of those objects that are available for retrieval by clients. In LDAP, the schema for an LDAP server defines all of the available object classes and attribute types that can be used in entries created on that server.

Search   LDAP operation that is used to retrieve entries from the DIT.

Sig (Signature)   In DNS, this record holds the digital signature of some other resource record.

Signature   In computer security, this is created when a message digest is encrypted by a user with his private key.

SOA (Start Of Authority)   In DNS, this record specifies information about the naming authority for a host. For example, it specifies the e-mail address for a contact for information about this host.

Socket   In TCP and other Internet protocols, is a communications channel that is opened between two hosts on some port. There is normally some sort of handshaking process that occurs before the successful creation of a socket.

SRV (Service Type)   In DNS, the record that specifies the location of the server(s) for a specific protocol and domain.

SSL (The Secure Socket Layer)   Allows for the creation of a socket over which encrypted and/or digitally signed data can be transferred between Internet hosts; is built on top of TCP.

Subtree   A portion of the DIT beneath a specific entry in LDAP.

T

Tagged Index Object (TIO)   Used in the Common Indexing Protocol (CIP). Each item in the TIO is given a specific numeric tag. All items with the same tag are presumed to have come from the same entry or record in the Directory.

TLS (Transport Layer Security)   The successor to SSL. It has the same goals.

Tree   See *Hierarchy*.

TXT (Text)   Allows the administrator to insert unformatted textual comments about the host in DNS.

W

WKS (Well Known Services)   A record that lists different well known services that have been installed on this host in DNS.

Index